THE
WILD GARDEN

THE
WILD GARDEN

VIOLET STEVENSON

WINDWARD

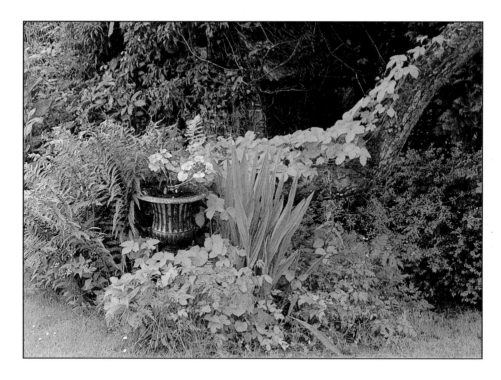

A FRANCES LINCOLN BOOK

CONTENTS

FOREWORD

In some ways when we create a wild garden we return to our beginnings, for the first gardens were made from plants brought in from the wild either because they were not to be found locally or so that they were near at hand when required for healing, medicine, cooking or some other purpose.

Those gardeners who created the first romantic wild gardens had no need seriously to consider conservation. Except where industrialization had wantonly trespassed, lanes, woodlands, heaths, meadows, marshes, ponds and streams were still much the same as they had been for centuries.

Now, however, there is a need for consideration, not only for many familiar and beloved plants, but also for the myriad creatures dependent upon them which are no longer commonly seen. Many of us who grew up in a less industrial world and a less farming-efficient countryside miss them. For a number of reasons we realize that we should not allow these plants to disappear. I hope that this book will show that it should not be difficult to stay the loss, indeed, will help increase their numbers.

Until quite recently, making a wild garden or a patch in a larger plot offered problems of its own. For example, since no conservationist should entertain the thought of lifting plants from the wild to bring home, where were the native plants needed to stock it to come from?

When I wrote *A Garden Full of Flowers* in 1968 I included a list of wildflowers worth growing and selected particularly only those which were listed among garden flowers in the seedsmen's catalogues and so were readily available to the gardener. There were 82 names! The list included many garden favourites such as wind flower, *Anemone nemorosa*; pasque flower, *Pulsatilla vulgaris*; Pyrenean lily, *Lilium nyrenaicum*; and snake's head lily, *Fritillaria meleagris*.

It is now possible to buy all manner of seeds and plants, too, of truly native species, even of those that have become very rare in the wild. Using wild-flower seed and with surprisingly little work, a dull and demanding lawn can be transformed into a flowery mead. Any piece of poor, unproductive land can be converted to a place of beauty.

A shrub border or a wooded building-site can become a flower-carpeted copse. Prefabricated shapes and easy-to-handle plastics enable the gardener to make a pond, the most quickly created form of wild garden one can hope to have, and a sure magnet for a wide variety of wildlife.

To create and run a successful wild garden, a change of attitude to both plant and garden beauty is demanded. When I was last in Australia, I was interested to find that gardeners there had begun to reject cultivars in favour of native plants. Even though some are not so showy, they have a natural beauty of their own.

Apart from the interest and joy of having native plants at hand and watching them grow, and the satisfaction of having found an easier way to manage the plot, the wild gardener also has the added pleasure of sharing it with a number of fascinating tenants, the number of which increases as the garden becomes wilder. For instance, once their season arrives, there are always butterflies and moths in my garden. As one would expect, since their caterpillars and many other insects are plentiful, birds also abound. The many nests we find and fledglings we see are evidence that all parts of the garden are their territories. That there are also many other little creatures present is shown by the unmistakable traces left here and there, noted as one walks by or disturbs soil and heaped leaves in a border or hedge bottom. Only small traces, but important proof that there is yet another bonus worth noting – no-one is alone in a wild garden.

WHAT IS A WILD GARDEN?

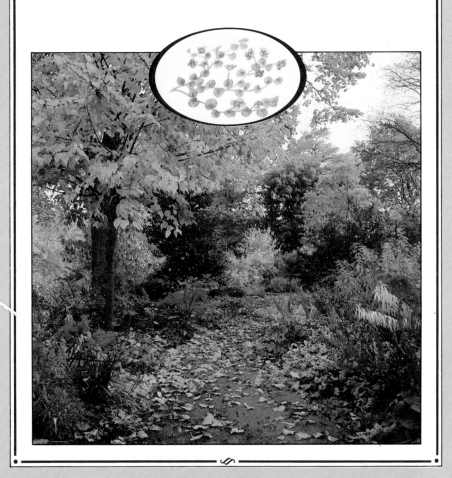

INTRODUCTION

Today's concept of a wild garden differs greatly from that of a century or so ago. A wild garden then was not a place for the care or protection of native plants for, after all, these still abounded in the countryside around. It was instead a contrived and romantic wilderness, a selected spot for those plants both novel and familiar, homesprung and exotic which, in spite of their beauty, would not fit into the precise gardening styles which then prevailed.

For centuries the vogue had been for controlled and very formal gardens. The plants, selected both for beauty and use, and later for novelty value, were grown in well-defined beds, which were most usually shaped to fit an overall geometric pattern, such as in the parterre. Although at first the plants within the beds were diverse, the ultimate ideal was that the decorative kinds should conform, for example be of uniform height, and that they should be ornamental at about the same time, flowering plants in spring and summer, to be replaced by evergreens in winter.

William Robinson and the wild garden

The man who tried to change this, and who indeed revolutionized British gardening by calling for informality in design and natural planting, was William Robinson (1838-1935), an Irish-born gardener of great imagination, drive and perhaps a certain opportunism. In 1870 he published *The Wild Garden*, where he wrote: 'My object . . . is now to show how we may have more of the varied beauty of hardy flowers than the most ardent admirer of the old style of garden ever dreams of, by naturalising innumerable beautiful natives of *many regions of the earth* in our woods and copses, rougher parts of pleasure grounds and in unoccupied places in almost every kind of garden.' (The italics are mine.) The gardens planted as Robinson advised were created in the grounds of great houses as a conceit, devised rather in the manner of the contemporary ferneries and grottos to delight and amuse guests. They were intended as an attractive and pastoral contrast to the disciplined bedding and seasonal displays of the 'trim' garden which Robinson so criticized.

Robinson used plants considered too coarse for the trim garden, and curiously, many of those he cites – paeonies, delphiniums and lilies – are in fact favourites of today's trim gardens. Moreover, many herbaceous borders and island beds in the average garden are assembled in the way visualized by Robinson for his wild areas. The great difference is that these are not tucked away in some glade but stand revealed in the middle of a lawn or by a house.

RIGHT *A leafy corner of a garden originally designed by Gertrude Jekyll, continues to typify her style. Apparently informally grouped, in fact each plant has been carefully considered. Under a canopy of native trees, among exotic conifers and others, including on the left the Japanese angelica tree,* Aralia elata, *the South American* Gunnera magellanica *rises majestically above a carpet of ferns.*

LEFT *Ground under trees cleared of too dense and coarse undergrowth offers an area in which some of the most charming wildflowers can be encouraged to grow. Little labour is required, other than in the removing of those interlopers such as brambles which would smother the smaller plants. There are subjects suitable for all kinds of soils, but local plants can best guide the new wild gardener. William Robinson might well have approved of this particular scene, as he wrote: 'a pretty plant in a free state is more attractive than any garden denizen'.*

Significantly, Robinson's influence was felt at a time when exotic plants were being introduced, many of them plants which could not be expected to conform to the garden fashions of that time. Furthermore, the plant hunters brought back vivid descriptions of the terrain and settings in which they had found their trophies growing. The plantsman, standing spellbound before an imported lily growing in a pot, imagined it in its native setting, and tried to create the nearest thing to it. True, in his own plot the trees overhead, the shrubs below and the ground cover beneath might be comprised of subjects of different genera from those of the immigrants' home land, but would they fundamentally be so different? Was it not possible to reach some compromise? And, of course, it was.

In native woodland and copse, the would-be owners of wild gardens set about creating delightful areas for the cultivation of exotics. Soon, with the import of plants ever-expanding, on the right soil and in the right climate, rhododendron, eucryphia, pieris, kalmia, magnolia and others either took the place of native oak and birch or mingled amicably with them. Thus the romantic wilderness became an important part of the great gardens. Some still exist and are still known as 'wild' gardens.

Gertrude Jekyll and the hardy flower border

Gertrude Jekyll (1843-1932), had great influence on the breakaway from the over formal. She admired the sweet simplicity of cottage gardens and her innovation was to bring new plants and old cottage favourites together, in borders away from wild areas, which she also planted in the Robinson manner. But with her painter's eye (for that was her training), she saw the pitfalls of the new gardening fashion, 'because it is understood to mean the planting of exotics in wild places, unthinking people rush to the conclusion that they can put any garden plants into any wild places . . . I have seen woody places that were already perfect with their own simple charm just muddled and spoilt by a reckless planting . . .'

On the whole she thought it better to leave the wood alone, but where it joined the garden to allow some bold planting of flowering plants 'as of Mullein in one part and Foxglove in another; for when standing in the free part of the garden it is pleasant to project the sight far into the wood, and to let the garden influences penetrate here and there, the better to join the one to the other'. But, her great contribution was to reinstate native plants to flower borders, planting them alongside newer cultivars and exotics.

Wild gardening in the grand manner

It is worth considering that except for the energetic and enthusiastic Miss Jekyll, few of the people who had their gardens restyled did the actual work

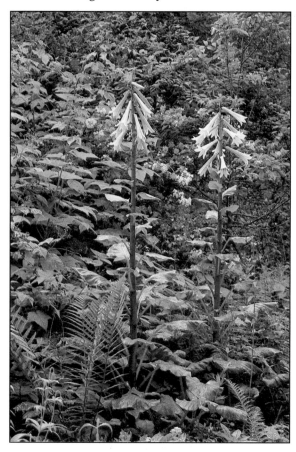

LEFT *The original concept of the wild garden was that it should delight and amuse, and should display plants not as they are found in nature but in a contrived natural setting. If indigenous plants were not spectacular enough, then certain others should be imported and set down among the most attractive of our native plants. Lilies such as this* Lilium giganteum, *one of Gertrude Jekyll's favourites, and many other species were to be seen in a woodland setting, framed perhaps by imported shrubs and fringed by both exotic and native ferns.*

themselves. This was left to the professional land-scaper and afterwards to the gardener (who by nature and training usually found it difficult to be anything other than precise and tidy). Miss Jekyll, in her woodland area, among other ploys had a pit dug 1.2m/4ft deep and about 3.5m/12ft across so that it could be filled with a carefully selected soil mixture, brought there by many donkey cart-loads, each holding three barrowloads, for her to grow to perfection her precious *Lilium giganteum*.

Even today many of the famous and great 'wild' gardens of the traditional romantic style are in fact intensively cultivated mainly because they contain or are intended to contain many exotics, the original habitats of which were in areas of rich, very humusy or acid soils which must be provided if the plants are to grow happily. So although the flowery areas were informal when compared with those of the past, they were seldom if ever really relaxed. It was not, I suggest, until professional gardeners became fewer and owner gardeners more plentiful that the majority of gardens took on as much 'sweet disorder' as they do today.

The ecological garden
Although the romantic wilderness is still an important, and desirable, part of the garden scene, some gardeners are moving into a rather different wild territory. In almost every country there now exists a lively interest in conservation and in providing a haven for native flora and fauna, rather than the display area for exotics and cultivars.

In my own garden, the native plants which I especially treasure are plants which once were common locally, many of which appear spontaneously in the garden, while others are rescued from the centre of a rough farm lane, from a building site or a field about to be sprayed with herbicide. I like to think that here in our garden is a little credit bank ready to pay out with interest if and when the time comes. These plants are symbolic of my personal concept of a wild garden, which is not just a wild place but which has become a place where wild plants and creatures are encouraged. The garden

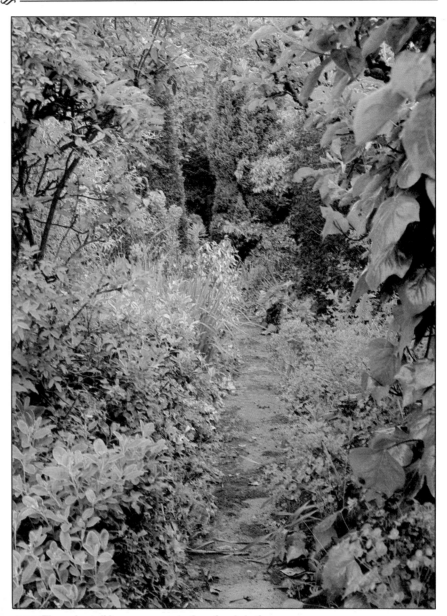

ABOVE *The modern wild garden may take many forms, but all include those plants which may be considered to be labour saving – those which on the whole can be left to grow their own way, layer on layer, nestling close together or even entwined, as they do in the wild. Informality is the rule. Straight lines are avoided or eliminated. Path and border edges are softened by an embroidery of sprawling and creeping plants.*

is very much under control, yet I believe it to be more wild than tame and it grows wilder all the time as yet another plant appears to have established itself and each day brings new sightings of wild creatures. I identified around 300 native plant species at the last rough count, and that did not include the many grasses and ferns.

Wild gardening – a more relaxed attitude

Since the time of Robinson's wild garden and Jekyll's mixed borders, the number of plants under cultivation has multiplied so considerably and the hybrids and varieties have so improved that few people wish to banish them. So where the gardener is more interested in the general appearance of the plot rather than its content, and where the cultivation of exclusively native species does not greatly appeal, then there is no reason why exotics and cultivars should not grow alongside native species quite happily, especially if the exotics are also attractive to wildlife. But, it is not generally realized that many of our familiar garden plants are in fact

BELOW *To convert a traditional garden to one with a wilder appeal, only few touches are necessary in the beginning. Foxgloves, among the most stately of our native species, mingle agreeably with most exotics and will seed themselves. Some garden shrubs can be supplemented by natives. Bushy and leafy perennials, creeping, climbing and trailing plants, will provide essential cover for wildlife.*

native. This point should be stressed, in case the novice gardener believes that 'wild' plants are limited to those seen around in great quantities at certain times of the year, such as dandelions and cow parsley, and often referred to as 'weeds'.

Furthermore, many 'exotics' are naturalized and some have been adopted by wildlife. For example, buddleia, a butterfly and nectar plant and a native of Chile, is found on waste land in many northern hemisphere cities, and rhododendron, of uncertain origin, provides excellent cover. The ivy-leaved toadflax, which takes a hold in the smallest crevices of town walls and often appears in country lanes, was introduced from southern Europe as a plant for hanging pots and baskets in the early seventeenth century. Introduced much earlier, the curious houseleek may have 'escaped' from rooftops where it was planted to ward off fire.

A NATURAL OASIS

Even the smallest of formal gardens, kept well groomed and constantly tended, will be demanding of time, labour and money. Unfortunately, there are other things, some less tangible perhaps, but to many people more precious, which are inevitably sacrificed in a perfectly maintained plot. So often, in spite of the wealth of bloom and colour, there is a feeling that something is missing. I sympathize with the three-year-old child, standing on the threshold of an immaculate billiard-table lawn, who turned to his hosts and told them kindly, 'We have daisies on *our* lawn.' And I have come to agree with the friend who told me, 'If there is no moss, for me there is no magic.'

Only gradually are people realizing that herbicides and insecticides used in the perfectly maintained plot lead to an all but sterile environment. And not only in gardens: so often in city parks and so-called environmental improvement areas the ground is sprayed to clear wild plants, only to be replaced by a monoculture – a single species of grass relieved by perhaps one or two species of trees – not as time-consuming as rows of bedding plants, but certainly more dreary.

No one quite knows what the long-term effects of persistent herbicide use will be, and this is perhaps the most important reason for discouraging that use. Once the gardener makes this decision, he or she will soon learn that it is extremely satisfying to leave nature to her own devices and see a succession of wild plants gradually introduce themselves, soon followed by a whole range of wildlife.

Bringing nature back to the garden

A wild garden depends very much on the personality of the gardener, and on his or her locality. Many urban dwellers will want to bring the countryside to town and fill their small gardens and backyard plots with a mixture of wild and exotic species, or perhaps produce a synthesis of wild species to remind them of their favourite stretch of countryside. Small urban gardens can be made to look striking, with ferns sprouting from shaded walls and different mulleins or clovers, for example, seeding among paving stones. In the suburbs, where there is usually more space available, the gardener can plan for continuity and mix plants of varied sizes, using a more casual blend of native and exotic.

If you have the motivation and the space, then you could create the ultimate wild garden – several different habitats merging into one, a situation that would be hard to find in real countryside. For example, a large garden could support a grassy meadow area, a small woodland copse or a natural

RIGHT *No matter how small or how urban, it is possible to create a wild garden in which water, living green leaves and a succession of flowers not only attract many forms of wildlife but provide also a delightful and restorative retreat.*

BELOW *Few places hold more charm than a flower-filled grass plot and few places are so easy to create. A mixture of grass and cornfield annuals sown in autumn or spring will become a delight the following summer.*

hedgerow, a butterfly border which could effectively simulate a roadside verge, with its multiplicity of plant species, and perhaps a pond. Depending on local conditions, the site might lend itself to a heath, chalk or rock garden. The possibilities are endless but the opportunities are there with so many nurseries now producing more native plant stock and seed.

As more and more of our countryside is taken over for agriculture or is buried under the concrete of a motorway or industrial development, gardens, in terms of the space they occupy, represent important potential sanctuaries for both plants and animals. This applies especially to small discrete habitats such as hedgerows, ponds and meadow. By creating and knowing how to encourage such habitats, the wild gardener plays an important ecological and conservational role. What may start as a hobby may even become an obsession, albeit a fascinating and worthwhile one.

A neighbour, a keen cottage gardener, shocked to find herb robert in one of my borders, commented in her country burr, 'Fancy *you* growing they!' When I explained that I was not growing them, simply allowing them to grow, she shook her head, uncomprehending. To her these were weeds, common wild plants, and she had not noticed that they were no longer common outside the boundaries of our gardens. This is the case with many wild plants in many localities. So what, indeed, is a rare plant?

In the United Kingdom many wild plants are now protected by the Wildlife and Countryside Act, 1981, some very strictly so, but I think it necessary to point out that the prohibitions refer to plants in the wild. Many of the species listed are in fact established garden plants, such as the lady's slipper orchid, *Cypripedium calceolus*. The wild *Gladiolus illyricus*, native to heathland in Hampshire and Dorset, is a near relative of *G. byzantinus*, which abounds in gardens near my home, though not yet in mine. In early summer, bunches of the flowers are often on sale in country markets. Other rarities have been in cultivation so long that they are found in many nurserymen's lists. Sometimes they are to be found on sale in gardens open to the public and on market stalls.

If those urban or suburban gardeners have doubts on the wisdom of growing wild plants because of the likelihood that they will be too 'weedy'-looking and will cause a nuisance to neighbour's gardens, compare the names in a flora with those in a seedman's or nurseryman's list. It should then become evident that there is a great range of beautiful wild species to draw upon, which have inhabited our gardens for centuries. Some of them are known affectionately as cottage flowers, plants such as cornflowers, columbines, loosestrife, heartsease and maiden pinks.

The wildlife bonus
A wild garden should be aesthetically pleasing and at the same time attractive to wildlife. Even people who cannot tell one bird from another and who

LEFT *Hibernating butterflies will stir in early spring. After so long a fast, once on the wing they seek energy-providing nectar. Few suitable garden plants blossom early enough, but there are some native species which do. The goat or pussy willow's catkins offer nectar to the butterflies and pollen to early foraging bees. Willows come in such variety that it should be possible to suit any garden.*

consider that most insects are pests will find that encouraging wildlife into the garden can open up new vistas and stimulate new interests. The garden will take on a new life of its own, not only during the spring with its surge of nesting activity. If you provide the right kind of food and shelter you can continue to attract wildlife through the year with groups of finches feeding on seed heads in the autumn, followed by waves of winter migrant birds that will gorge themselves on carefully planted berry-laden trees and bushes.

You will be amazed how quickly animals of all kinds will respond to selective planting. Even the addition of one native species can make a lot of difference, such as an early-flowering goat or pussy willow which will provide a rich source of nectar and pollen to insects newly emerged from hibernation. A single cluster of pussy willow catkins may contain an assortment of hoverflies, bees, moths, and butterflies. Later in the year the willow's fluffy seeds provide a fine lining for nests.

Not everyone in town welcomes the country invasion. Where for neighbourly harmony's sake or perhaps for other reasons the gardener wishes to present a well-groomed garden, it is still possible to help in the maintenance of wildlife. In my own 'trim' borders near the house, many kinds of native and naturalized plants grow happily with the more cultivated kinds, so easily in fact that they often have to be pointed out to visitors. A butterfly border of native plants can be both pretty and neat (see pages 50-51). It can also be supplemented by nectar-rich exotics so that it conforms to the general idea of a flower border.

The wildlife aspect of wild gardening is especially satisfying for those people who spend a good deal of time at home – young children or the elderly, as well as the infirm who may be confined for long periods.

A change of approach
New gardeners may have few problems in setting to and starting a wild garden, but more traditional gardeners like myself may need consciously to

encourage a more relaxed frame of mind. Think of it this way: if, during a normal working day, one is continually subject to a strict routine, then why impose a similar pattern on a place which has nothing to do with one's work? It certainly can be invigorating to get out the mower or hoe after a day at the office but all this energy can, with a wild garden, be channelled into more constructive rather than destructive occupations. There is always plenty to be done in creating a wild garden before you arrive at the right aesthetic and ecological balance; and if you are to attract wildlife, you must set up as many nooks, corners, shrubs, climbers and shelter belts as you can. But, while introducing native species, there is really no reason at all why you should dig up favourite cultivars which can easily fit into your scheme.

LEFT *Many garden perennials, like these lupins, will quite happily become naturalized. If they are left to seed themselves, they gradually revert to type, which of course presents no problem to the wild gardener. Umbellifers push their way into many gardens. Beautiful but invasive, they grow quite well among other plants and are most effective where they can be given an area to spread and colonize.*

ABOVE *Wild gladiolus,* Gladiolus illyricus, *a protected plant in the wild, and a near relative of the cottage garden G. byzantinus.*

A solution to poor soil

Frequently the creation of a wild garden, however romantic the term may sound, may in fact be the most practical way of dealing with a fallow piece of land. Not all houses are surrounded by a plot of best top soil. In the traditional flower garden, and certainly in a vegetable or fruit plot, the gardener often sets about altering the type and quality of the soil in order to grow favourite plants or a greater range of them, or to produce heavier yields of food crops. In wild gardening we should not be so concerned with altering the soil; rather we should be more concerned with finding plants to suit it and in maintaining its condition for as long as possible. This means that we avoid going against the grain by adding fertilizers or artificial manures, and leave it, as much as is practicable, to nature.

Do not be despondent, therefore, if your soil is poor and you cannot afford to enrich it. Many wild plants flourish best where the soil is poor. Take, for example, the management of grass in a flower meadow. When the long grass is cut it should not be allowed to lie. It should be cleared by raking and removing it from the site as soon as possible. This is because when mown grass is left to rot it is gradually incorporated into the soil below and becomes a form of organic manure which will increase the nutrient value of the soil. This will suit some plants, especially grasses, but other meadow plants will find enriched soil unsuitable and their numbers will decline. While some species die out, others, not always so welcome, are likely to appear in great numbers. (See pages 56-67 on wildflower meadows.)

Soil quality can be tested in the first year by roughly broadcasting some of the cheaper seed bought from traditional seedsmen rather than from wildflower specialists. Shirley poppies, a variety of the wild red one, and cornflowers are examples. Once it is appreciated how well these grow and how profusely they flower by this rough and ready method, the gardener is likely to be encouraged to go to a little more trouble on the same soil.

ABOVE *Dappled shade, rather than the dense canopy offered by some trees, provides ideal conditions for many plants which have handsome, long-lasting foliage. To avoid competition with any tree roots near the surface, before planting raise the area in which they are to grow.*

LEFT *Where the ground of a new garden is well covered with vegetation, wait to see what plants flower or thrive before completely clearing it.*

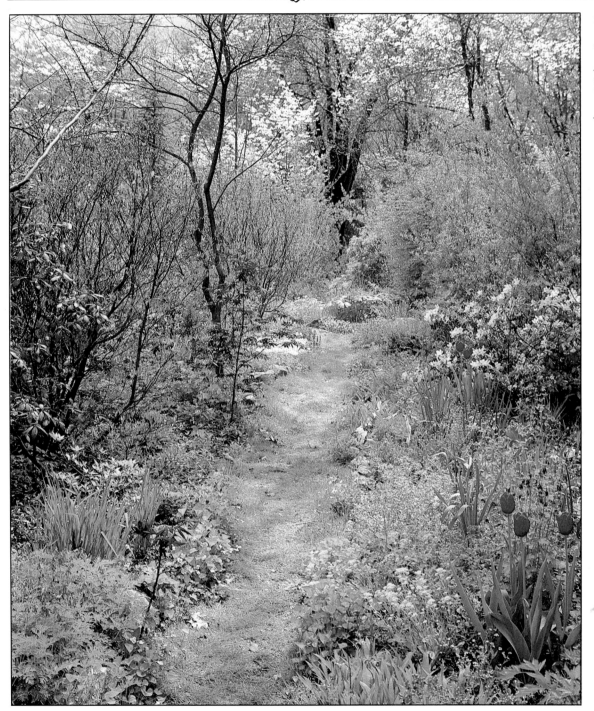

LEFT *Diversity is essential in a wild garden if there is to be year-long interest. The wider the range of plants, the more fascinating their display. Often plants currently at their peak will mask the spent forms of those which are gradually fading from the garden scene.*

ABOVE *Found in sheltered places in some gardens, the lady's slipper orchid,* Cypripedium calceolus, *is almost extinct in the wild in Britain.*

19

New ways of seeing wild plants

While some may think that a plant in seed is drab, others see beauty in its new form, texture and fecundity. Certainly a truly wild garden will never give the months-long display of floral colour expected from say, petunias and begonias. It is often possible to plant in such a way that the eye can be taken from fading spring-flowering plants and directed to those that bloom in summer or autumn. In winter, especially in frosty weather, spent stems take on a new beauty and significance, being either covered with sparkle or visited by seed-seeking birds.

Some plants will go through their annual cycle very attractively and usefully if their seeds and fruits are of value to wildlife. Others may not please the more tidy-minded gardener. Those of mine which grow alongside cultivars and other garden plants and are likely to become straggly are usually trimmed, often with pleasing or unexpected results. Red campion and toadflax, for instance, after seeding stems are cut away, will usually continue to bloom, albeit less luxuriantly, sometimes deep into winter. However, a permanently tidy or disciplined plant such as a large fern or some berried shrub will always divert attention at the critical season. Late-blooming nectar plants are also good for this purpose, plants such as *Sedum spectabile*, michaelmas daisies or golden rod, aliens it is true but all extremely attractive to late-foraging butterflies and other insects.

A garden to relax in

Conservation and sentiment apart, there is another valid reason why more people are turning to a less formal way of gardening and from there to wild gardens. House owners are not automatically skilled gardeners, and there are many people with gardens who actively dislike gardening chores but nevertheless want to have attractive plants at hand. Such people are obvious candidates for wild gardens, for upkeep can be kept to a minimum. This view may run counter to expectation, but, once set up, a wild garden can be almost self-

maintaining. And if your plot is not as tidy or well-groomed as visitors might expect a garden to look, you can always say with honesty, 'It's supposed to be wild.' Instead of censure, usually a genuine interest is aroused, especially if the gardener can then point to an interesting butterfly or nesting bird to show the benefit of non-interference.

With imagination, your garden can be transformed into a tranquil oasis, not only for wildlife, but for yourself. There are few things nicer than to relax in your own garden, and if it has a wild feel about it, you get additional satisfaction – perhaps from a shaded corner with foxgloves busily visited by bees, or from the wonderful confusion of the twining stems of hops and bryony rambling over a hedge or fence. It is easy to forget, too, just how much children like wild patches of garden to play in, where there are places in which they can hide. Perhaps many of us need this, a modern counterpart to the old medieval walled garden, with its arbours and secret places, a garden that shuts off and is a respite from the cares of the world.

ABOVE *What might be an eyesore in a neat, well-groomed plot can prove to be an asset in a wild garden. A tree stump often houses a diversity of wildlife. This one will soon be hidden from view as the fern fronds extend and as the honesty seeds itself. But why go to the trouble of cutting down a dead tree? Leave it and drape it with attractive climbers, to provide nesting and roosting sites.*

PLANNING THE WILD GARDEN

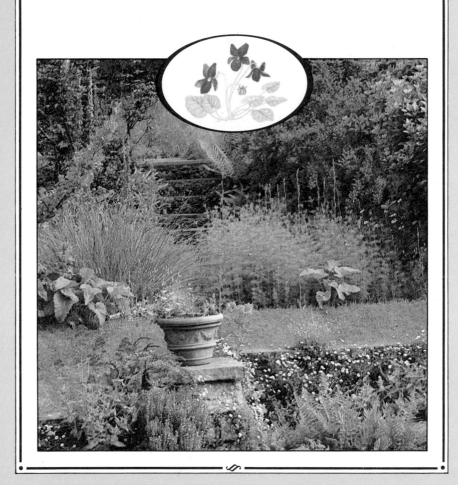

AN UNHURRIED APPROACH

The great thing to remember about creating a wild garden is that it should not be hurried. Take time. As with any garden, one is well advised to spend the first year taking stock and planning gradually. Too often, when confronted with an uncultivated building plot or an established but overrun garden, the new owner impulsively sets to work, clearing it of all vegetation that he or she considers to be ugly or that is labelled 'weeds' by popular opinion. These plants are often purposely and ruthlessly destroyed by the application of some virulent weedkiller, or a great deal of hard labour goes into eliminating them by hand. When making a wild garden, these impulses should be subdued. Many of the plants that are despised or even feared horticulturally are essential to the lives of living creatures. The stinging nettle (see page 52) is just one example. If the gardener is not familiar with wild plants it is a good plan to spend a season or two identifying those which grow spontaneously, and then checking their usefulness in both bird and insect books. If the plants prove to be unattractive visually yet are well worth saving, allow them to grow somewhere out of sight. The bramble is one example. Spread over an area it can be an unsightly nuisance, but its importance for wildlife (see page 48) means that you should try to look at it in a new light.

Similarly, if you acquire a site that has been newly cleared, whether it once sustained shrubs, trees, grass or was waste ground, wait and see what appears in the spring. Since the topsoil will have been disturbed, and especially where subsoils have been raised, there will be an upsurge of growth from seeds which have lain dormant, possibly for years. Once light and moisture reaches them, the seeds will germinate and the seedlings grow vigorously, often in great numbers.

This is why waysides where new roads have been built are often covered with scarlet poppies; their oily seeds remain viable for many years. A similar spontaneous show once happened in my own garden when we purchased an adjoining piece of land. When it was worked for the first time, the ground was smothered with a crop of corn chamomile, *Anthemis arvensis*. An unexpected show of this kind might be welcome in a new garden, for it has in it the beginnings of a flower meadow. However, not all seedlings that appear in this way are as attractive or as welcome as poppies and daisies. If you are unlucky there may be one or two dominating species only which will need to be cleared or at least drastically reduced.

If, on the other hand, the soil is very poor and unproductive, and the site has little to commend it so far as beauty and special features are concerned, consider taking a short cut. You could establish a water and waterside garden. Aquatic plants will grow rather more quickly and luxuriantly than land plants in a similar situation. Alternatively, especially where the soil is either exhausted or unresponsive, cover the area with a good layer of gravel and make a gravel garden. Surprisingly, but as all who own a gravel path or drive will know, a great variety of plants elect to grow in the medium. Purposely planned and planted as a wild garden, it can be used to great advantage. Stone could be used instead of gravel, especially if you live in an area where flat local stone abounds. Pave some areas informally, and fill the spaces with plants, which will soon spread to colour and cover the stone. See also chapters on water gardens, pages 108-113 and on rock gardens, pages 114-120.

RIGHT *The introduction of a selection of distinctive foliage and native plants into a smart town or paved garden need not lead to an untidy or unkempt appearance. Yellow-flowered corydalis in the left foreground readily grows in cracks between stones. Thyme, opposite, which will self-seed freely in pavings or gravel, scents the air and attracts butterflies and bees. The variegated flag growing in the little pond is a variety of the plain green-leaved wild type.*

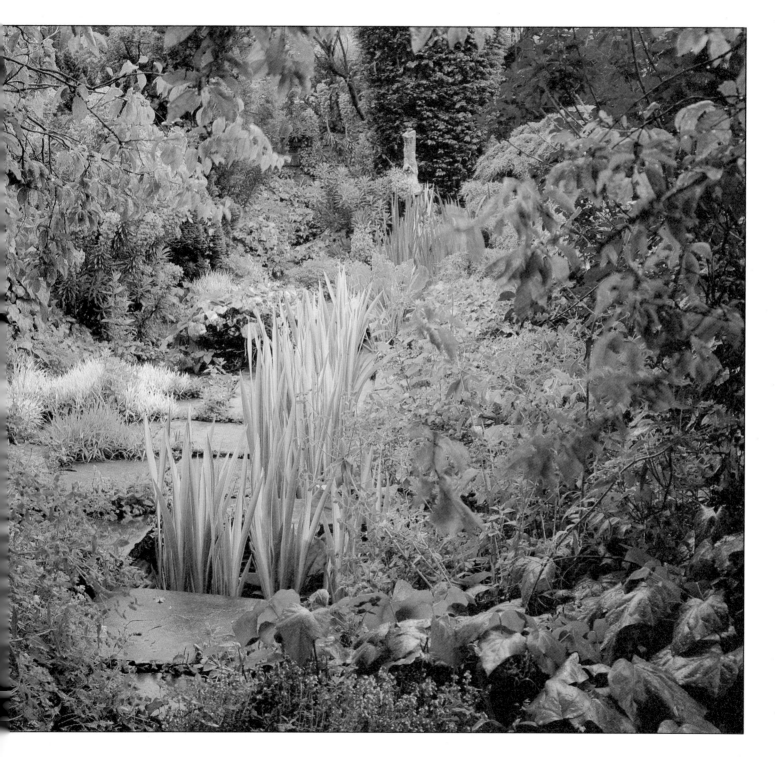

THE SITE

Besides the all-important matter of soil type (see pages 32-33), there are other site factors that you need to take into account before deciding what kinds of plants to grow and how to distribute them. These include aspect, sun and shade, wind exposure and shelter, drainage and the general lie of the land, such as whether it is flat or sloping.

A windy site offers problems. Take note of the direction of the prevailing wind. If trees grow in the vicinity, these should give a guide, for the treetops inevitably become sculpted by a strong prevailing wind. It is important to establish shelter in a windy site: in a small garden even one large shrub or a group of trees will help in this respect, and evergreens are particularly useful. Take care not to shut out the sun when you plant windbreaks and shelter screens of trees or shrubs. If this is likely to happen, plant the trees and shrubs in interrupted groups rather than a single dense line. And these trees and shrubs play more than a weather-protective role: they give birds cover and nesting sites. (See also native plants for shade, page 42.)

If you live in an area subject to frosts, try always to avoid the creation of a major hollow or valley in your landscaping. Frosts tend to roll downhill and will settle in and fill a dip in the land to create a frost pocket. With a sloping garden always try to leave a gap in fencing, walling, hedging or other boundary at the lowest point, so that the frost can continue to roll downhill rather than becoming trapped and causing damage.

Adapting a traditional garden

Where a gardener's aim is to change the nature of the existing plot and create a wild garden instead, obviously it will not be possible to start from scratch. Existing plants, particularly trees and shrubs, may have sentimental value or may deserve respect because of their age. Or, if you live in a town, there may be prohibitions on felling mature trees. But it should not be difficult, whatever their country of origin, to fit trees into your wild garden scheme. Some trees can be suitable as supports for climbing plants, and so provide a quick means to a more natural and informal scene, especially if native climbers are used.

The substitution of a native shrub or tree for an exotic species can make a remarkable difference, especially if the native is common in the locality. There is a fine range of native shrubs and trees, all of which have an important ecological role, often one which an imported species cannot understudy. On the other hand, exotic climbers may prove more effective in terms of fast growth and cover than a native species. *Clematis montana* is especially vigorous and has the bonus of masses of pink flowers in the spring.

However large or small the garden, the transition from traditional to wild can be stepped, beginning with concentrating the garden plants near the house, and then designing the rest of the garden so that you are led gently into a wild area. You can begin by introducing some natives into the borders at a point further from the house so that they grow among the exotics and the cultivars – columbines, red campion, Jacob's ladder and many campanulas.

The grass areas can follow a similar theme, that is, mown frequently near the house, a little shaggier and mown less frequently further away, perhaps embroidered with white clover for honey bees and prunella and speedwell for delight, and then on to full flower meadow (see pages 56-67), cut just twice a year. This is much the method followed in my own garden.

If there is space, a little group of shrubs and trees can be constructed, accompanied by suitable herbaceous plants, ferns perhaps, or if there is enough shade, Solomon's seal, lily-of-the-valley, forget-me-not and London pride. There are also ways of extending the wild area visually. A shrub

ABOVE *Solomon's seal,* Polygonatum multiflorum, *also known as David's harp, is a native of woodland.*

RIGHT *Where a traditional garden exists, the gardener is advised to take time over its conversion. Many of the existing plants can be left to grow alongside any native species to be brought in. Some, like the yellow potentilla in the foreground, may in fact be indigenous. Fruit or other trees can support native climbers and also be attractively underplanted with native and exotic ferns and other shade-loving plants.*

border, screen or hedge can be made to take on the semblance of the margin of a wood, where ferns and woodland plants can reach out into the more formal garden areas, fringing them discreetly.

A patch of wild garden

Where a driveway leads to a house, the land on either side could be used as a wildflower border. There is something very refreshing about turning off from a busy road to find oneself immediately among cool, leafy climbers and country flowers. Much will depend upon the width of the drive borders – there may be space for a series of levels, with trees, shrubs and ground covers. Or, the border may be wide enough only to house a colony of ferns and, say, bluebells in spring, foxgloves in summer and perhaps colchicums and cyclamen in autumn and winter.

In most gardens there is a compost heap and a utility area tucked away out of sight. Visitors' steps are usually steered away from it. If this portion was to be enlarged, it could become a wild area where the more informal plants, nettles perhaps or long grass, could be allowed to grow. It could be hidden by one or more native shrubs – a holly, blackthorn, wayfaring tree or guelder rose, growing on ivy-covered, leaf-littered ground.

Sometimes it is possible to annexe a strip of land to use as a wild plot. Often there is, or could be, a little piece of no man's land outside the garden proper, even flanking the road or pavement, perhaps at the foot of a boundary hedge, wall or fence. In my own case there is such a strip out in the lane which leads to the house, on the far side of a wall. In this overspill strip are allowed to grow a great assortment of plants, most of which were originally selected because they are the food plants of certain butterflies. These were brought from other parts of the garden and transplanted. Others, such as the garlic mustard, *Alliaria petiolata*, host among others to the orange tip butterfly, have just dropped in. Each year the range of plants increases as the native species, their seed dispersed by wind, birds or some other natural means, become established

among those that were planted. Most are welcome. Thistles, for instance, attracted masses of beautiful goldfinches one year. But one finds that borders of this kind, which are very much on view to those who visit or pass the house, may need a little more grooming than most wild plots, mainly because certain plants which find their way there are very invasive and become dominant, docks and couch grass, *Agropyron repens*, for instance.

Banks and ditches

Where a grass bank lies either outside or inside the perimeter of the garden consider whether or not it should be kept carefully mowed and groomed. Hot and sunny or cool and shady, it can prove to be a splendid habitat for a varied range of plants, and need not present an untidy appearance. A cool, shady bank can hold many of the little early-flowering spring bulbs: aconites, snowdrops, crocus, scillas; tiny wild daffodils, bluebells, fritillaries, combined with violets, primroses, self-heal and other low-growing meadow flowers.

On a sunny bank other meadow flowers will flourish, those with the shortest or sprawling stems usually being most suitable. Whether for chalk, lime or clay soils, lady's bedstraws, clustered bell-flower, cowslip, harebell, self-heal, field scabious and ox-eye daisies are examples.

A ditch, which by its very nature is likely to be moist at certain times of the year or in some cases certain times of the day, offers yet another site for improvement and exploitation. Fern-lined sides topped with carpeting, moisture-loving plants, will transform what is usually intended as a utility feature into a charming one without diminishing its purpose.

Accommodating existing garden features

A wall, particularly if it is an old one, can become a wild plantation in its own right, for it will support a wealth of plants if encouraged to do so. Such a wall garden also offers a safe haven for many forms of wildlife. A dry-stone wall can be a good setting for alpine plants and will prove to be an attractive

ABOVE *The tallest of all native bellflowers, the giant bellflower,* Campanula latifolia, *is found growing wild on hedge banks and in open woods on limestone. Its shoots may be cooked like spinach.*

and interesting feature the year through.

In the same way a hedge can be made to play a more important ecological role. If it is already a 'wild' hedge – that is, made of native plants, hawthorn or beech perhaps, it should not be difficult to transform it into a more fecund hedgerow, with many plants growing at its foot and some creepers within it. As in so many cases, the local flora is a

FROM TRADITIONAL GARDEN TO WILD

This garden is being gradually transformed from traditional to wild, and favourite exotics and garden plants mingle happily with the native species. Plants grown in tubs near the house are selected to attract butterflies and moths, and make the link from house to garden. The potted plants here are thyme, nicotiana, geranium and petunia. From the steps, you go down past the rock garden where alyssum, thrift and campanulas grow among the heathers. The lawn here is kept fairly short, with some meadow flowers grown around the edges and opposite the pond. A bird feeder is attached to an overhanging branch from the next door garden, and buddleia and lilac attract insects. From the pond area, the garden takes on a wilder aspect, with the grass becoming meadow-length and, at the end of the garden, quite long, where it offers a haven for insects and small mammals. Here also grow plants to provide food.

1 Wild Cherry, *Prunus avium*
2 Cornflower, *Centaurea cyanus*
3 Buddleia, *Escallonia macrantha*
4 Species rose, *Rosa* sp.
5 Sweet flag, *Acorus calamus*
6 Bog arum, *Calla palustris*
7 Marsh marigold, *Caltha palustris*
8 Holly, *Ilex aquifolium*
9 Smokebush, *Cotinus coggyria*
10 Russian vine, *Polygonum baldschuanium*
11 Hazel, *Corylus avelana*
12 Brambles, *Rubus* sp.
13 Lilac, *Syringa vulgaris*
14 Lawson cypress, *Chamaecyparis lawsoniana*
15 Rowan or mountain ash, *Sorbus aucuparia*
16 Foxglove, *Digitalis purpurea*
17 St John's wort, *Hypericum* sp.
18 Crab apple, *Malus pumila*
19 Nettles, *Lamium* sp.

good guide to what to grow, but it is also pleasing to introduce some species which are not so common, perhaps violets, primroses, ground ivy for early spring, creeping jenny for summer, tall hedge garlic and honesty for butterflies. Ferns and periwinkles will provide an evergreen mixture.

If there is an existing hedge of some garden shrub – conifers, privet or lonicera – it can be embroidered and at the same time recharged by introducing a few native plants here and there along its length. (See page 137 for planting a native hedgerow.) My own gappy hedge, consisting largely of elderberry, is gradually being thickened with little seedlings of hawthorn and holly found growing in the garden from seed obviously dispersed by birds. Alternatively, introduce climbers: the two bryony species, white and black, which produce attractive berries and handsome foliage, vine-like hops or, so long as the soil is not acid, clematis. Ivy, which seems willing to grow in any kind of soil, when encouraged to climb and mingle will prettily decorate a hedge. Where it is practical, the hedge can support larger climbers, wild roses or blackberries for instance.

Enhancing the site
Artificial mounds and banks, apart from adding interest to a flat site, offer good shelter. Even a metre's height will provide a surprising amount of protection and, well-planted, can become an attractive feature. In my own garden, which is very exposed and flat, occasional mounds and banks have been made here and there to give shelter from the cold north and east, the latter because certain early-flowering plants need shielding from the morning sun following frosts (a precaution not so vital where native plants rather than slightly tender exotics are concerned). A bank gives plants a deep root-hold, which means that tall plants as well as shorter, close-carpeting kinds can be grown on it. Plants can 'borrow' height this way. A metre-high bank, for instance, will 'lift' a plant considerably, giving it greater importance in the landscape. Thickly planted with shrubs, some

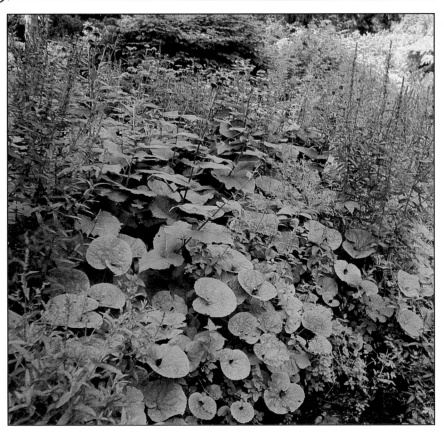

evergreen, a bank makes an effective windbreak.

For the gardener who is growing native plants, a long mound running east-west offers two useful sites. One is in full sun and the other in shade. If such a bank can also be situated where it can give shelter, the benefits are manifold. The north face need not offer any problems. There are many plants for such a site: periwinkle, ivy and ferns will keep it green all winter, hellebore and snowdrops will pattern it with flowers in spring, while a great number of little flowering plants which enjoy cool, shady conditions, such as creeping jenny, bugle, celandine, and cuckoo flower, will carpet the floor and produce blooms in spring and summer. (See also page 99 and page 125.)

Sometimes, where there is the space and the setting, the bank can be cut away to make a little

ABOVE *Both natural and artificial banks can be clothed attractively whether they lie in sun or shade. Where the shade and the root soil are both deep, some of the moisture-loving plants, such as the tall purple* Lythrum *seen here, will grow luxuriantly and will mingle with shade-loving kinds. Where there exists plenty of cover, a bank offers a good home for fauna as well as flora.*

cliff, a backdrop for certain plants to grow at its foot, or in little bays cut into its face. When planting a bank, whether it is steep or not, always begin at the top and work towards the bottom.

More plants can be grown on a terraced slope than on one which is simply steep and they can be grown much more attractively. Many will spill over prettily to the lower levels while some will grow in the crevices of whatever materials are used to support the terraces. These can be rock, peat blocks which are ideal for acid soils, tree trunks or boughs and turves. All of these have been used at some time or another in my own garden. Freshly dug turves are turned upside down so that the grass part is buried and set in place, first in a row, straight or curving, and then one over the other in the same way as bricks are laid. Soil is then brought level with the root portion of the turf and the terrace planted as soon as possible. The grass gradually rots but the turves stay intact for a long period, long enough for roots of other plants to grow into them and to hold. (See also page 125 for the peat block method of supporting a terrace.)

A very steep slope can be covered with spreading plants, rather than be closely planted. The exotic *Cotoneaster horizontalis* set at the foot will lean close to the surface as it grows upwards. This plant also bears blossom attractive to bees, berries for birds, dense foliage and useful nesting sites.

The creeping willow, *Salix repens*, can be planted at the top of a slope and will gradually extend its prostrate stems over the summit and will cascade down the slope, meeting and merging with plants from below. Other climbing or carpeting plants can also be used to the same effect (see pages 38-40).

ABOVE *The cuckoo flower,* Cardamine pratensis, *is a plant of damp meadows yet it often grows in great drifts of colour along country road-sides.*

LEFT *Columbines, cranesbills and sweet cicely provide a succession of flowers among the diverse leaves which cover this bank so attractively. Perennial plants ensure that the display is continual and those flowers which seed freely such as the columbine, ensure that the mixture is constantly rejuvenated. Some plants, and these are examples, accept almost any aspect – shady, semi-shady or sunny.*

Paths in the wild garden

Pathways once established are difficult to eradicate and therefore the gardener is advised to proceed with caution before deciding the course a path should take. Walk around your plot to get a feel as to where your proposed pathways should be set. It may take months, even the four seasons to decide upon the position, the nature and indeed the role of the path.

Quite often once a pathway has been planned it is best to use the materials at hand. A simple natural panning of the surface may suffice, as in a woodland, where the fallen leaves are trodden and flattened. Suggestions for more permanent paths suitable for the wild garden are on page 128.

There are few gardens which do not yield a crop of stones, uncovered as the gardener plants or cultivates the ground. These can be used as path foundations or surfaces, in the sure knowledge that the material is local and is likely to be in harmony with the setting. Shingle and other small loose stones and gravel make admirable surfaces. Although some of these may look new and even garish when first applied, they soon settle down.

A sunken path can add to the charm and interest of a wild garden. It could become a little dell, enchanting when passing through a rock or alpine area. In a woodland garden one can make a path which runs below the general level of the ground in much the same manner as an old woodland track, its soft border mulched naturally by annual leaf fall. Sides of sunken paths, well drained and warm, provide ideal conditions for certain flowering and leafy plants and ferns.

Where possible, the path should wind in such a way as to direct one's steps to places or plants of interest, or to points where the garden or the surrounding landscape can be seen from an advantageous or unfamiliar angle. Paths which lead to some hidden, secluded or unexpected feature of great interest, give the garden charm and an element of mystery.

For those who are making a meadow or orchard flower garden, one of the simplest of all paths is a passage made by a mower, its width being the same or perhaps double that of the swathe cut by the machine. This kind of path is also practical because it is so much more pleasant to walk in short grass after heavy rain or dews than to try to pass through long grass. Such a path, sometimes called a 'ride', needs to be mown fairly regularly.

One way of softening paved paths is to allow certain plants to grow between the stones. Low-growing and creeping plants are best, although once the gardener no longer keeps these paved areas immaculately weed-free, a surprising range of self-sown plants will appear. To crowd out any

BELOW *Grass, ferns and ground cover plants growing at the edge of a woodland path will help define its shape and direction. If these are trailing or creeping kinds, they will need cutting back from time to time so that they do not cover the surface. It is wise to keep pathways narrow. Foot traffic is often then sufficient to keep the surface clear without the need to hoe it clean or to use chemical weedkillers. Plants growing on a path can make it slippery.*

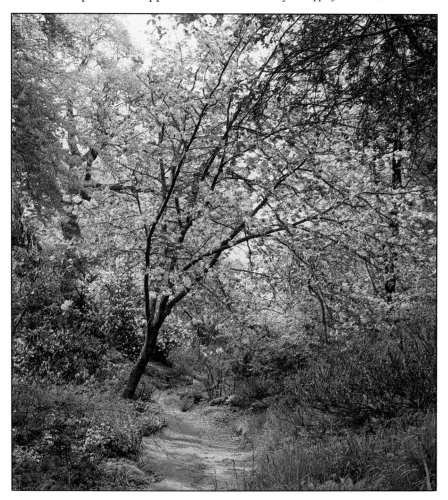

unwanted weeds, sow seeds of your own choosing between the cracks of larger stones. Where they are smaller, remove a paving stone here and there, plant that area and allow the plant to establish its own colony. Several varieties of thyme are ideal for this purpose and have the advantage of smelling sweetly when trodden upon. Shaded paths can be planted with wood avens, periwinkles and bugle.

Guard against making a path too wide, at least in the early stages of creating the garden. This is particularly important when a path runs through a woodland or bushy area. If kept narrow enough, foot traffic alone should keep the path clean.

Beware, too, of raised paths, even an inch or two above the level of the surrounding ground. These can prove hazardous to the very young and the elderly. The same applies to shady paths covered with moss which can prove extremely slippery.

A MEANDERING PATH

Points of interest in a garden can be emphasized by a winding path. From the terrace before the house, a gravel path runs between a low hedge 1 and a border of herbs 2, before entering a small copse 3. The path then opens out for a sitting area by the pond 4, and then continues past a meadow area 5. It leads back to the house as short cut grass, passing a border planned to attract butterflies 6.

ABOVE *A delightful plant for bordering a path in a wild garden is the Welsh poppy, Meconopsis cambrica. A cheerful yellow colour, it grows well in either sun or shade, and flowers all summer long. It seeds itself freely, even in the dry cracks between paving stones, and helps the path blend in to the informal setting of the wild garden.*

SOIL TYPES

Those who are hoping to create a wild garden need to understand that much of the advice given for dealing with soils in traditional gardening practice is not of great value or consequence to them. Sometimes, a little soil alteration may result in being able to grow a great number of species and so may be justified, but on the whole, since wild gardening is also intended in the main to be trouble-free gardening, the principle should be to go along with whatever soil exists rather than try to change it.

In the landmass of Europe, a limestone subsoil predominates and where this occurs it influences the soils which lie upon it and, therefore, the wild flora and the kinds of cultivated plants that can most easily be grown. In North America the reverse is true and acid soils predominate, so we find that many of the continent's indigenous plants, favourite garden plants in other parts of the world, are mostly what are known as calcifuges, lime-haters.

Acid soils

Acid soils are not all of the same type. Some may be peaty, others so rich in decayed organic materials that they are almost so. Some may be sandy, some clayey and heavy. Some may be very dry or liable to become so under certain circumstances, some moist and even boggy. Sometimes a part of a cultivated garden which has been generously and continuously mulched with organic manures and composts may have become acid. Simple soil testing (see page 122) will reveal this condition.

Acid soils offer the gardener the opportunity to grow a wonderful range of native plants, for many of the rarest and most beautiful subjects grow on this type of soil, although some need particular habitats prepared for them. On very acid soil, a plot could be made to support a miniature heath (see pages 78-85). Acid soil can also support a special kind of woodland, the plants of which are quite unlike those found in woods on limy soils.

Alkaline soils

Contrary to widespread belief, it is possible to make a garden on chalk. Certainly it offers problems but one should keep in mind that some of the most treasured European wildflowers grow on chalk and also that chalk is not so very far removed from limestone. The latter has an abundance of

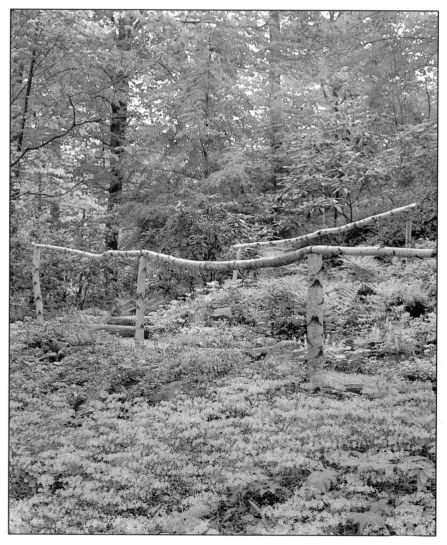

BELOW *Garden rhododendrons confirm that soil is acid here. The lovely little* Phlox divaricata, *from north-east America, has creeping rhizomatic roots which aid it in carpeting the ground, a characteristic of many plants favouring acid soils.*

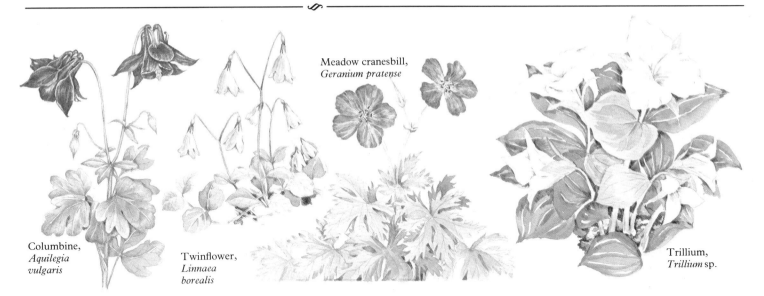

Columbine,
*Aquilegia
vulgaris*

Twinflower,
*Linnaea
borealis*

Meadow cranesbill,
Geranium pratense

Trillium,
Trillium sp.

inorganic material within it, while chalk is either lacking or very poor in other content. However, although gardens on chalk have a very shallow top-soil, they can support a variety of plants.

In the wild, on a base of limestone rock, plant material accumulates over a period of many years, producing a layer of acid humus. Despite the lime beneath and if the layer is deep enough, some calcifuges will grow, the crowberry, *Empetrum nigrum,* for example. This natural phenomenon can be simulated in rock gardens where the gardener wishes to grow many diverse species of similar habit but differing soil requirements.

Neutral or mixed soils

Where gardens exist on neutral soil, that is one which is neither acid nor alkaline, often many species of plants preferring both soil types will flourish. Some plants are very adaptable, for example, in my own garden, herb robert grows freely in every part of the garden – in alkaline un-cultivated ground, in well-fed borders alongside cultivars, in the well-manured vegetable patch and on the acid peat mound.

When calcifuges are to be grown on neutral soil they will grow better for a little assistance, and there is no contradiction in importing extra peat to increase the soil's acidity.

Woodland soils

The soil beneath trees and shrubs is bound to be influenced by the spent leaves which fall upon it. If this soil is of poor quality, that can be an advantage so long as the plants are given some help at planting time (see pages 134-5). Where trees have been standing for a long period, as in a natural wood, the leaf layer may be very deep and each year's layer will be in a different condition from the one above or below. The state and even the rate of decomposition varies according to the type of trees contributing to the leaf layer.

Woodland plants are adapted to grow in this loose, leafy litter. Many of them (for example the wood anemone) have creeping stems or rhizomes, which can not only store up food but work their way through the litter grasping what small particles of leaf soil they can find for sustenance, thus spreading the plant further and further afield.

Where the gardener hopes to introduce some woodland or woodland plants, it is necessary to establish woodland soil. Import leafmould for planting and mix with good soil compost.

ABOVE *Although a remarkable number of plants will grow quite happily on ordinary or neutral soil in the garden, in the wild they tend to appear only on specific types. For instance, the four wildflowers shown here all have different tastes, the meadow cranesbill preferring clay, the lovely twinflower the acid soils of pinewoods, the North American trillium, or wake-robin, a well-drained, humusy woodland soil, and the columbine, lime. By identi-fying the wild flora around you (or the garden plants in the neighbourhood), it should be possible to gain a general idea of your local soil.*

33

WHAT TO GROW

New wild gardeners would be wise to realize that a bluebell-carpeted woodland, or a spacious heather garden, or a waterfall and babbling brook plus their attendant plants are not transformations that can be achieved instantly – at least, not without the expenditure of a considerable fortune. Even if the necessary time and labour were expended, and the appropriate plants carefully installed, the picture would hardly look natural, let alone wild, for several seasons however much care was taken over random planting and natural curves. Nature works relatively slowly. The changes in our own garden have been gradual, but the gardener can hurry nature along.

In the wild, plants form colonies naturally, often growing in such numbers that they make drifts of colour and areas of different textures, perhaps among grass or in the shade beneath trees. Where one or two plants of the same species already exist in a garden, it is often worth propagating more to add to the group. Where the gardener hopes to establish a colony of plants from scratch, they have a better chance of survival if all the plants available are grouped fairly thickly in one patch; when you distribute individual plants widely over a larger area, the colony is likely to become invaded by a stronger, unwanted species (see page 44). Do not zone the plants too thickly, however; allow one species to merge into another at the edge of the group – even if the neighbour is grass. Left to go their own way, plants will usually do this, but you have to give new plants you are introducing a fighting chance.

Don't hesitate to plant thickly. In the wild most plants jostle each other. Often in many gardens one finds that the ground tends to become closely covered in spring when a great variety of little flowering bulbous plants colonize the sites under or between shrubs and trees and then once these have faded becomes bare for the rest of the year. These early flowering plants seldom object to

other kinds growing above them. Their flowers will push their way up through the foliage of such plants as thymes, heathers, creeping jenny, ivy or the seedlings of biennials such as foxgloves which bloom much later on. They also have the effect of masking any untidy phase in those which have bloomed earlier.

If the gardener wishes to grow established garden plants among the wild ones, they will mingle better if the garden plants are species rather than varieties or cultivars. Most varieties are a part of man's work, although some do occur in nature. All species are wild plants somewhere. Usually species mingle with species attractively, even when their countries of origin are far apart. It is fortunate, for those who admire diversity in plants, that the species from one type of terrain in

RIGHT *The thicker the plants are allowed to grow, the more quickly the wild garden takes shape. Some, like the yellow Welsh poppies at the centre, and many umbellifers such as the fennel in the foreground, will prove ubiquitous, gradually moving to other places about the garden. Usually where they choose to grow they look most at home.*

BELOW *To create a wild look in some part of the garden, allow some of the 'weeds' to grow unchecked. It helps conserve many forms of wildlife if the grass grows long right up against shrubs and trees.*

one country will, so long as the climate suits, usually grow quite well in the appropriate soil of another. This means that a plant species from North America, such as dog's tooth violet, is likely to settle down in northern Europe, and, happily, migration of plants in the opposite direction is also possible. Some species are extremely adaptable, such as those of many of the poppy family, and all those plants that have 'escaped' into the wild.

If you hope to sow seed of native species, it is possible to find many of them simply by going carefully through a good seedsman's lists and looking for species rather than varieties. For instance, among the pinks in one leading firm's list of 'garden plants', you can find *Dianthus gratianopolitanus*, the rare Cheddar pink. By searching under other flower names you will find more native species. However, certain firms (see page 168) now concentrate on supplying wildflower seed only, and the number of species listed grows every year.

At the time of writing there are 62 plants in the UK which are so rare in the wild that picking them, and even collecting seed from them, has been made an offence punishable on conviction by a maximum fine of £500 a plant. A list of these plants is on page 160. Another 317 species are endangered, threatened or rare in the British Isles, and seed from these plants should not be collected. At the same time, under a different Act, it is an offence for anyone without the permission of the owner or occupier to dig up any wild plant, although this does not prevent seed collection. Since it is obviously difficult for most people to keep nearly 400 species in mind, and since there are merchants offering 'safe' seed of most of these species, it is best to buy from them.

Trees and shrubs

It is possible to buy fairly mature trees and shrubs. Even just three or four, set well apart, will give both shelter and cohesion to smaller specimens planted between them. Evergreens are good furnishers.

Choose plants which produce significant blossom to attract bees and other insects, followed by

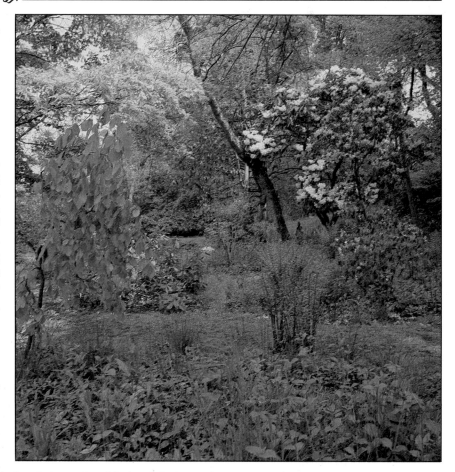

berries or other kinds of fruits such as mountain ash, *Sorbus aucuparia*, wild cherry, *Prunus avium* and hawthorn, *Crataegus monogyna*. The neat *Amelanchier canadensis*, the American shadbush, known in Britain as the snowy mespilus, prettily coloured in autumn, produces little fruits much appreciated by blackbirds.

Of a lesser height than any of these, plant sloes for the first white starry blossom, hazel and sallow for early catkins and a wild or species rose to add to the variety of blossom and fruit.

We found that it was well worth planting some trees as seedlings, and 25 years later these are now some of the tallest specimens in the locality. Trees and shrubs planted as more mature specimens

ABOVE *On acid soils, where rhododendron species and varieties provide colour mass, native shrubs and trees planted among and below them will both soften their effect and provide more suitable plants for the conservation of wildlife. Deciduous species will cast the dappled shade enjoyed by many herbaceous flowering plants and ferns in summer and, before their leaves develop in the spring, will allow in the daylight essential for spring flowers.*

LEFT *The handsome, hardy, European spurge,* Euphorbia wulfenii *(also known as E. veneta), visually dominates a great many other plants, most of which, like the spurge, will furnish this garden space for most of the year.* Corydalis, *ivy in variety, cotoneaster and several different conifers mingle closely with one another. On the wall is growing the ivy-leaved toadflax, a little long-naturalized plant.*

ABOVE *Often found on wasteland, mullein,* Verbascum thapsus, *grows to 2m/6ft 6in. There are many beautiful species and varieties.*

seemed to stay fairly static for a year or two, after which they began to race away.

Creating close-knit communities

The secret of creating a permanent impression is to plant closely, to cover every inch of ground, which, after all, is what wild plants do. Use grass to act as a stand in, if needed, while other plants are being collected.

In one of my own fairly shaded borders topped by a giant walnut and shorter hawthorns, liquid-ambar, buddleia and buckthorn, sweet scented woodruff is allowed to spread where it will, sharing the ground as it emerges in the early spring with daffodils and other bulb plants, followed by bien-nial, self-seeding forget-me-nots and the much taller sweet rocket, and then later by foxgloves and the autumn colchicums.

In other places I rely on woodspurge which so readily fills any empty spaces. In the area below three old lilac trees this plant merges agreeably with a low-growing, winter-flowering evergreen, the exotic *Mahonia aquifolium*. This is an excellent under tree plant thriving where most others fail. One quality which endears it to me is that its thickly clustered, honey-scented yellow blooms are there ready for the first foraging bees, butter-flies and others. For guidance on other species to plant below and between trees, see the chapter on woodland gardens, pages 68-77.

Ground cover and carpeting plants

If the soil and site suits them, so many plants will spread over the ground covering it attractively and at the same time keeping other plants at bay. Bugle, a fast-growing perennial with blue flowers in early summer, throws out creeping growths and soon covers a wide area. It is a good plant for sites in deep, moist shade, although it will also furnish the ground at the fringes of trees and shrub groups. On light, calcareous soils in the wild it is often associated with the yellow archangel, *Lamium galeobdolon*, otherwise known as the yellow dead nettle, a charming and endearing plant which will soon make itself at home in the wild garden.

An unusual little violet with deep purple leaves as well as flowers, *Viola labradorica*, which likes a reasonably damp and shady spot will quickly colonize itself. In my own garden it has even left the shade and settles down among the rose bushes in what should be a formal bed.

Periwinkles, the lesser *Vinca minor* and the greater *V. major*, are ideal carpeters even for large areas and for shady banks. They provide a good dense cover for wildlife also. These two have produced many varieties which differ in leaf and flower colour from the types.

A species which birds sow in my garden is the woody nightshade or bittersweet, *Solanum dulcamara*. Although this plant is described as a climber it also trails and creeps over the ground attractively, covering the soil with trails of angular leafy stems bearing clusters of purple flowers followed by bright red shining berries.

It is worth remembering that other climbers, such as honeysuckle and wild clematis, can be used to trail over and carpet the ground.

Self-propagating natives

Most annual and biennial plants will, once established, and so long as they are not dead-headed, set seed and reproduce themselves freely. In filling the space around the parent plant, the seedlings will grow to create an attractive ground cover – although this might threaten neighbouring plants. If so,

restrict the new growth early. My own method is to decide how much space can be spared for a single species, take out the weaker seedlings and then to leave the new plants alone, and not, as one would do for a traditional garden, thin them out. This propensity of some plants for self-seeding can be very helpful to the new gardener who must begin with only a few specimens, for, where the parent plants are initially spaced a good distance apart, by dropping their seed the following autumn, the spaces in between will be filled by the next year.

In my own garden, red campion insists on growing among cultivars in a mixed border. It does look well there, but, since it is a woodland plant, it follows that I should transfer some seedlings to where bluebells and other field layer species grow. In another place the little St John's wort, *Hypericum perforatum* (syn. *H. vulgare*) grows so freely

ABOVE *Few plants offer more flowers to the square inch than the carpeting and mat-forming thymes. They are very versatile and spread freely, revelling in light, well-drained soil and sunshine. They can be used to top a wall, cover rocks, fill cracks between pavings, carpet floor between heathers, soften gravel, and even be used for a pungent-scented lawn. The native thyme,* Thymus drucei, *has produced a great many varieties with white, rose, crimson, mauve and purple flowers.*

that it has led me to search for other hypericums, both native and exotic. One of these. the berry-bearing tutsan, *H. androsaemum*, favoured by birds, now freely seeds itself in many places.

Several native species will seed freely between paving stones or along paths, such as the welsh poppy, herb robert, speedwell, sweet marjoram, forget-me-not and violets.

Not all plants depend upon seed to multiply. Some have creeping rootstocks. The lily-of-the-valley, for instance, makes its way across a piece of ground by way of a thick underground stem which produces two new leaves each year a little further from the point of origin. Such stems are known as rhizomes. Rhizomatous plants include the garlic-scented ramsons, herb paris, Solomon's seal and wood anemone.

Others employ quite different methods. The rare yellow star of Bethlehem, *Gagea sylvatica*, can reproduce itself vegetatively by means of tiny

ABOVE *The red campion,* Melandrium rubrum, *growing with flag irises here, has long been accepted as a garden plant, especially in its double form. In the wild it also favours mixed company, often mingling with bluebells and purple orchids. It makes itself very much at home in gardens in wooded areas. There, and in the wild, it frequently crosses with the white campion,* M. album, *to produce a hybrid known as* M. x dubium, *with pink flowers. The white campion also produces a double form which, like that of the red, does not come true from seed.*

RIGHT *Low-growing plants can be encouraged, or allowed to increase, so that they carpet the ground. A most attractive effect is created if several different types are grown. Gradually each little colony will contrast and complement the other, often merging prettily, a tendency demon-strated by this pretty little phlox, an American species,* Phlox stolonifera, *which as its specific name explains, has its own method of propagation.*

bulbils which it produces in the axils of its leaves. These can be sown like seed, for when they fall to the soil plants are produced from them.

Besides seeding freely, blackberries reproduce themselves by stolons. When the tip of an arching stem touches the soil it will make and take root. This explains how a bramble bush, if allowed, will in time become a great mass of growth, simply because the outer curving branches root into the soil and so spread the plant. These rooted branches can be detached from the parent plant and used as individuals and transplanted elsewhere.

Climbers

In the wild, climbing plants use trees as support, most species growing happily one with another. In order to make the most of every bit of space, and to populate the plot with as many plant species as possible, one may profitably follow the same theme in the wild garden. In the garden, however, the plant associations can be by design rather than by accident.

The sweet-smelling wild honeysuckle, attractive to some butterflies and moths, is often as much in evidence in wild hedgerows as it is in woods. It is a good plant to choose for clothing deciduous trees or to soften a formal hedge made perhaps of a single species, but it also looks well in holly. Wild roses and hops are also good choices for clothing hedges, and the yellow-leaved variety of hop looks most handsome when seen against dark leaves – try growing it against a purple-leaved hazel.

The native *Clematis vitalba*, traveller's joy, is a grand climber for soils on lime or chalk, given a little initial help. Its long, fairly weak stems become entwined one around the other, gradually thickening and toughening. If either this clematis or any of the sturdy exotic species of clematis are to be grown against a tree, be sure to select a tall, sturdy specimen as host for small trees and shrubs may soon become smothered. Given height, clematis really can climb, even to a height of 15m/50ft – they will live for 50 years, too. These plants may need help in their early days for they do not climb

by using their tendrils or by twining their stems around a support, but by curling their leaf stems quite tightly around whatever they might happen to meet – even stems or leaves of their own plant. The weight of stem on stem will often pull the plant mass to the ground. Try fixing a cylinder of wire netting, 1m/3ft high, close around the base of the tree or subject being climbed, to encourage the stems to grow upwards. There are a few exotic species which could be used in partial shade, such as the violet-blue Chinese *C. macropetala* and *C. tangutica*, with flowers a pale or deep yellow colour, and the fragrant mediterranean *C. flammula*.

The two kinds of bryony both have handsome leaves, the black bryony's being heart-shaped and highly glossed, as are its berries. These are particularly beautiful, changing from green through an analogous colour range to bright red, their clusters thickly studding the twining stems like enamelled beads.

Once again some exotics can play a part. For instance, many grape vines will assume beautiful hues in the fall, such as Virginia creeper and its near relatives. All combine especially well with the Russian vine, *Polygonum baldschuanicum*, so that

ABOVE *The lovely native dog rose is very variable and has produced other forms with flowers richer in hue, larger in size, even stronger in scent than the type. These and other single-petalled rose species, including climbers, fit beautifully into many wild gardens. Most also provide handsome fruits, the rose hips, which are not only decorative in themselves but rich enough in flesh and seed to attract many wild creatures.*

Field rose,
R. arvensis

Burnet rose,
R. pimpinellifolia

Sweetbriar,
Rosa rubiginosa

Downy rose,
R. tomentosa

Dog rose,
R. canina

foamy white flowers contrast with flaming foliage. Any of these can be used to drape a tall tree. Consider them also for a fence so that for a while at least it resembles a living leafy structure rather than a static artefact.

Roses

Fortunately, rose species abound in the wild in the northern hemisphere; in Britain alone there are a dozen or so species, many of which have produced varieties. The lovely dog rose, *Rosa canina*, with its exquisitely formed buds, once so very common in hedgerows, is a must for a wild garden. However, it is very variable, with blooms coloured from rose to white. Some plants found growing in the wild produce blooms much deeper in colour or a fragrance much stronger than their neighbours'.

Where one species of wild rose grows, it is likely that some of the other native species would thrive. All of them are to be valued not only for their flowers but for their hips (or heps), which can be very showy. The hips of *Rosa villosa*, the apple rose, are round and rich in colour; the blooms are a deep rose pink. The pretty little creamy white field rose, *R. arvensis*, has small red hips and

purple stems. This species will grow in shade. The burnet rose, *R. pimpinellifolia*, grows near the sea, while the sweet briar, *R. rubiginosa*, which prefers calcareous soils, has deliciously scented leaves and lovely pink blooms, followed by round hips. The downy rose, *R. tomentosa*, will grow on chalk.

Most people want roses in a garden, and roses of one type or another appear to be tolerant enough to grow almost anywhere. However, not all rose varieties, for example hybrid teas or floribundas, would be acceptable in a wild garden. On the other hand, a species rose (single not double petalled), even an exotic, is likely to look quite at home. A plant of *Rosa rugosa*, originally from Japan and China, is in one of my own wild patches. Twenty years old, it is now several feet in diameter and grows happily enough nestled close to a frame of native shrubs and trees.

Obviously, where a traditional garden is being converted to a wild garden, and rose varieties or hybrids already exist, compromises will have to be made. One ploy is simply to leave them unpruned, treating them as shrub roses. I have tried this with a traditional bed of modern varieties, simply tidying the bushes in the spring.

WILD ROSES
The ubiquity of Rosa canina *indicates that it accepts ordinary soil and can adapt itself to slight variations. The other species shown here are more specific in their soil requirements.* R. tomentosa *is found growing on chalk;* R. rubiginosa *on chalk or limy soils;* R. pimpinellifolia *on dunes and sandy heaths, while the trailing* R. arvensis *prefers the humus-rich soil of shady wood margins and hedgerows.*

Planting for shade

Shade is mostly an asset in a wild garden although some trees form such a dense canopy of foliage that they block out daylight from the ground below sufficiently to allow only a few species of plants, mostly early-flowering kinds, to grow freely. A greater diversity of plants, such as columbines, foxgloves and lilies, can be grown on the margins or at the limits of shade.

Deciduous trees cast the densest shade in summer, some, beech for instance, much more than others. Under such a canopy, it may be necessary to concentrate on planting those species that reach their peak in autumn when the leaves are thinning or in spring before they open. Many of these are bulbous types, the classic example being the bluebell.

Where a border of lower growing plants is to be made at the margin of a wood or near a tree or trees and shrubs, the outer edge of the border can be made to follow the line of shadow cast at mid-day. This ensures that all the plants in the border will be shaded for some time each day. Also, if a mown path through a meadow adjoining trees is made to follow this line of midday shadow it will appear much more inviting during the sunniest and hottest periods of the day.

A deep canopy of leaves may keep the ground below fairly dry, but plants growing near the edges of the trees' spread may be subjected to heavy drip during rainy periods. Not all plants tolerate this. One reason why the exotic hosta or plantain lily was so often to be seen in romantic gardens is because it is very tolerant of drip.

Planting for colour

Colour in a wild garden may be more subdued than that of, say, park bedding schemes, and certainly the flowering period of individuals will not be so long as that of the seedsmen's hybrid annuals. Even so, colour displays can be planned. One way is to allow some plants to occupy a good area of ground and so create sizeable drifts of colour; there is more on this subject in the chapter on meadow gardens, pages 56-67. It is also possible to plan little patches of seasonal colour so that one species follows another in bloom.

Having enjoyed through the winter the red and green of holly, the swathes of red bryony berries in the hedgerow, the orange berry-filled seed pods of the gladden iris, and the ever-present rosy hues of winter-flowering heathers, I look forward to the first aconites planted in little patches here and there, the little wild daffodils now colonizing a bank and grass, the bluebells and cuckoo flowers

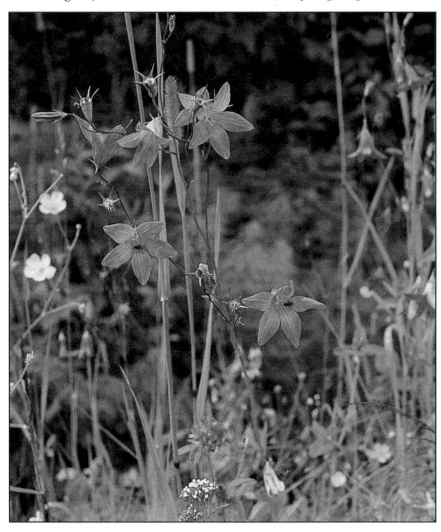

BELOW *Found growing wild in only a few localities in England and Wales, the spreading bell flower,* Campanulata patula, *which grows up to 1m/3ft, is found in herbaceous borders in many gardens. A biennial plant preferring shady places to open, sunny ones, it flowers in late summer in Britain, often continuing until the autumn. In the wild it is more commonly found growing in or near woods.*

under the copper beech, the germander speedwell in the paving and the red campion in the border. But the year really begins with snowdrops. They spread and appear everywhere, but in my garden in one place they are part of a plan to give contrast of colour, form and texture. They cover the ground below a dogwood, *Cornus sanguinea*, a species that has dark red stems which in spring, while they are still bare, become a brighter hue. Rising up from a carpet of white flowers with a thicket of silver-white honesty seed stems in the background, this plant is seen to great advantage. Willows also have good coloured barks, conspicuous in winter.

Another dogwood, *Cornus mas*, flowers in early spring and presents a mass of tiny yellow flowers. Beneath it grows a carpet of primroses and violets. See also fine foliage, page 94.

For those who enjoy really flamboyant colour in plants, none perhaps can excel the acid-loving rhododendron or eucryphias in splendour. However, few individual flowers are more gorgeous than paeonies, easily grown plants that prefer soil with lime content and are tolerant of either sun or shade. One, *Paeonia mascula*, has become naturalized on Steepholme, a little island in the Bristol Channel where it was brought by monks for medicinal use in the Middle Ages. Other members of the same family are equally tolerant. In my own garden a seedling of the beautiful yellow-flowered *Paeonia lutea* is now a quarter of a century old and some 2m/6ft 6in high and as broad.

The South American fuchsia species such as *Fuchsia magellanica* have naturalized themselves in parts of Ireland and other parts of Britain, where they are often used as hedge plants. They will thrive in ordinary soil if it is deep and rich.

Statuesque plants

Few of my wild garden plants give as much pleasure as the foxgloves, most of which by pure accident are of the white variety, plants so sophisticated in appearance that to call them 'wild' seems impertinent. Beginning with just half a dozen plants, the garden now holds several colonies of

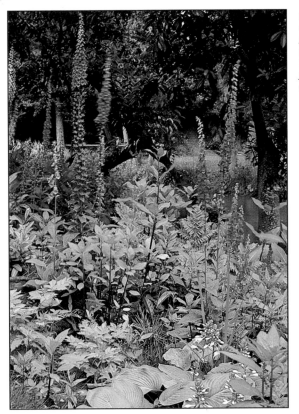

them, for they seed freely. A large foxglove may produce a million seeds of which only a minute quantity grows into plants. Tall spicate shapes of this kind – monkshood and mullein are two others – bring a more stately quality to a wild landscape, especially if they are set in showy groups rather than just one or two plants spaced about the place. If possible, grow them with a plant with flowers in a contrasting form, angelica for instance. In some ways sweet cicely is preferable to angelica, which can be choosy about soils and positions, preferring a moderately damp situation.

Plant shapes are important in a landscape, especially in a small garden. The thistle, which has both beauty and architectural value, can be used to good effect. The towering cotton thistle, *Onopordon acanthium,* with its woolly-covered leaves and stems, is a handsome addition to any garden.

LEFT *A variety of leaf shapes add beauty to areas in a wild garden, one reason why the exotic hostas are so popular. The foxglove like most spicate flowers provides a contrast of shape.*

ABOVE *Sweet cicely,* Myrrhis odorata, *grows to 1.5m/5ft high. Its leaves smell of liquorice.*

CREATING A NATURAL GARDEN

From time to time, especially when they are not in competition with other plants, some species grow too exuberantly and will need to be subject to some measure of control (see page 138). An isolated country gardener can be fairly uninhibited in his or her choice of plants, but even here it may be necessary to consider farmer neighbours who may not particularly relish a plot within their area where plants such as dandelions and thistles are allowed to seed unchecked. In such cases some balance should obviously be sought. Problems arise mainly where one species of plant is allowed to dominate, but where the plant population is very mixed, troubles of this kind are not so likely to arise.

Many plants, for example, germander speedwell, soapwort, white deadnettle and toadflax, can be kept under control by cutting away the seed stems before they become mature and forking up the roots or smothering them by using the newspaper method (see page 139). Some perennials, too, will need to be controlled, such as creeping bellflower, named from its underground creeping runners, and also celandines which crowd out other species.

Sometimes, seed wanders and plants are found growing in quite a different part of the garden from that originally intended. This can be a nuisance. Often a wild plant appearing spontaneously in this way among cultivars in a border will look enchanting while it is young and in its early stages of flowering. But, in the rich soil of the border, the plant begins to grow so fast that it becomes gross and will smother the plants around it if left alone. It is best pulled out before it becomes too dominant, but after it has been allowed to make a decorative contribution.

Wild plants and self-maintenance

In an ordinary well-tended garden, herbaceous plants are spaced well apart and not jostled by neighbours, and their faded stems are removed at the end of the year. This means that they have no support for their new growth, and they have to be staked or supported in some way; thus twigs, canes or metal frames are used to encourage the shoots to grow upright.

By contrast, plants in the wild retain their spent stems unless the area has been grazed or mown. Sometimes the stems of one plant will help support plants of another species. The young growth pushes up through other vegetation, often using it as a means of keeping its frail stems upright, and holding flowers aloft in the sunshine and in the flight path of insects. In meadows, particularly, the support plants are grasses. When a grass plant invades a cultivated flower border and is removed, the result is often a floppy unattractive flowering plant which had up to that time used the grass as a natural support. So what is the wild gardener to do? He can either tidy stray grasses and then stake plants to provide support, or let the plants go their own way. Thus a climbing plant, a vetch for instance, will use a neighbouring plant for support. Some plants will flop and sprawl, and why should this matter? Plants that sprawl on the ground also cover it. And a sprawling plant will disperse its seed more widely than a plant that has its stems growing neatly and vertically. In the early stages of plant colonization this is obviously important. Do not be concerned, either, if one species seems to collapse into another. Usually the plants sort this out quite well on their own and what has been the scene one year is not necessarily the same the next.

Pruning and clipping

For appearance's sake, many groomed gardens are dependent upon the blade in some form or another: mown grass, clipped hedges, flowering plants dead-headed or cut back after flowering; shrubs and trees annually pruned. Often over-pruned. But, admiring the countryside in spring and seeing the wealth of blossom of, say, hawthorn in England or dogwood in North America, one is tempted to

RIGHT *Bluebells grow beautifully in grass. Because flower stalks and foliage should be allowed to die down naturally, the grass which has grown unmown since autumn should not be cut again until after midsummer. Usually the uncut grasses, in flower by that time, are attractive enough, but where the gardener would prefer more colour, other later-flowering plants can be grown to follow the bluebells.*

ask, who prunes them? There is no answer, yet no well-tended garden plant can really surpass them in abundance of blossom.

Plants left alone still flower and fruit, but in their own time and in their own way. In some seasons they will be better than others and this is to be expected.

The owner of a wild garden, therefore, need not be over-concerned with the niceties of pruning. Those wild plants which flower should not be dead-headed for it is planned that they should produce seed. Hedges that house birds and other animals should not be too frequently cut – once a year should do. See also page 138.

Towards an ecological balance

Sometimes the number of seedlings which appear on what was assumed to be a cleared site can be alarming. Yet if the gardener is not familiar with the plants and so long as he or she can bear to do so, once again it is prudent first to identify species that have appeared rather than to set about destroying them. (Apart from anything else they are likely to be a good guide to the type of soil and its condition, see pages 122-123). By selecting the more attractive plants common to your garden, you will be speeding the process of arriving at a good ecological balance for your neighbourhood, as well as helping the species you have deliberately introduced from outside to increase their numbers.

Since the garden itself is so obviously an interference with the natural pattern of plant ecology, we cannot really hope to achieve a perfect natural balance but it should be possible to help more than we do at present. Take, for instance, the simple and widespread practice of spraying aphids to 'clean' plants. Because they are likely also to be present on the plant or in the area, we are also likely to spray the larvae or the adults of those insects which naturally prey on them at the same time as we destroy the aphids. This is so whether we use modern chemical sprays or the old fashioned soap sud solution. Insecticides and other pesticides are deadly not only for the target animal, say a wasp,

but for the other insects that wander into the treated area, and this may include interesting solitary moths that add to the rich spectrum of insect life typical of a well-planned garden.

It may take a bit of courage to stop using these 'garden aids', but after the initial onslaught, say by aphids on your unsprayed roses, there is generally an increase in aphid predators such as certain hoverflies, ladybirds and lacewings, and in birds such as tits which soon clear up the flower buds to redress the balance.

It is understandable that a gardener should be prejudiced against those insects which unpleasantly smother parts of a plant and sap its strength, as aphids do, or which, like so many grubs or caterpillars, consume most of its foliage, leaving it tattered and unlovely. Yet how often in normal seasons do we see a truly wild plant quite so devastated? The only reason for this surely must be that there exist more predators in the wild.

One hopes for a 'natural' method which could be used in all kinds of gardens, but so far the biological control of plant pests is effective only under certain controlled conditions. See also page 140.

ABOVE *Even a few simple means will help gradually to restore the ecological balance in a garden. Although a pond may be present, one or more bird baths placed about, kept clean and regularly filled, will attract many species of birds, for they also provide drinking water. Once inside the garden, and so long as plants are not sprayed with insecticides, they will stay and search for food, usually to return again and again. Some will seek nesting sites.*

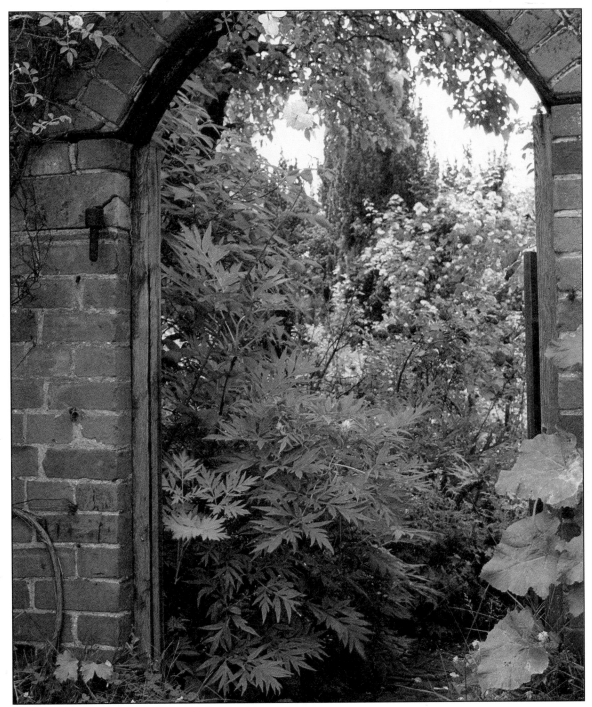

LEFT *Confined and sheltered gardens sometimes offer a refuge to the less endearing forms of wildlife. Aphids, for instance, will settle on many kinds of plants. Roses are particularly attractive to them. The insects form unpleasantly thick masses on young shoots, sucking the sweet sap, weakening and sometimes even killing them. Fortunately, the aphids provide rich food for nestling birds. The parent birds collect the pests diligently, eventually diminishing their numbers.*

AN ENVIRONMENT FOR WILDLIFE

Whether you like it or not, and unless you still use pesticides, your garden already serves as an important refuge for wildlife of all kinds. Most people would include here birds, bees and butterflies but would discount nocturnal and dawn feeders as well as the multitude of under-stone inhabitants which all make up the surprisingly complex mix of animals that reside in or are visitors to the garden.

To be conscious of the role your garden plays in attracting wildlife, try and look at it as a series of distinct, interlocking habitats. For example, the lawn, often short-cropped and sterile looking, could soon be turned into an open clearing cum-meadow area alive with grasshoppers. A hedge is a kind of miniature thicket and, of course, if you are fortunate enough to have mature bushes and trees, you have a ready-made copse or wood on your doorstep. To these you could add a series of micro-habitats: a wall, for example, functions in a similar way to a rocky outcrop and the numerous crevices are soon colonized by plants and insects as well as nesting birds.

Also helpful are those plants which grow in such a way that they sometimes seem as snug as a house. One reason why it is not a good thing to tidy plants in autumn is because, combined with their own faded stems, leaves which have blown against them and grass or climbers with which they may have become intertwined, they offer good, warm, even windproof cover. One of these is the blackberry or bramble of which they are so many species, sub species and varieties growing wild that here they will considered as just one kind of plant. The fortunate thing, especially for those who live far from the immediate countryside, is that the host of insects which visit wild brambles do not refuse the cultivated kinds.

In gardens where space does not allow the plant over the years to produce the great natural dome of a mature bramble, it should be possible to grow the 'canes' trained against a flat framework of supports and wires situated perhaps at the side of a path or at the end of a plot. Grown this way the plant can be kept under control.

Even a trained plant such as this should attract a great diversity of insect life which visits the plant during many stages of its life, seeking leaves, shoots, blossom and fruits, fresh or decaying. So far as butterflies are concerned, speckled wood, ringlet, hedge brown and the beautiful white admiral are four that visit the flowers for nectar, while the pretty little buff-arches, peach blossom and russet-coloured fox moths among many others will come to lay their eggs upon the leaves.

Raspberries also attract a great variety of insects. Beautiful jade-green spiders are almost always to be found on them. Where there is sufficient space, a stand of raspberries would be well worth growing.

Your compost heap, if maintained properly, doubles up as a dung heap and rich bed of leaf litter. It is especially rich in decomposers – mites,

LEFT Sedum spectabile, *a hardy succulent perennial from China, blooms at the end of summer when it attracts many different species of butterflies. The grass,* Festuca ovina glauca, *is a variety of sheep's fescue often used as an edging plant in formal gardens, and offering seed and cover in wild ones.*

RIGHT *Water in a garden attracts all forms of wildlife. Leafy cover at the margins ensures protection for vulnerable creatures, such as tiny frogs, leaving the water for the first time. Newly emerged dragon and damsel flies can climb the tall leaves growing above water level as they prepare for their first flight.*

fungi and bacteria, and also worms and insect larvae which are sought after by birds and small animals. Hedgehogs, for instance, are attracted to this rich insect store, especially during cold weather.

Feeding and reproduction take up a large part in the life of any animal, be it an insect or mammal. Your garden should therefore have as many food plants as possible and at the same time provide a sanctuary in the way of trees, shrubs and climbers. These will provide shelter for overwintering insects, nest and roost sites for birds and protected cover for small mammals such as shrews and voles.

The emphasis of any garden should be on variety and, with wildlife in mind, the more nooks and crannies you can provide, the more chance you have of attracting a greater variety of animal life. At the same time you should establish or improve nest sites for birds by putting up nest boxes, well out of reach of cats. If you have a thick hedge, you can improve it by planting climbers until you get that wild tangled effect which will attract birds to nest in the deepest recesses.

Multipurpose plants and food webs

Many common plants are useful in that they fulfil several functions as far as wildlife is concerned. Take the holly and the ivy, which, paired as they are in the Christmas carol, serve as the larval food plants of the holly blue butterfly, a woodland insect, now common in parks and gardens. The females of the spring brood lay their eggs among the flower buds of holly while the next generation in the summer choose the unopened buds of ivy. If either plant needs cutting back, obviously, in order not to destroy a colony of these insects, the holly should be pruned between late summer and spring, and the ivy trimmed between late spring and summer.

Both plants also provide year-round cover, the holly in particular is a favoured roost site for small birds and is also an excellent nesting site as the leathery prickly leaves render it virtually cat-proof. The leaves of holly are very often disfigured by the larvae of the holly-leaf miner fly. In early spring these larvae are sought after by blue tits which scour the leaves for the tell-tale pale blotches made by the the insects. In autumn, the bumper crop of red berries produced on the female plant acts as a magnet to birds, especially the blackbird and its relatives.

Ivy has the advantage of flowering late in the year, providing a rich and possibly final feast for hoverflies, wasps and bees. You may also get the occasional comma butterfly.

With butterflies and moths in mind

Those who bemoan the fact that no butterflies ever visit their gardens, and a surprising number of people do so, are usually not aware that in spite of the garden being well furnished with blooms, there is nothing in particular to entice the insects or prompt them to linger. The first point to remember is that butterflies live in two distinct phases, the caterpillar and the adult. Each requires different foods, namely nectar-rich flowers for the adult butterflies and a particular kind of foliage for the larval stages. From the gardener's point of view, it is extremely rewarding to grow the flowers, and to see, year after year, a build-up in the number of visiting butterflies. For the caterpillars, first learn which are the best plants to grow for which species of insect, and what particular species might be induced to establish itself in your area.

Sometimes you may accidentally introduce a plant with butterfly eggs on it into the garden. This happened when some mullein plants taken from a friend's garden were found to be covered with the caterpillars of the mullein moth; fortunately, although the plants were initially ravaged, enough grew to set seed.

A sunny flower filled border

A good start in the creation of any wild garden is a border of plants attractive to both bees and butterflies. Most gardens will already have a sunny flower border and it takes relatively little effort to modify this for wildlife, so that it serves as a rich source of nectar from spring through until late autumn.

BUTTERFLY AND BEE BORDER
Because of the nectar they produce, some flowers attract a great number of insects. For short-lived species such as butterflies, nectar is a source of energy rather than food. Other insects seek pollen. A garden furnished with such flowers will be well-populated.

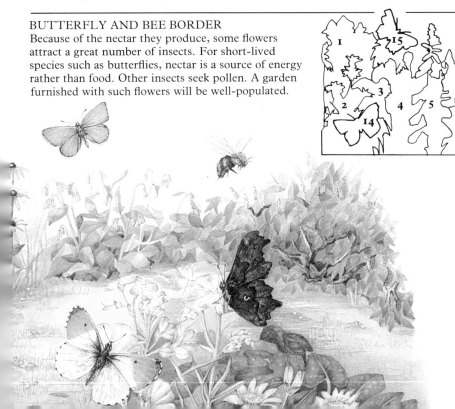

1 Goldenrod, *Solidago canadensis*
2 Michelmas daisy, *Aster novae-angliae*
3 Yarrow, *Achillea millefolium*
4 Teasel, *Dipsacus sylvestris*
5 Foxglove, *Digitalis purpurea*
6 Comfrey, *Symphytium officinale*
7 Cornflower, *Centaurea cyanus*
8 Rose-bay willow herb, *Chamaenerion angustifolium*
9 Black-eyed susan, *Rudbeckia hirta*
10 Virginia cowslip, *Mertensia virginica*
11 Cuckoo flower, *Cardamine pratensis*
12 Sage, *Salvia officinalis*
13 Lesser celandine, *Ranunculus ficaria*
14 Tortoiseshell butterfly
15 Comma butterfly
16 Red admiral butterfly
17 Fritillary butterfly
18 Blue butterfly
19 Orange-tip butterfly
20 Bumblebee

Your border, although designed primarily to attract bees and butterflies, will also lure many other insects. Among these, hoverflies will be most noticeable, darting about from flower to flower. These insects are not only interesting to look at, often banded yellow and black, but they should be encouraged because many of their larvae feed voraciously on aphids. Because they have only short feeding mouthparts they are particularly attracted to flat, open flowers, especially those of the daisy family. The larvae develop in a number of sites including rotten wood, so if possible it is a good idea to leave one or two felled logs in situ to aid your hoverfly population; however, the larvae of a few species of hoverflies can do damage to bulbs.

Bushes

Many shrubs and bushes are rich in nectar, some much more than our native plants. Among the favourites are the early summer small-flowered *Buddleia alternifolia*, and the pale mauve and white forms of *B. davidii*. Their flowers act like magnets to butterflies. On a sunny day they become crowded with coppers and fritillaries. Bumblebees and long-tongued hoverflies also lap up the rich nectar source. Some moths, such as the old lady (a large moth with beautifully patterned wings in dark brown and beige), will visit the flowers at night. Sadly, the lovely deep-coloured cultivars are not so effective. If more than one buddleia is planted, a longer period of flower can be obtained by cutting only one back; the uncut one will still flower first. Since these plants self-seed freely and are now escapes in both town and country, all the better reason to incorporate them into wild gardens.

Escallonia virgata, one of the hardiest of this genera, from Chile and other parts of South America, is also a great favourite in my own garden where a few bushes have been allowed to grow wild. On a fine summer's day, a plant in blossom can be thick with many different species of butterflies and bees, all sipping in harmony among the pale pink flowers.

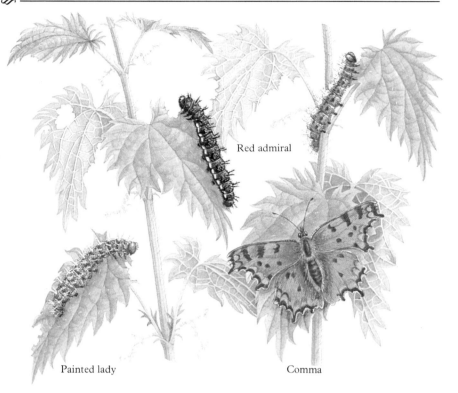

Red admiral

Painted lady   Comma

Nettle culture

The nettle is in vogue again, not for its fibres that were once woven into a cloth nor for its shoots eaten by country folk, but because the caterpillars of three attractive butterflies, the small tortoise-shell, the peacock and the red admiral all feed on nettle leaves. Before extolling the virtue of this plant, many people judge it as unsightly and I suggest therefore, that if you have a small garden and you want to experiment with nettle culture, that you relegate your nettle patch to the end of the garden, bearing in mind that butterflies will only use young nettle growth in full sunshine. The eggs of these butterflies are laid in the spring and the caterpillars should have left by the end of June, to pupate away from the nettle plant. If the nettles are cut down to just above the ground, new growth will attract a second generation of small tortoise-shells. If unchecked, nettles can become rampant. See page 139 on management of them.

ABOVE *Stinging nettles are food plants of the caterpillars of some of our most beautiful butterflies. The painted lady will sometimes take them as an alternative to the preferred spear thistle, but for others they are the essential source of sustenance. Cut the plants down in midsummer so that they produce young shoots ready to receive the eggs of the late broods of these insects. This practice also prevents the nettles from making quantities of seed.*

PLANTING SUCCESSFUL WILD GARDENS

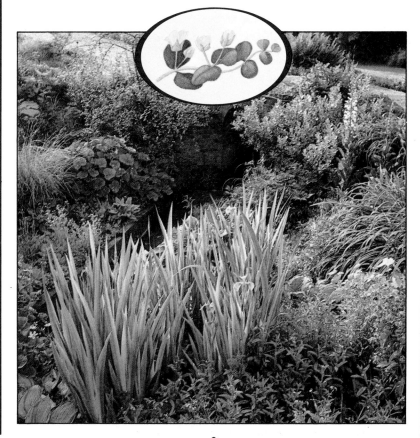

A CHOICE OF RURAL SETTINGS

Whether you are adapting a traditional garden – or perhaps starting a new one – or whether you want to make a special garden feature to show off wild plants, you will find many ideas for developing the potential of your garden, whatever its scale, terrain and soil type, in the chapters that follow. Here, wild plants can be seen and enjoyed on their own, or in carefully thought out groupings of native and naturalized, or native and exotic.

Any lawn can be translated into a meadow garden, with old-fashioned wildflowers in a sequence of blooms for most months of the year. Where an orchard exists, the gardener has the perfect site for a meadow garden and the late summer – early autumn routine of the second grass cut will ensure that the area is mown and convenient for fruit harvesting.

It might be that the house stands on a wooded plot or, particularly if the house is on a new site, on one that was once wooded. In this case, the soil could already be right for the gardener to exploit the situation and create a picturesque wildwood. This can be underplanted with shrubs and an attractive carpet of varied plants.

On land which adjoins heathland, where the soil will be acid, it is possible to create a heath garden in which the many members of the heather family, the taller shrubs and trees as well as the shorter, ground-covering heaths, would provide colour and interest every day of the year, for most are evergreens. They include some of the rarer wild plants, such as the trailing bear-berry, the glossy-leaved cowberry, or if the site is damp and shady enough, the ivy-leaved bellflower. If more variety is desired, then there are many other native plants which will grow along with the ericaceous kinds. Silver birch, in particular, looks delightful rising up from the coloured heather carpet.

An attractive green garden can be made using different species of hardy ferns, distinctive grasses and green-flowered plants such as hellebores, spurges and others. There are many suitable native species and, here, ivy varieties can play an important role, either as ground covers or as climbers. Such a garden offers year-round interest, and might be particularly suitable for an enclosed courtyard or very shaded plot.

A green garden could merge with, or be part of, a wild herb garden. Handsome angelica, tansy and mints will furnish the shadier, moister places, with sun-lovers such as fennel, marjoram and thymes attracting butterflies.

Water gardens offer great scope to the imaginative gardener, for there are so many lovely native aquatic plants, which are more versatile than exotic floating water lilies. Where a pond is not a practical option, perhaps because young children use the garden, most of these waterloving species could be grown in a small artificial marshy area.

The characteristics of a rocky or very stony site can be easily exploited by making a scree, alpine or gravel garden since most of the essentials, such as sharp drainage, already exist. Where the soil is sandy, plants need to be chosen carefully if they are to thrive. There are many suitable attractive species, both native and exotic, particularly Australian species which should do well. In frost-free areas a 'desert' garden with succulents such as *Mesembryanthemum edule*, the Hottentot fig, which is naturalized in Britain, and even cacti is not beyond the bounds of possibility.

RIGHT *A weedy lawn left unmown so that existing plants and grasses can mature and flower will become a meadow garden. Other plants can be added to those already present as time goes by. Any part of the lawn which for some reason needs to be kept more closely mown can be flower-decked in springtime. Daisies, cowslips, self-heal and other plants which form rosettes pressed down on the grass are able to withstand summer mowing without irreparable damage and so live to flower another year.*

WILDFLOWER LAWNS AND MEADOWS

ew features of the landscape are as beautiful as a 'flowery mead'. Until a few decades ago, such meadows full of flowers were a common sight in the countryside. Daisy-spangled in spring, the well-cropped grass then rapidly became covered with a rich carpet of cowslips or dandelions once the cattle or sheep were moved off. Buttercups followed in early summer, quickly succeeded by the oxeye daisies, sorrel, clover and quaking grass, that together brought such a sweet fragrance to the swathes of hay cut in midsummer.

Nowadays, sadly, such floristically rich grasslands can usually be found only on slopes too steep to cultivate or in isolated corners of the countryside which modern agriculture, with its fertilizers and herbicides, has failed to reach. Perhaps more unfortunately, the loss of this attractive habitat, with its great variety of nectar-producing flowers, has contributed to a decline in the butterfly population, and the loss of some species.

Wildflower meadows can, however, be recreated quite easily on a much smaller scale in gardens everywhere, even in the centre of a town. Today, there are a number of seedsmen ready to supply a range of suitable seed mixtures of native meadow grasses and wildflowers.

The area set aside for wildflowers and meadow grasses need not be flat: it could be a boundary bank, or a bank sloping down to or away from a more formal lawn, or any steep ground as long as it is accessible and not too large for hand-scything.

Not everyone has precisely the same understanding of the term 'flowery mead' or wildflower meadow. For me, there are three types of wildflower lawn or meadow. The simplest is an area of existing lawn where the broad-leaved plants (weeds to the purist lawnkeeper) have been encouraged to reproduce and a few wildflowers have been introduced. I find these lawns more attractive than the best-kept velvety sward. If well managed, they can resemble the pretty front lawns you see in Switzer-

land and Austria – themselves derived from the Alpine flower meadows. There, the myriad hues of speedwells, field daisies, cowslips, primulas, cuckoo flowers and self-heal jostle in uncut grass in the spring sunshine.

For the more romantic, and for those with a strong interest in conservation, a spring-flowering meadow lawn or a small-scale summer meadow might be created on virgin ground using specially selected mixtures of wildflowers and grasses.

Although there is nothing to prevent you from creating a wildflower meadow which will flower throughout the year, you will find the meadow easier to maintain if you divide the proposed area into two sections: one for spring flowers, some of

RIGHT *The poorer the soil, the more colourful the meadow flowers. Species such as the yellow loosestrife and foxgloves growing close to the trees have a richer soil and deeper shade and so grow in a different environment.*

BELOW *Annual cornflowers and poppies, typical flora of a pre-herbicide cornfield, are mainly represented here by their garden varieties, such as Shirley poppy in the foreground. Left to seed themselves they will in time revert to the species.*

which grow from bulbs so that the grass must be left uncut until midsummer, and one for summer flowers, where the grass is cut early in the year and then left until late summer. I have done this in my own garden where the area beneath a large copper beech holds a spring-flowering meadow lawn which comes into bloom before the beech leaves form a dense canopy. Beyond them, stretching down the garden, the summer meadow flowers grow among the feathery plumes of the grasses.

To some, the term 'wildflower meadow' conjures up an image of drifts of scarlet poppies, blue cornflowers, yellow corn marigolds and, perhaps, purple-pink corn cockle. These are really inhabitants of the pre-herbicide cornfield, amongst the annual cultivated crop of oats, wheat or barley. If you want to create a small patch of old-fashioned cornfield flowers, it should be kept separate from the wildflower meadow for these annual species require quite different cultivation.

Bear in mind, though, when planning a wildflower meadow, that most species of meadow flowers do best on poor soil. Rich soils are to be avoided as they promote the growth of vigorous grasses like the perennial rye-grass which tends to dominate other species of wild grass and smother the very flowers you hope to encourage.

Some people go to great lengths to create patches of poor soil on which to sow their wildflower meadow, removing existing turf and the good soil immediately beneath before sowing with a wildflower mixture. If your garden soil is generally too rich to favour a wildflower meadow, I suggest you put the area down to grass using a fine grass seed mixture, but then leave it largely unweeded, apart from removing by hand any invasive perennials like fat hen, docks and thistles. In a couple of years' time, provided the grass is not fertilized and the clippings are religiously removed when it is mowed, the soil will gradually become poorer and some of the more interesting wildflower species can be introduced. In the meantime, you can try introducing some of the less fussy species – bistort, black medick, oxeye daisy, knapweeds, columbines and white clover, for example.

Adapting a formal lawn

If you are toying with the idea of making an informal flower lawn out of part of your existing lawn, and you are in no hurry, then you might consider the approach I took in my own garden. I simply let the grass in a small area at the end of the garden grow, completely untended, for one year, to see which plants would flower. I eliminated some which grew too abundantly – dandelions appeared in great profusion – and in doing so made space for species I wished to introduce. I dug out each unwanted plant, carefully removing all the root (dandelions have deep root systems), to prevent it reappearing, and replaced it with a new plant.

The first rule, if you are trying to encourage wildflowers to grow in an existing lawn, is to stop using any weedkillers or fertilizers. Broad-leaved plants such as daisies, cat's ear, speedwell, white

MEADOW FLOWERS THROUGH THE YEAR
You could make a calendar of meadow flowers, for there is one or another in bloom for most months of the year. In mild winters, there will be a few daisies and dandelions which, like many others, spread their leaves tightly against the ground, thus claiming their living space and preventing grass from closing in and smothering them. Others each have characteristic ways of pushing their way through the lengthening grass so that their flowers are in the sunlight and fully visible to pollinating insects.

1 Field daisy, *Bellis perennis*
2 Dandelion, *Taraxacum officinale*
3 Germander speedwell, *Veronica chamaedrys*
4 Meadow buttercup, *Ranunculus acris*
5 Cuckoo flower, *Cardamine pratensis*
6 Cowslip, *Primula veris*
7 Lesser trefoil, *Trifolium dubium*
8 Common cat's ear, *Hypochaeris radicata*
9 Oxeye daisy, *Leucanthemum vulgare*
10 Field scabious, *Knautia arvensis*
11 Birdsfoot trefoil, *Lotus corniculatus*

RIGHT *Lawn weeds allowed to grow naturally may be considered anti-social in the suburbs, perhaps, but they are heavenly in the country. Dandelions* en masse *provide pleasure for people and food for wildlife. Bees will find pollen and honey in abundance from blossom above and meadow flowers below. Later, gold-finches and other birds will enliven the scene as they feed from dandelion seeds.*

12 Yarrow, *Achillea millefolium*
13 Self-heal, *Prunella vulgaris*
14 Pyramidal orchid, *Anacamptis pyramidalis*
15 Meadow cranesbill, *Geranium pratense*
16 Lady's bedstraw, *Galium verum*
17 Common centaury, *Centaurium erythraea*
18 Common mallow, *Malva sylvestris*
19 Common restharrow, *Ononis repens*
20 Feverfew, *Chrysanthemum parthenium*
21 Field gentian, *Gentianella campestris*
22 Greater knapweed, *Centaurea scabiosa*
23 Dyer's greenweed, *Genista tinctoria*
24 Meadow saffron, *Colchicum autumnale*

59

A MEADOW GARDEN IN SUMMER

A wild meadow garden is divided into different zones for management and colour. Paths can be defined simply, by close-mowing the grass. Low-growing lawn plants flower in the more regularly mown area near the house, though this area is left unmown for several weeks from midsummer to give all the species a chance to bloom. Herbs in pots and nectar-rich flowers grow on the sunnier side, though the hedgerow of native species (hornbeam, holly and wild privet) is heavily scented with honeysuckle. Beneath the oak, the fading stems of bulbs in the spring-flowering area indicate that the time has come when the grass here may be mown.

At the junction of the paths is a miniature 'cornfield' where poppies and other 'weeds of cultivation' grow, providing a blaze of colour. Beyond, in the summer meadow, are knapweed, yarrow, fritillaries, hawkbit and other members of the dandelion family, together with apple and plum trees and a crab apple. Tucked away, at the end to the left, is an area of very rough grass and nettles which also conceals the compost heap.

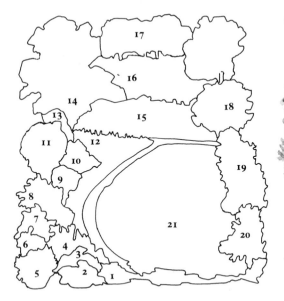

1 Thymes, *Thymus* sp.
2 Marjoram, *Origanum* sp.
3 Sage, *Salvia* sp.
4 Rosemary, *Rosemarinus officinalis*
5 Lavender, *Lavandula* sp.
6 Michaelmas daisy, *Aster novi-belgii*
7 Black-eyed susan, *Rudbeckia hirta*
8 Rose, *Rosa* sp.
9 *Alchemilla* sp.
10 Periwinkle, *Vinca minor*
11 White lilac, *Syringa vulgaris*
12 Spring bulb area
13 Old man's beard, *Clematis vitalba*
14 Oak, *Quercus* sp.
15 Cornfield border: poppies, *Papaver rhoeas*, and cornflowers, *Centaurea cyanus*
16 Summer meadow: fritillaries, *Fritillaria meleagris*; knapweed, *Centaures nigra*; yarrow, *Achillea millefolium*; cat's ear, *Hypochaeris radicata*
17 Fruit trees
18 Hawthorn
19 Hedgerow with honeysuckle, *Lonicera periclymenum*
20 *Clematis montana*
21 Flowering informal lawn: daisies, *Bellis perennis;* speedwell, *Veronica chamaedrys;* dandelions, *Taraxacum officinale*

clover, self-heal and birdsfoot trefoil can be encouraged by mowing the grass only every fourteen days or so throughout one growing season, with the mower blades raised to leave the grass height at 8cm/3in. In early summer, stop mowing for four to five weeks, to allow the flowers to bloom and set seed. In the autumn, spring-flowering bulbs could be introduced into the lawn, planted in groups and drifts, to provide welcome early colour for next year.

Whether you want to have a spring display of flowers, or a succession of flowers through the summer and into autumn, you will need to introduce new species. One, or a combination of, the following methods can be tried.

If you wish to sow seed, you must first rip away the surface of the grass with a steel rake or spiked harrow. Remove any debris and sow the chosen seed mixture in autumn (see page 134).

You can introduce small pot-grown plants directly into the turf, if your budget allows and the area is not too large. Plant them in groups, having first removed pot-sized patches of turf, which can be done most successfully using a bulb-planter (see page 133). Again, it is best to plant in autumn to prevent the plants being smothered by more vigorous grasses. But, if you are prepared to keep them well-watered, you can plant at any time.

If you or a friend already have a well-established meadow area, you could transplant small chunks of turf from it into an existing lawn to diversify the plants. This has also been done experimentally on bare soil using turf from an area about to be quarried, arranging the turves in a spaced chequerboard pattern, and sowing a meadow grass mixture around them.

ABOVE RIGHT *The 'Alpine meadow' comes in many forms depending upon the terrain and the indigenous flora. Not all are to be found on mountains. Here an American hillside, where flowers are allowed to grow anywhere, is just one delightful example.*

RIGHT *Unweeded lawns in spring will produce an alpine meadow of a different pattern, with field daisies, speedwell, dandelions and others which will flower each year, even if the grass is regularly cut in summer – so long as it is not treated with weedkiller.*

LEFT *The garden at Great Dixter is one of the most famous of English gardens and its present owner, Christopher Lloyd, one of the century's great gardeners. A beautiful and unusual feature through which the house is reached is the meadow garden. Here among the grass, a rich flora from spring to autumn includes narcissi, orchids, fritillaries, oxeye daisies, colchicums and autumn crocuses.*

BELOW *A meadow mixture can become richer and richer, not only because of species continually introduced by the gardener but also by those seeds and spores brought in by insects, birds, animals and wind. Often some plants, for example orchids, do not appear until others, such as fungi, are also present. Gardeners lucky enough to have old grassland nearby may have many pleasant surprises in store.*

Creating a new wildflower meadow

If you decide to make a wildflower meadow on fresh ground, there are several ways of tackling it. Don't forget, however, that the soil should be poor for best results. It is probably cheapest to create a fairly large wildflower meadow area from seed, but for a smaller area you might consider a mixed sowing and planting approach (see below, and page 134).

Whichever method you adopt, it is essential to clear the ground completely, getting rid of all invasive perennial weeds, like couch grass, docks, nettles and elder. You can either dig the site over with a fork, removing all the perennial weeds, including the roots, by hand or, for a larger site, you could spray with a herbicide such as glyphosate and then use a rotovator to turn the soil over. Before sowing or planting, the soil should be broken up and free-draining. It can then be raked over to a firm and fine tilth, as you would for a lawn.

Autumn is the best time of the year to sow a new meadow as there will be adequate moisture in the soil. Also, the cold winter months will help to break the dormancy pattern of some of the seeds, ensuring that a larger number will germinate than if sown in spring (see also pages 130-131).

If you are using a packeted mixture of grass and wildflower seed (or seed that you have collected yourself), mix it with several times its volume of damp sand, so that it is distributed more evenly during sowing. The grass and wildflower mixture is normally sown sparsely, using about 4 grammes per square metre ($\frac{1}{6}$ oz per square yard). I would recommend broadcasting the seed by hand, but if you are sowing a large area you could use a hand operated lawn fertilizer spreader to do the job. Again, first mix the seed with sand. After sowing, the seed should be raked in or, on a small plot, lightly covered with soil and trodden in.

An alternative method for small areas is to sow the grasses only and introduce the wildflowers as plants. You can start by sowing the seed of the meadow grasses in round patches over the proposed site. The following spring, when any patches of bare soil are visible, you can introduce the wildflowers which you have raised in nursery beds (see page 131).

Using seeded hay

Hayfield mixtures from species-rich meadows can be purchased from some seed merchants. This will consist of a mixture of chaff and seed, and the quantity to sow depends on how clean the seed and chaff mixture is. It is important to follow the seed merchant's recommendations. Another method, used with good results in Holland and Sweden, is to use the hay itself, from species-rich meadows. If the hay is loose-baled when still green, most of the seed will remain attached to the seed heads. The hay is spread loosely over the surface of the proposed meadow area in autumn, and left to decompose. Seed from the hay will then germinate the following spring. The quantity of seed from one

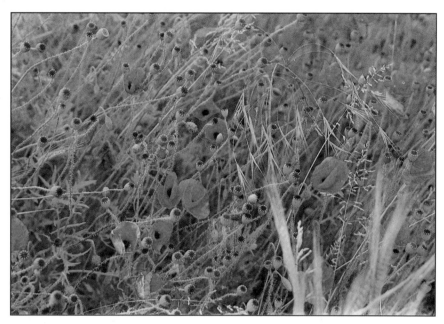

bale of species-rich hay can vary from around 150-200g/5-7oz – enough for sowing an area 30m/198ft square.

Choice of flower and grass seed

If you buy packeted wildflower meadow seed mixture, it will normally contain up to 20 species of wildflowers and up to half a dozen different grasses. Specialist firms produce seeds suitable for different soil types and drainage conditions, and it is important to follow the advice in their catalogues and buy seed to suit your own conditions (see also charts pages 142-145). Some distinguish between spring- and summer-flowering species. Most grasses are very adaptable and will grow anywhere, although some species do best in certain soil conditions. You may find that the number of species of grass in the bought mixture is not as great, nor the grasses as attractive, as hoped for. Generally, the mixture can easily be augmented by sowing seed of any pretty grasses found growing wild in your locality. But beware – some grasses can be a nuisance. Tall, aggressive grasses like tall fescue, *Festuca arundinacea*, cocksfoot, *Dactylis glomerata*

ABOVE *Unclean seed is one reason why cornfields produced such colourful flowers; the seeds came in with the grain. Another reason: because cereals are an annual crop, soil is disturbed before sowing and after harvesting, thus inhibiting the growth of perennials which would ultimately smother the annual flowers. Nowadays, clean seed and herbicides combine to prohibit the growth of annual flowers, like poppies, on farms.*

and Timothy grass, *Phleum pratense*, should be avoided, as should all agricultural cultivars of rye grass, *Lolium perennei*. On chalky soil, one of the least welcome grasses is the false brome or tor grass, *Brachypodium pinnatum*, as it tends to dominate other species. Before adding wild grass seeds to your meadow, it would be wise to check first with a conservation body that they are suitable for your soil conditions and local climate.

Many people who have kept formal lawns are unfamiliar with flowering grasses and you may find it worthwhile to let a small area of a formal lawn go uncut for a season, just to see the appearance of the mature grasses. You may be surprised how lovely some of the grass 'flowers' are, and how much the plumes vary in length, shape, texture and hue. You might also consider incorporating some of the more exotic grasses in your meadow mixture. Once these grasses have become established, they should seed themselves and spread, flowering year after year (see also pages 90-93).

Cornfield border

Should you decide to establish an old-fashioned cornfield flower border to your meadow area, you should adopt the same soil preparation methods as you would for sowing the wildflower meadow. After sowing, you must periodically remove any dominating perennials that find their way there, to prevent the annuals being smothered by them. Provided you leave the area uncut until after the seed heads have ripened, the flowers will reseed themselves. For a longer flowering period the following year, remove some of the seed heads after harvesting in late summer and store the seed (see page 129) for sowing the following spring in seed trays or seed beds. Flowers sown in spring will bloom later than those produced from seeds falling to the ground *in situ* in autumn. For rarer species of cornfield flowers, it is probably best to raise the seed in seed beds or seed trays to ensure germination. Some specialists offer a collection of colourful cornfield flowers – poppies, cornflowers, pheasant's eye (*Adonis annua*), and corn cockle – all of

which are now rarely seen in modern arable fields.

It would be worthwhile including some of the lovely annual grasses, both native and exotic, such as quaking grass and hare's tails (see pages 150-151). Some of the farm cereal crops, like oats, wheat and barley, can be mixed with annual cornfield flowers and the grasses mentioned above. Although not wild plants, the seed of the cereal crop will be appreciated by wildlife. The natural sowing time is again autumn.

Nurse crops

Many wild grasses grow slowly and may take a while to get established. Slow-growing forms are usually preferable because they are easier to manage, but for aesthetic reasons you may wish to put in a fast-growing 'nurse' crop which will germinate quickly and then die back, allowing the permanent species for the meadow to replace it. Westerwolds rye grass (a form of *Lolium multiflorum*) is used for this purpose over large areas, but only on soils with low fertility (chalk or clay) as it tends to grow too strongly on richer soils, and is therefore not recommended for gardens. Instead, the usual cornfield mixture (see above) could be used, but should be

ABOVE *The practice of planting bulbs in grass in gardens has long been known as 'naturalizing' them. Certainly they can look attractive when grown this way, but where the grass around them is kept closely mown, hardly natural. Where the grass is not only allowd to grow but is also filled with little flowers the garden varieties take on a much less sophisticated appearance.*

cut before the seed heads have fully ripened.

The nurse crop must be cut before the seed has formed, otherwise it will reseed itself the following year. The sowing rate for the nurse crop is still experimental but 30kg a hectare has been used for commercial operations, and less might be used successfully. (Packets containing just 500g/17.5oz are available, and are cheap compared with wildflower seed.) They are worth using when a quick, cheap cover is required and have been used successfully by various conservation bodies when establishing flower meadows.

Managing the wildflower meadow

Grass cutting is a tiresome chore and you may think, if you are trying to create a really wild corner of your garden, that you can escape it altogether. If you gave the plot over to nature and left the grass uncut or ungrazed year after year, the ground would simply revert naturally to scrubland, as the seedlings of shrubs and trees tend to dominate most other species.

It is not possible to lay down hard-and-fast rules for cutting a meadow since much will depend on the nutrients in and moisture content of your soil, as well as on the species of grasses and wildflowers that it contains. There will also be considerable seasonal differences. General guidelines can be given for the three types of lawn or meadow that I have previously identified: the informal flower lawn, the spring-flowering meadow lawn and the summer-flowering meadow.

Mowing an informal flower lawn has already

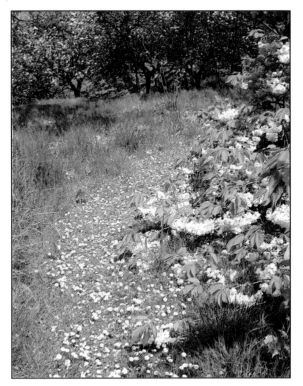

LEFT *Primrose paths are legendary, but daisy paths may be easier for some gardeners to establish. One of the most cherished of all flowers (and Chaucer's favourite), it is also the most persecuted by lawn enthusiasts. It has a role to play in wild gardens not least because it blooms so early in the year and stays so late into the season.*

BELOW *A spring meadow can be in flower from the early months of the year with the first bulbs, and continue flowering to midsummer with oxeye daisies, cowslips, cat's ear, self-heal and cuckoo flowers. Around or a little later than midsummer (depending on the season and appearance of the flowers) mow the meadow and remove the hay. Either keep mown at 10cm/4in, or leave for a second crop.*

MOWING REGIMES
1 Spring meadow

Mid-spring to summer   Midsummer   Later summer and autumn

2 Summer meadow

Early summer   Midsummer to autumn   Autumn

LEFT *For a summer meadow, mow the grass regularly throughout the spring at 7.5-10cm/3-4in and then leave uncut from midsummer to autumn. The taller wildflowers such as field scabious and greater knapweed, will be ideal as a breeding ground for butterflies. Mow the hay in autumn and take off.*

been discussed (see page 61). For a spring meadow, where you are concentrating on a spring show of flowers, leave the grass uncut until midsummer – haymaking time. Cut it once then and leave it uncut until autumn.

For a summer meadow – and summer flowers come in greater diversity than spring ones, and attract more insects – I would cut the grass regularly in the early months of the year and then not cut it again until the summer flowers are over in late summer or even autumn. Some species will flower twice, and you may need to give it a second cut in late autumn. Alternatively, leave it until early the following spring, and cut when the weather is not frosty or too wet.

Meadow grass, and even informal lawn grass, should never be cut really short. The only area to be so treated would be a path leading through it. The grass should be cut about as short as it would be if grazed and you can either use a hand scythe to do the job, or a mower with the blades set to about 8cm/3in. At this level, the broad-leaved plants will not be ruthlessly destroyed and light and air will still reach them.

BELOW *Few flowers are as endearing as oxeye daisies or marguerites – to give but two of its many popular names, evidence that it was once much more familiar than it is today. Shallow-rooted, it will thrive on the poorest of soil.*

Although all long grass mowings should be removed from the meadow to prevent fertility from building up, you will find the work less arduous if you allow them to lie and dry out on the ground for a few days. It makes them much lighter to handle.

Never let grass cuttings rot on the meadow. If they are left lying on broad-leaved plants they will damage or kill them and if they are allowed to stay *in situ* and enrich the soil, it will be less welcoming to meadow species.

Although infrequent mowing or scything sounds easy compared with managing a lawn, and even if you use a mower to do the work, collecting up the long grass mowings is laborious. For a large area, however, it might be worth hiring or borrowing a small garden tractor and also using it to cart the mowings away on a trailer. Since, in this case, the quantity of mown hay will be too great to compost, you may well find friends with animals who would be glad of it.

Wildlife in the meadow

Summer's meadow flowers come in a much greater diversity and attract more kinds of insects to their nectar than do those of spring. The most attractive include scabious, marjoram, dwarf thistle, meadow saffron and oxeye daisy. (Knapweed is additionally useful because the dead heads are much sought after by seed-eating goldfinch, bullfinch and greenfinch.) Insects continue to visit the meadow until cold slows down their activities, and the long grasses afford a safe place for the pupae of moths and butterflies to hibernate.

A grassy area grown for butterflies as well as for its flowers should be rough cut twice a year, once at midsummer, when the first flush of flowers is over, and again at the very end of summer, to tidy up. But even then, leave some long grasses, round shrubs at the edges of the meadow area, for instance. By this method, the caterpillars are left undisturbed to pupate and hibernate. Always allow cut grass to lie for a few days before raking it up so that any caterpillars, larvae and other creatures have time to find a new refuge on the living

Salad burnet, *Poterium sanguisorba*

Oxeye daisy, *Leucanthemum vulgare*

Marjoram, *Origanum vulgare*

Red clover, *Trifolium pratense*

Dwarf thistle, *Cirsium acaule*

grass left standing in the meadow or elsewhere.

Among the many butterflies and moths that use grasses as larval foodplants, the browns are most common, especially the meadow brown which lays its eggs on various species of meadow grass. Another easily enticed grassland butterfly, the common blue, will breed only on birdsfoot trefoil, black medick or clover.

Now that the grass grows long, one of my great joys is to stand on the mown path and look around, to try to identify the ever increasing numbers of butterflies, moths and other insects which come to the graceful grasses and winsome flowers alike. I also hope to glimpse one of the small mammals that find a retreat there, such as bank-voles, pygmy shrews and hedgehogs.

ABOVE *Bees collect both pollen and nectar for honey, but butterflies and moths and other insects come to the flowers simply to sip. Each tiny floret of clover, daisies and thistles holds a minute store of sweetness. Marjoram which like some thistles blooms late in summer attracts late brood butterflies. Salad burnet attracts pollen beetles and hoverflies, although it holds no nectar.*

WOODED GARDENS

Few wild places are as enchanting as a little wood, but if you have only a very small garden you may have to remain content with a small tree or two and an assortment of shrubs. However, if your plot is large enough, and certainly if it was once part of a wood and vestiges of woodland remain, you might feel inclined to create your own wooded area. It is no great problem to use an existing shrub border, a few trees or even one great tree, an orchard or the remains of one, even a mixed hedge-row, as a basis for this type of garden and to build on that, bringing in other trees, shrubs, climbers and smaller plants to complement those which already exist and to help build an ecologically viable plant community. Some of the native fruits could be grown: sloes, wild or bird cherry (the latter a neater, smaller and hardier tree than the former), as well as crab apple, service tree and rowan, all of which will attract wildlife and fill the scene with special seasonal beauty in spring and autumn. With these can be grown certain exotics, for instance the North American shad bush as well as its near relation the medlar, from the Caucasus. This will increase the profitability of the plot and will at the same time add to its content and interest. Fruit blossom, lovely to look at and often among the first flowering, is a great attraction to early-foraging insects.

If you want to plant a proper woodland from scratch, you must be prepared for it to take time – a couple of decades rather than a couple of years. Where no large trees already exist, you should not rush ahead and plant them, but concentrate on the underwood first. On the outer edges of your area, plant young specimens of light-seeking shrubs, and shade-tolerant species within. Once these have had at least a couple of years to become established, start introducing trees. This method has the advantage that the wood can be planned gradually, and by following the sequence that occurs in the wild, will give a much better long-term result.

Where you want a clearway, shrubs can be cut back to ground level or 'coppiced' (see page 138). The ground can be carpeted with woodland plants while you decide what trees you want and where best to position them. In this way, the mature woodland profile can be built up, and you can be sure that it will soon attract a variety of wildlife.

It is good practice to use leaf litter and chopped bark as mulches for your new woodland plants (see page 124), as these naturally organic materials not

RIGHT *Layers of fallen leaves gradually decompose to produce leaf soil, rich in humus, well-drained yet moisture-retentive, an ideal rooting medium for many lovely plants.*

BELOW *A glade is enchanting when carpeted with flowers, such as these bluets from North America, which are free-seeding annuals.*

only help to sustain the vitality of the soil, but also help support many forms of life – beetles, woodlice, chafers – which find shelter and food beneath. In a similar spirit, already established trees should be provided with roosting boxes for birds.

If there are fallen trees or branches to be cleared, take some pieces of them into your new woodland area and leave them to rot there. Rotting wood, with its considerable population of insects, fungi, mosses and lichens, also has an important role to play. Even one or two logs, taken perhaps from your fuel store will help. In my own garden I grow ferns around them which helps to keep the soil moist.

The woodland profile

Every wooded country, indeed each geologically different area, has its own type of woodland, often with four layers of plants (though one or other of the lower layers may be barely present in certain woodland types). The traditional oakwood is a good example of this four-tiered structure.

At ground level are the mosses and liverworts which will be more in evidence where the soil is shaded and damp. Above these are the herbaceous plants growing in what botanists call the 'field layer'. The third layer consists of shrubs together with the climbing plants, and finally, often covering all with a dense leafy canopy, grow the trees. Though interdependent, each layer has its own part to play and contributes to the whole woodland scene. If the gardener follows this pattern, the result is sure to be pleasing. The floor of the wooden garden becomes prettily covered with a diversity of earth-based foliage and flowering plants, from which rise up climbers, some weaving through the stems of other shrubs to the higher branches of the trees, some, like ivy, creeping first over the floor until a tree trunk is reached, others cascading to the ground, forming screens or hides.

Oaks are native to or naturalized in many countries throughout the world. Some species are deciduous, some evergreen. Most will grow well in a deep, loamy soil; some species are not lime-tolerant. The two British deciduous species are

fairly adaptable. The pedunculate oak, *Quercus robur*, favours clays and heavy loams, while the sessile or durmast oak, *Q. petraea*, which produces stemless acorns, grows in sandier, shallow soils. (This species also tolerates some acidity in the soil.) Obviously, in the wild, each species covers a different kind of shrub and field layer. For instance, while quite often the pedunculate oak is associated with a hazel shrub layer, hornbeam is often to be found growing under the sessile oak. Generally, the undergrowth of each is quite varied, depending on the nature of the rock beneath the soil, altitude and light intensity.

BELOW *Handsome bracket fungi and lush emerald green mosses grow upon and attractively mask a mass of rotting wood which in turn sustains a considerable population of lesser wildlife.*

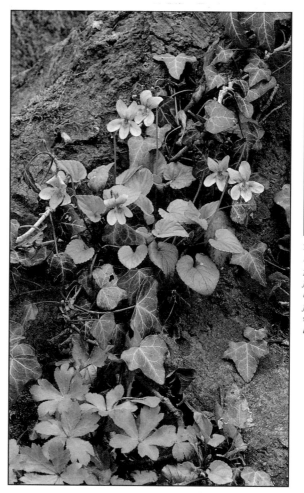

LEFT *Scentless but beautiful, the dog or wood violet, a plant of the open woodland, favours sloping land and banks, flowers and seeds freely and clothes the ground with pretty heart-shaped leaves.*

There is no need for an oak to dominate a small garden at the expense of many other plants. This tree is considered to be one of the best 'mother' trees. Its roots go down quite deep, thus presenting little, if any, competition to the near-surface rooting plants which grow readily in its shade. This applies to shrubs and field layer plants alike. Those who have oaks in their gardens can grow a wide range of plants in the deep humus that forms beneath them.

Of the early-flowering field-layer plants, the first is dog's mercury, *Mercurialis perennis,* and lesser celandine, *Ranunculus ficaria* (both of which are invasive and would need controlling) followed by wood anemone, *Anemone nemorosa*, bugle and, where the ground is moist, ramsons. All these species reproduce freely, some by creeping roots. Before the tree canopy thickens in late spring, there are primroses, bluebells, woodruff and violets, especially *Viola riviniana,* which sometimes has a second autumn flowering. Of the rarer species, try growing oxlip, *Primula elatior* (similar to the cowslip, but preferring the moist shade of woodland), herb Paris, moschatel, *Adoxa moschatellina,* and wood forget-me-not, *Myosotis sylvatica.* On acid soils, some of the woodland exotics could be grown, such as the North American trilliums, especially wake robin and dog's tooth violet. There is also the native late-blooming wintergreen, *Pyrola minor,* and the charming twinflower, *Linnaea borealis.*

The birch tree probably offers the wild gardener a greater scope than many others because of its adaptability. The two woodland birch trees native to Britain, the silver birch, *Betula pendula,* and the downy birch, *B. pubescens*, with whiter bark, grow readily in poor soil, whether calcareous or sandy acid soil (the birch is said to be one of the quickest colonizers of sandy heaths), on gravels as well as on any ordinary or even rich soils. Many beautiful cultivars can be readily grown, such as *B. jacquemontii* and *B. papyrifera.* Their elegance can be truly appreciated if the trees are well-spaced, with the ground below thickly carpeted with plants.

The alder, *Alnus glutinosa,* one of the last to lose

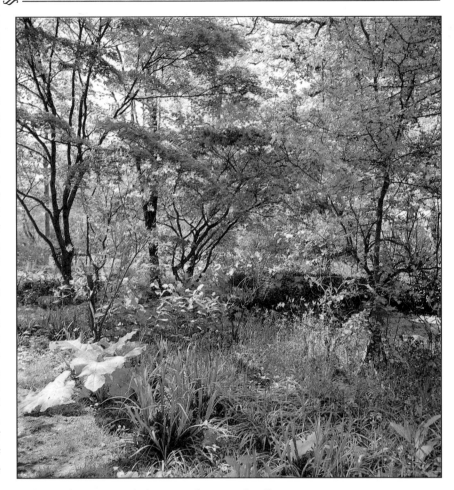

its leaves in autumn, belongs to the same family as the birch. Although it will grow quite well in drier sites – I have a young beauty in a little copse being created at the end of my garden – it is most often seen in moist places, even by the waterside. It is the dominant tree in damp woods where it is associated with ash and birch. The grey alder, *A. incana*, is a useful tree for growing on very difficult soils, and is used in land reclamation schemes.

Trees for the smaller garden
While a garden may be large enough to contain a little woodland, it may not be really large enough to give space to the true forest trees. Though not

ABOVE *Many species of woodland flowering plants can be grown in the soft, dappled shade cast by shrubs and small trees. Where the leaf canopy is formed by large trees and is likely to become very dense in summer, creating deep shade, those kinds of plants which flower in spring before the trees are in full leaf or in autumn when the leaves begin to fall are best grown.*

very large when first planted, the day will come when they reach great proportions. In this case it is more prudent to select smaller trees or the larger understorey shrubs, those which seem to hover between being a bush or a tree, such as hazel, hornbeam and guelder rose. (I have hazel trees in my woodland and hazel shrubs in my hedgerow.)

If these little trees play the role of the top storey, there are still many other shrubs that can be grown as attractive and useful understorey plants. There is also a bonus. Since the foliage canopy of these smaller trees is unlikely to be as dense as that of the larger trees, the field layer can be extremely varied and at times truly colourful, much more so than in a densely canopied wood. I suggest that the more varied the canopy trees, the better so as to provide different zones of light and deeper shade.

There is no reason why natives and exotics should not be mixed if this is what the gardener would prefer. I have visited many attractive small woodlands where exotic species such as maples, magnolias, pieris, arbutus, Turkey oak, American dogwood, rhododendrons and others are seen to mingle attractively with an assortment of native trees. These often shelter a correspondingly mixed undergrowth of shade-tolerant plants.

ABOVE *The oxlip,* Primula elatior, *is like a giant cowslip, but like the primrose is found in woody areas and not in meadows. It hybridizes with both of them.*

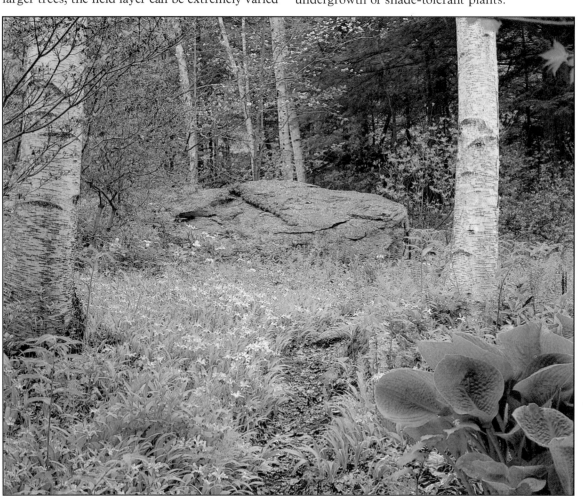

LEFT *Many exotic species fit attractively into a native setting and of them all, the woodland plants possibly look most at home. Here, filling a role which in spring in a British wood might be played by anemones, bluebells, primroses or violets, are the starry flowers of* Iris cristata, *the crested dwarf iris, a flower of the eastern United States,*

A WOODLAND GARDEN

A woodland garden in which the trees are neat, small species mingling with the shrubs, and with native climbers on the boundary fence, will together produce blossom, fruits and foliage necessary to many different forms of wildlife. In this garden, a curving path leads to a pond in a clearing, and crosses it by means of a timber bridge. Rustic seats overlook the pond, close by a wild cherry, so that people can sit and watch the water and pond life. The path continues towards a hide in the guise of a summerhouse draped with honeysuckle. Going back towards the house, now treading in grass, you pass alongside a woodland border where many different kinds of woodland and wood edge flowering plants carpet the ground, beneath as well as between the trees: violets, *Viola* sp.; primroses, *Primula vulgaris*; star-of-bethlehem, *Ornithogalum umbellatum*; wood anemone, *Anemone nemorosa*; periwinkle, *Vinca major*; wood forget-me-not, *Myosotis sylvatica*; foxglove, *Digitalis purpurea*; greater celandine, *Chelidonium majus*; lily-of-the-valley, *Convallaria majalis*.

1 Whitebeam, *Sorbus aria*
2 Bramble, *Rubus* sp.
3 Holly, *Ilex aquifolium*
4 Blackthorn, *Prunus spinosa*
5 Hawthorn, *Crataegus oxycanthus*
6 Guelder rose, *Viburnum opulus*
7 Field maple, *Acer campestre*
8 Hazel, *Corylus avellana*
9 Wayfaring tree, *Viburnum lantana*
10 Wild service tree, *Sorbus torminalis*
11 Wild privet, *Lingustrum vulgaris*
12 Hornbeam, *Carpinus betulus*
13 Black bryony, *Tamus communis*
14 Silver birch, *Betula pendula*
15 Alder buckthorn, *Frangula alnus*
16 Old man's beard, *Clematis vitalba*
17 Small-leaved lime, *Tilia cordata*
18 Elder, *Sambucus nigra*
19 Downy birch, *Betula pubescens*
20 Dogwood, *Cornus sanguinea*
21 Mountain ash, *Sorbus aucuparia*
22 Crab apple, *Malus pumila*
23 Wild cherry, *Prunus avium*

My own little wood, still very much in its early stages, is of necessity influenced by those trees which already existed, and those planted when the garden was first made, when a wild garden was not a part of the plan. There are the original Turkey oak, copper beech, small-leaved lime, 'Aurora', variety poplar, apple, plum, quince and eucalyptus spread about. Now, among these older trees, others are gradually being established. Most of them are raised from those seedlings (known as 'volunteers' by farmers) which appear, usually unwanted, about the garden. When they are a few inches high, the plants are lifted and transplanted in the wood area. Meanwhile, I raise others from seed I have collected or from cuttings, or I buy saplings from nurseries (see pages 129-132). It might seem, when one looks at the tiny plant which has come from, say a cotoneaster or pine seed, that it will take years for it to grow to a good size, but it is both surprising and reassuring to know that, once these little plants have reached two or three years, they will quickly catch up with and overtake older bought in nursery stock. Examples of some useful plants for the woodland garden that can be obtained in this way are alder, aspen, field maple, blackthorn, wayfaring tree, pine, willow, hazel, holly and guelder rose.

One can buy a whole range of tree seedlings, usually 2-year old, from nurseries. They are often sold as 'hedging' plants and are cheap, but as they are usually expected to be sold in quantity, some negotiation may be necessary. Where understorey plants or garden boundary plants are required, these trees and shrubs can be grown into one another as they do in the wild. In this way they can provide a useful screen or windbreak for those other, perhaps choicer, plants in your wood area.

Shrubs and climbers

The shrub layer of a wood contains the plants with which we become most familiar, for they are near at hand, growing more or less at our level. These we can touch and in turn they touch us as we pass by. They need careful choosing because they are

the plants which add so much to the character of a woodland interior. We are likely to be more aware of them than we are of the trees which create the canopy above them. Fortunately, there are many shrubs both native and exotic which readily accept woodland conditions and which will grow either in the deepest shade at its heart or in the lighter shade at its margins, or maybe in clearings within.

One of the simplest ways of furnishing a woodland is to allow some dominant shrub to grow. Hazel comes to mind because it so often occurs in a wildwood. It will grow on any loamy soil, and a varied field layer will grow quite luxuriantly beneath it.

ABOVE *Where a traditional-style garden ends in a wooded area, existing garden plants mingled with the wild ones help to merge the two areas. If the plants sprawl informally, even flamboyant kinds such as yellow alyssum – when in flower, softly grey in leaf alone – will suit the scene. It helps to interplant them with some of the old-fashioned garden plants that are really native species, such as forget-me-nots.*

Elder, *Sambucus nigra*

Wild cherry,
Prunus avium

Holly,
Ilex aquifolium

Snowberry,
*Symphoricarpos
rivularis*

Mountain ash, *Sorbus aucuparia*

However, most gardeners prefer to collect and grow a wider range of plants than a single species. Where there is a certain amount of moisture or where the shade is really deep, as it can be on some north-facing margins, the guelder rose will thrive. Here also can be grown the common or purging buckthorn, *Rhamnus cathartica,* and the alder buckthorn, *Frangula alnus,* both host plants to the brimstone butterfly. The alder buckthorn is not to be confused with the alder tree which could be grown in the same site. Other shrubs for heavy shade include box, spurge laurel, butcher's broom, bird cherry, tutsan, privet, the exotic *Mahonia aquifolium,* holly, juniper and yew.

Some of the plants designated as small trees can also be grown as shrubs under woodland conditions. Good examples are pussy willow or great sallow, *Salix caprea* and the field maple. In any case, where any of these small trees are planted as shrubs, they can be kept under control if they threaten to grow too large, by being cut back from time to time (see page 138).

Climbers can play an important part in a wooded area. Since these are fairly fast-growing, they can be used to furnish existing trees quickly to give them a more informal and sylvan look. It is better if the support tree has had two or three years to become established. (See also pages 38-39.)

ABOVE *Holly, elder, cherry, rowan and snowberry, five fruiting wild trees or shrubs which brighten the woodland scene. Some fruits are taken by birds as soon as they are ripe, others not until the weather is harsh. North American snowberry, naturalized in Britain, is a favourite of game birds and of bees, for this plant like all the others serves wildlife and the gardener in more ways than one. All have blossom which supports bees or other insects and also brings beauty to the garden.*

Although it is classified as a climbing shrub, ivy will efficiently cover the floor of a wood, especially in heavy shade where other plants are less likely to grow. Remember that the deeper the green and the tougher the texture of a leaf, the more it can tolerate shade. This applies to all kinds of plants. (See also pages 38-39.)

Evergreens

Although the list may seem short when compared with the exotics listed in a nursery catalogue, there is in fact much more variety in native evergreens than is at first apparent, sufficient to provide the gardener with a diversity if this is wanted. Ivy, juniper, yew and holly in particular, as if aware of their singularity, have all produced a great number of varieties. Some of these are extraordinary and differ considerably from the type in their habit and appearance. For instance, a juniper variety may be prostrate, a yew columnar, an ivy rigid, a holly smooth-leaved or with foliage smothered in prickles like a hedgehog. They differ also in leaf size, shape and colour, particularly in variegation. This diversity provides an assortment of specimens which might just suit a gardener's particular needs, so it is well worth while visiting a tree or shrub nursery or an arboretum to see what is available before deciding to remain with the type only.

In Britain, there are few native conifers, yet the presence of these plants in a garden is desirable, since many of them, the pines for example, provide splendid windbreaks, while those thickly clothed with foliage provide cover for nesting birds. Exotic conifers are varied enough for there to be species to suit every kind of soil.

Hedgerows and woodland edges

Very old hedgerows, which contain a diverse collection of species, are thought to be remnants of ancient wildwood. As the land was cleared for farming, a line of trees and shrubs was left to mark boundaries or for shelter. Once laid, a good thick hedgerow would soon be formed. The micro-climate of a hedge is therefore not dissimilar from conditions in a wood – there exists shade, humidity and shelter for both plants and creatures.

If you wish to make a wild hedge, plant it fairly thickly (see page 137). Local hedgerows should guide you to the species most suitable to grow, but most native species will do well on ordinary soil. One of the joys of my local hedgerows is the field maple, the leaves of which persist long after others have fallen. Grow this with hawthorns, guelder rose, dog rose, holly, wild privet, buckthorn and, if you don't mind it suckering, blackthorn. I grow this last because I love to see the first blossom in the hedge. I remove the suckers with a 'lopper', pushing this down into the soil to sever the root.

Where space does not permit a wooded area or copse in the garden, an existing border can often be widened and given a woodland appearance. It can be planted as though it were the edge of a wood. If the border is near a hedge, the woodland effect will be easier to create, especially if the hedge is of mixed species. If you stake one main stem of each hedge species so that it grows above the hedge top, it will not be long before you have a series of little trees – hawthorn, oak, willow, blackthorn and holly among them, perhaps.

ABOVE *Rosebay willowherb,* Epilobium angustifolium, *is a tall perennial found commonly in woods and on heaths and wasteground.*

BELOW *Common in woods of the north temperate zone, wood sorrel,* Oxalis aceto-sella, *has a creeping root and so will soon spread and carpet an area of shady, moist woodland garden.*

On the fringes of the woodland border or hedge-row, grow ferns, campion, spurge, meadow geraniums, willow herb, foxgloves, mullein and honesty. According to soil conditions, the pretty field rose and other climbers can grow.

Where the soil at the wood edge is moist but not wet, yellow deadnettle, yellow loosestrife and its low-growing relative creeping jenny, purple loose-strife, monkshood and tansy can be grown.

Where the soil becomes dry, stony, or gravelly, the bloody crane's bill, various St John's worts, the naturalized rose of sharon, *H. calycinum*, and *Hypericum montanum* can be encouraged to grow.

On acid soils, woodland edge plants such as bilberry and other low shrubs of this family, ling, and heathers can form the basis of a mixed community into which ferns, woodsage and other Labiates could be introduced, many of them wild herbs.

In some gardens it may be the woodland edge which is most on view, in which case the gardener will wish to make it look as attractive and as inviting as possible. Remember that a densely foliated plant will set off one which is more delicately structured, a spreading plant can be grouped against or at the foot of a thin or columnar one.

A woodland border can solve a problem for those gardeners who regret that so much of their plot is in shade. Perhaps a neighbouring tree is so large that it creates a leafy barrier to the sun along part of the garden boundary, or perhaps a high wall projects a harsh shield against sunlight, at least for much of the year. However, plant a woodland edge and the high tree presents a ready-made sylvan backcloth. The high wall, once creeper covered, would seem less aggressive, and the foliage it carried would merge with shade-loving shrubs, which, in turn could frame a field layer, as bright and interesting as mine is.

LEFT *A thicket of ivy offers a secluded nesting site for the wren. Holes or cracks and crevices in banks, walls and woodpiles and dense bushes are other favoured places.*

RIGHT *A border can resemble a wood margin for, given the same conditions of leafy soil and shade for some part of the day, the same kinds of plants can be grown. Those of the field layer include many with handsome foliage which in turn give shade to smaller plants below.*

HEATH AND HEATHER GARDENS

The heather family, the Ericaceae, consists of some 1500 plant species that thrive in peaty, acid or slightly neutral conditions. While many people associate heathers with cool northern hillsides, the greatest number of species occur naturally on the windswept tablelands of South Africa, and indeed most heather species do best in exposed gardens with a mild yet blustery climate.

Heather gardens in which an overlapping patchwork of different heather species is created have long been popular. However, they can look very contrived and formal which is not the effect you should aim for in creating a wild heather garden. Most ericaceous plants are low-lying, slow-growing shrubs and are therefore seen to advantage in a contoured landscape, discreetly clothing a slope, and forming soft, cushioned areas between rocks.

Contours, which create a more attractive landscape, can be created by growing plants of different habit and height. One can begin at the lowest level and if there should be a depression in the land, this can be exploited. Grass pathways or open spaces can be made with the grass kept short, or creeping plants can be used as ground covers. Thymes grow well on the same types of soil, and a creeping thyme lawn can be a most attractive and colourful feature, and extend the season of floral hues.

Apart from heathers, there is a wide range of ericaceous plants available for planting, such as cranberry and other berry-bearing bushes as well as the more natural-looking azaleas and smaller rhododendron species. There are also a host of non-ericaceous companion plants that do well in acid conditions and that will fit well into a heathland scheme, for example, many of the brooms, and conifers, such as junipers, which make a good vertical contrast to the prostrate heather forms.

Many members of the Ericaceae are evergreen in habit, although green is by no means the predominating colour, for the fading stems of blossom and the young tips of the foliage create a perpetual variety of hue. When evergreen heathers are mixed with deciduous species, such as bilberry, a rich harmony of colour is created.

Calluna vulgaris, sometimes known as 'ling', is the common heather which from late summer covers moors and marginal woodland banks with a glorious pale purple-pink. Native to eastern North America, Asia Minor, and northern Europe, it is the only British representative of its genus. *Calluna* is variable, some stiffly erect and bushy, others sprawling and prostrate. The very closely related ericas (*Erica* spp.) are also confusingly known as heaths or heathers.

Heather gardens

Most heathers grow best in a peaty acid soil and it is therefore best to dig plenty of moist peat into your bed and spread a further layer of peat onto the newly dug surface so that this can be worked around the roots. Although it is possible to create artificial peat beds when gardening on an alkaline soil, in the long term this is not worthwhile as a substance called iron sequestrate must be applied to prevent a yellowing (chlorosis) of the leaves, a problem that gets more acute with the years.

There are certain attractive cushion-forming plants among the peaflower family, Papilionaceae, for example, which can be used to give the impression of little hillocks. (See plants for dry heaths, below.) Rising above these, taller shrubs and trees will add both interest and beauty to the landscape.

If there are to be heathers planted below the trees and shrubs, try to get them in at the same time. This will avoid disturbing any growing roots at a later date. This means also that all the plants can be cared for in their early days and both can quickly adjust to each other while they are still young. It is often much more helpful and less damaging if a deep mulch of peat or compost is first spread and the young plants rooted in this.

Plants on this type of soil tend to dry out

ABOVE *Ling,* Calluna vulgaris, *covers moors and woodland banks and margins on acid soil, flowering in late summer. Like the nearly related heathers or ericas, it is a favourite bee plant.*

RIGHT *A slope on acid soil is an ideal site for a heather garden. Apart from anything else, each plant is so well displayed, whether it sprawls on the ground or grows upright among a mass of others. Birch trees harmonize beautifully with these evergreen plants, in winter their silver barks providing a soft, glistening contrast of colour and texture. Some heathers such as the Irish heath,* Erica mediterranea, *become really bushy, growing as tall as 1.5m/5ft or more.*

speedily if they are not kept watered until they are obviously established and capable of looking after themselves. It is advisable for as long as two years after planting and especially at times of drought to keep a close eye on the new inhabitants to make sure that the soil in which they are growing is sufficiently moist.

Young heathers appear to do best when they are planted close together, so where only a few plants are available it is helpful to fill small areas and then extend these as more plants are obtained.

If there is an elevated area in the garden, it could be made into a rock garden or a rock hill. If it is associated with a pond or perhaps a water course, this would suit acid soil areas very well, as the presence of water helps to dispel any dry, arid impression which can sometimes haunt a heath in summer. Those ericas and other species which tolerate a hotter, drier situation could be grown on little plateaux made for them on the mound.

Colour harmonies

In some cases, on acid soils, there may exist little woodlands or copses in which rhododendrons dominate. Aged and mature plants often grow to be quite large. So far as I know, rhododendrons have little importance in native wild life, though where grown thickly the shrubs obviously provide cover. Indeed, it is said that the ponticum rhododendron was originally introduced into Britain – and planted to provide cover for game. It can be too dense in growth for those who wish to see a more varied landscape and may need to be thinned.

Popularly known as azaleas, but really rhododendrons, there are some deciduous American species which lend themselves attractively to the wild heather garden. They colour the landscape in late spring and early summer with blossom and with coloured foliage in the autumn. The North American flame flower, *Rhododendron calendulaceum* (syn. *Azalea calendulacea*), and the fragrant western azalea, *R. occidentale,* and the Pinxter flower or pink azalea, *R. nudiflorum,* are examples. A Japanese species, *R. japonicum* (known to many

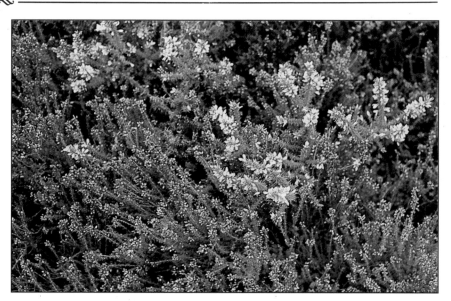

gardeners as *Azalea mollis*), is a great favourite for informal gardens.

Rhododendrons grow best under thinly planted trees such as oaks, where the light dappled shade protects the blossoms from intense sunshine so that they are not too quickly spent. They look delightful on the edge or in a clearing of a wood.

Heathers for milder aspects

Many gardeners with neutral or limy soil make successful cultivated heather gardens mainly because there are two species, *Erica carnea,* a native of the limestone Alps, and *E. mediterranea,* the Irish heath, native to Galway and south-west Europe, which are actually tolerant of a very little lime in the soil. Both of these species, like *Calluna,* have given rise to many commercially raised varieties. The Irish heath grows to 3m/10ft in time, and flowers early.

E. vagans, the Cornish heath, native also to south-west Europe, flowers right through the summer until early winter, but it is less hardy than the Irish heath and so should be grown only in climates where the winter is mild. It is a straggling shrub, 1m/3ft in height, with thick bushy racemes of small pale purple-pink flowers. Its cultivated

ABOVE *Abundant on heaths in the wild, gorse, furze and broom with their conspicuous yellow, pea-like flowers are often found complementing the rosy-purples of heather and ling. Gorse, Ulex europaeus, is the species shown here, and where more yellow is favoured, nurseries sell varieties of different species of ericas which have vividly-coloured foliage. When purple flowering varieties are also grown, together they make a brilliant patch of colour.*

forms have flowers of deeper and clearer colours.

Taking its name from an Irish saint, *Daboecia cantabrica,* St Dabeoc's Heath, looks a little like an outsize heather. It differs from the true ericas in that its corolla falls from the stem, while those of ericas remain, turning to many lovely russet hues – particularly striking when wet with rain or mist. This heath flowers through the summer months and is a striking plant when in bloom. There is a variety *D. alba* from Connemara as well as *D. bicolor* which has three-colour forms on the same individual – some purple, some white, some purple and white! Like the Cornish heath, this species is apt to become damaged in severe winters although it does seem to have good restorative powers. Any damaged part should be cut away once all danger of frost is passed.

Ericaceae for wet conditions

Those species which need constant moisture, such as the bog heather or cross-leaved heath, *Erica tetralix,* can be grown most successfully by the water's edge, although none of the heathers will thrive in a completely waterlogged situation. Where there is no natural water, arrangements should be made for the plants to be watered in

A HEATHER GARDEN
Heather colours can be naturally soft or vividly vibrant. So many of the native green-leaved species have produced varieties with bright flowers and foliage. Some flower through summer until late into autumn: *Erica vagens* 'Mrs Maxwell' **1**, and the bell heather, *E. cinerea* **2**, its variety *E.c.* 'Alba minor' **3** and *E. mackaiana* **4**. Ling, *Calluna vulgaris,* flowers similarly: *C.v.* 'Golden King' **5** and *C.v.* 'Silver Queen' **6**. Purple thymes **7** carpet the ground. Behind are *C.v.* 'H.E. Beale' **8** and *C.v.* 'Peter Sparkes' **9**. Other shrubs are broom, *Cytisus scoparius* **10**, *Hebe* **11** and *Juniperus horizontalis* **12**. On the right are cowberry, *Vaccinium vitis-idaea* **13** and its relative bilberry, *V. myrtillus* **14**. Between the strawberry tree, *Arbutus unedo* **15**, and the birch, *Betula* sp. **16** is St Dabeoc's heath, *Daeboecia cantabrica* **17**, and gorse, *Ulex europaeus* **18**.

some way. The soil can be kept in the right condition by the use of a trickle irrigation system, which can be bought and operated as necessary.

This heath forms a spreading plant, anything up to 50cm/20in high, with downy young shoots and rose-pink flowers from summer until late autumn. It has many lovely varieties in cultivation, all of which greatly resent dry soil, a fact which is not often appreciated by those who buy on impulse from garden centres. More straggly than the cross-leaved heath, the Dorset heath, *Erica ciliaris,* has larger, deeper coloured flowers from midsummer onwards. It is also a procumbent shrub, rarely exceeding 30cm/12in in height.

Described as an attractive carpeting plant in heath and woodland gardens, the cowberry, *Vaccinium vitis-idaea,* one of the Ericaceae, has obviously earned the approval of traditional gardeners. It grows wild on peat moors. It is a dainty evergreen creeping shrub with small but tough leathery-green leaves with paler undersides. Its flowers, which bloom from late spring, are very pale pink and bell-shaped. They are followed by small, edible red fruits. Similar plants forming small bushes include the whortleberry, *V. myrtillus,* and the cranberries, *V. microcarpum* and *V. oxycoccus,* all of which need ground moisture and humidity. Here also can be grown the evergreen marsh andromeda, *Andromeda polifolia,* a plant which is also sometimes grown in lime-free humus in gardens, although its varieties are most likely to be seen in cultivation. It is known as bog rosemary. *A. polifolia minima* is almost prostrate.

Among these moisture-loving acid soil plants, is the aromatic *Ledum palustre,* a plant of the northern lands of America, Europe and Asia, with terminally clustered and wide open flowers so unlike the general bell shape of most of the members of the Ericacea. It is a broad, thick-set evergreen bush, 1m/3ft high with dark green leaves which are rusty-coloured and tomentose on the undersides. The flowers are creamy white. It has been cultivated in our gardens for many years and is popularly known as Labrador tea.

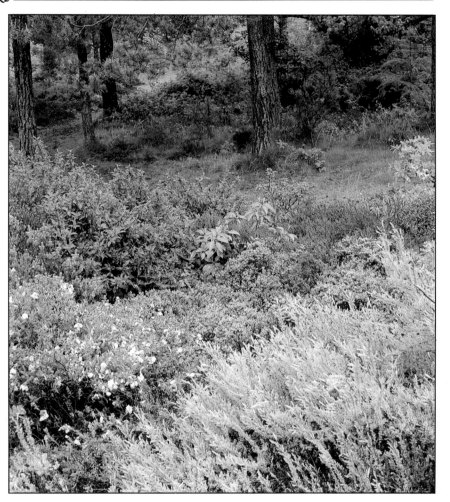

Other plants for moist and wet acid sites

The beautiful bog asphodel, *Narthecium ossifragum,* which produces orange-yellow lily flowers in midsummer, many on one stem, is a creeping perennial some 15cm/6in high. Actually, this species will grow in ordinary soil in moist beds and borders, as well as in the margins of a bog or pond. Its variety *americanum* has smaller flowers and narrower leaves.

For those who seek wild rarities, there is the lovely creeping harebell or ivy-leaved bell flower, *Wahlenbergia hederacea* (sometimes known as *Campanula hederacea*). It needs a peaty site and

ABOVE *Where the shade is never dense, the margin of a wood on acid soil provides an ideal area for an assortment of shrubs – both natives, such as the yellow-flowered gorse, or exotics, such as cistus and rhododendron. All can be attractively mingled with native heather and ling. Where space permits, they can gradually spread outwards to make a heather border where the taller species can give way to those which grow closer to the ground.*

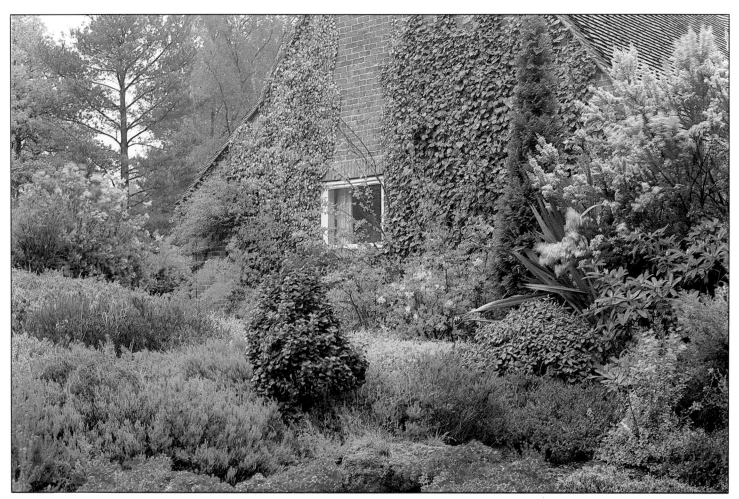

should be kept moist in dry weather. Gardeners recommend that it is best established by sowing seed on living sphagnum moss.

Another uncommon plant, of damp mountain sides, rather than the damp woodland edge, is the petty whin, *Genista anglica,* a dainty 60cm/24in high little 'broom'.

Plants of dry heath

Bell heather, *Erica cinerea,* also called purple heather or fine-leaved heath, often forms wide stretches of drier heathland and makes for an attractive ground-cover shrub, up to 60cm/24in

high, for a dry heathland display. The flowers are a dark crimson-purple and appear from summer through until late autumn.

The bilberry, or whortleberry, associates well with heather and is worth growing for its lovely autumn hues. One of the delightful features of heath gardens is that you can expect such fine colours in both autumn and winter.

Often overlooked in traditional gardens, even though it is a beautiful shrub, the evergreen gorse is eminently suitable for a garden of this nature. It grows quickly, can be grown from seed and attracts both birds and insects. It is often in bloom at a time

ABOVE *A house which seems to have grown up from its garden, an effect enhanced by the thick cover of ivy varieties which clothe its walls. The heathers which reach right up to it, covering large areas with free-flowering evergreen plants need little further attention once they have become established. Such a garden becomes both labour- and wildlife-saving since it provides so much undisturbed cover. There are many other shrubs which can be planted among the heathers.*

when there are few other flowers, thus offering nectar to any early foraging butterfly. The common gorse, *Ulex europaeus*, is mainly spring-flowering, but it often produces bloom erratically at different periods. There is a dwarfer autumn-flowering species, *U. galli*, and a smaller one still, also autumn-flowering, *U. minor*. These dwarf gorse are cushion-forming. When smothered with their bright yellow flowers, they complement wonderfully the purples of the heather, as do others of their tribe.

The closely related common broom, *Cytisus scoparius*, is a glorious sight when in full flower. It has a variety, *C. prostratus*, which some botanists regard as a subspecies.

All these plants are members of the peaflower family. Less well-known members, also suited for dry heath conditions, include the uncommon hairy greenweed, *Genista pilosa*, which has small yellow flowers and downy seed pods and blooms from spring to autumn.

Of the smaller flowers, the violets are especially attractive and seed freely once established. The dog or wood violet, *Viola riviniana*, is often found growing alongside the heath dog violet, *V. canina*, with bluer though paler flowers. This species is also confusingly known as dog violet. (It was so named by Linnaeus when the term 'dog' was used for certain common flowers.) A true heath violet is *V. lactea* with pale milky blue flowers. It is not

BELOW *Spring-flowering bulbous plants, such as these daffodils, can look attractive planted among heathers. However, one of the great qualities of the latter is that they cover the ground with colour throughout the year for the plants are seldom just plain green. Their flowering shoots provide colour for months on end, becoming tinted as the buds begin to form and gradually taking on a deeper hue as the flowers mature. Most of these persist and fade to warm russet colours which may continue until the new shoots arrive.*

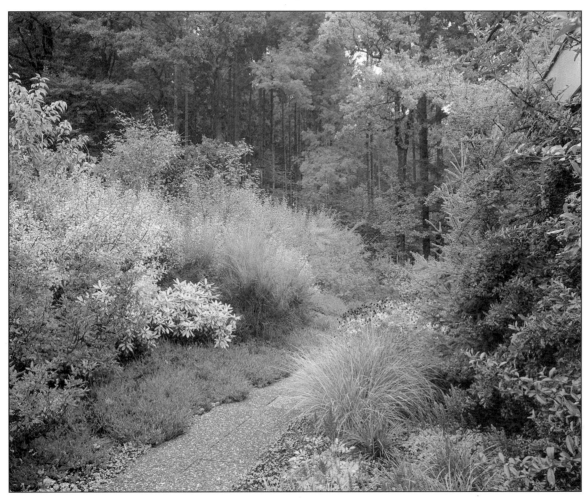

LEFT *A beautiful woodland border in heather country. While the ground is closely covered with heathers, many different kinds of shrubs and plants,* Pyracantha, Amelanchier, Cytisus, Rhododendron *and* Astilbe *among them, grow up above their level, their fruits or fox-coloured seed stems contributing to the general colour harmony and contrasting splendidly with the evergreen, coniferous background. Besides being such a visual delight, an area like this provides a useful environment for wildlife, for there is both food and shelter.*

ABOVE *Less hardy than some species, in mild climates the Cornish heath,* Erica vagans, *flowers from midsummer to late autumn. It has produced several varieties, different in colour and appearance from the type.*

unusual for these three species to grow together and to cross-fertilize, thus producing hybrids which may sometimes be sterile, sometimes partially fertile.

The beautiful harebell, *Campanula rotundifolia*, makes a lovely addition to the flowers of dry heath, with its loose trusses of nodding blue flowers.

Plants for rocky outcrops

Where stone is combined with acid soil conditions it should be possible to grow the bearberry, *Arctostaphylos uva-ursi*, a dwarf, trailing, shining evergreen shrub found on scree slopes on moorland.

Rock, carefully positioned, can help to create the atmosphere of a moor or heath. One or two large pieces placed with care are often much more effective than many small pieces assembled in a rock garden or dotted about. Used in unison with a tree, or group of trees, a piece of rock can look most dramatic. Sometimes, by grouping two rocks, it may be possible to give the impression that the tree is growing from a cleft in the single rock. The same ploy can be used on a smaller scale on a rock hill when smaller, perhaps prostrate shrubs including heathers and some conifers can be used. (See also Rock gardens, pages 114-120.)

FERN AND FOLIAGE GARDENS

A north-facing border, or sometimes the north side of a wide border, or a tree-shaded path might appear to pose a problem when planting a garden. Yet, this is often an ideal site for an all-green garden of ferns and grasses. And there are many other kinds of plants, both native and exotic, that have handsome foliage that can be pleasantly mingled with them.

Ferns and grasses growing together create a pleasing harmony of green shapes and textures which are often overlaid with other hues according to the season or to the variegation of a variety of species. They are delightful subjects for bordering woodland walks, and for fringing woodland and shrub borders, or for furnishing shady or partly shaded places.

Where only part of a garden is used for wild species, ferns and grasses can be planted to fill it in summer while, in early spring with these two not yet really active, smaller plants such as primroses, violets and celandines could be planted to carpet the ground between the green plants. When the flowering plants are fading and no longer decorative, the growing grass and ferns will mask them.

Ferns and grasses add a light touch to some of the denser plants such as holly, ivy and other evergreens (including rhododendrons), whether they are grouped immediately below and around them or in the spaces in between. Ferns of different species, with various heights and forms, will look most attractive, and tall ferns will add their charm where trees and shrubs cast a dappled shade.

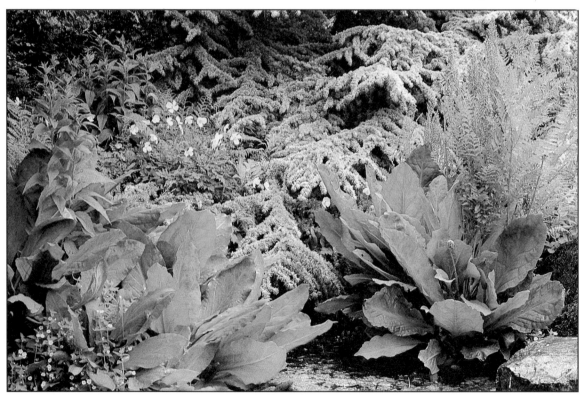

LEFT *The handsome leaves of* Lysichitum americanum, *sometimes called skunk cabbage, follow its giant yellow arum-like flowers. It is a fine plant for the waterside or for damp places where (to the right) the royal ferns,* Osmunda regalis, *also flourish. Both plants furnish the scene for many months, the fern gradually assuming lovely russet hues as the year end approaches. In the background is* Cedrus atlantica.

RIGHT *The large-leaved ivy beyond the arch and the variegated box to the left are just two examples of varieties of two native evergreen species which have many diverse forms. Both provide splendid cover for many forms of wildlife. The little ivy-leaved toadflax growing in the wall and the yellow-flowered* Corydalis *are two species which seed freely. Foliage in the foreground is of* Bergenia *from Asia, some species of which are hardy.*

Ferns

One of the most useful qualities of ferns is that they will grow well where most flowering plants fail, and although most require moisture, some will flourish in dry situations. In dense shade, even in that cast by overhanging tree branches which drip heavily in rainy weather, you can grow a fern garden or simply plant one or more species in groups. Most of the buckler fern family, Dryopteris, which has a world-wide distribution of a great number of species, are suitable. One of the most familiar is the handsome male fern, *Dryopteris filix-mas,* which survives even in dusty town gardens. Given shelter, it will remain almost evergreen and prove a handsome tenant to border and woodland alike. The exception for deep shade is *D. villarsii.* This is one of those ferns which will grow in sunny, dry and even exposed places.

Among the most ancient of plants on earth, ferns grow wild all over the world and there are thought to be some 10,000 species. Obviously not all are hardy in the northern hemisphere. Some of the fern families are very large. The polypody, the largest, has some 170 genera and possibly as many as 7,250 species distributed over all parts of the world. Most of the North American fern species

A COURTYARD FERN GARDEN

In a corner of a tiny paved town garden, water is more than an ornamental feature. Most importantly, it cleans and humidifies the air around, thus generating the ideal micro-climate for native ferns and other moisture-loving plants. Gardens of this nature are so often shaded by neighbouring buildings. Fortunately many foliage plants will accept the shade. The darker the green of their leaves, the more tolerant of it they will be. If, on the other hand, the yard is sunny, then take advantage of all shade, even that which at some time of the day is cast by tall, leafy plants such as the royal and lady ferns and Solomon's seal. As they grow, they can protect the carpeting species.

1 Scented water lily, *Nymphaea odorata* 'minor'
2 Sweet flag, *Acorus calamus*
3 Creeping jenny, *Lysimachia nummularia*
4 Pendulous sedge, *Carex pendula*
5 Violets, *Viola* sp.
6 Thymes, *Thymus* sp.
7 Bog arum, *Calla palustris*
8 Lady fern, *Athyrium filix-femina*
9 Male fern, *Dryopteris filix-mas*
10 Parsley fern, *Cryptogramma crispa*
11 Solomon's seal, *Polygonatum multiflorum*
12 Ivy, *Hedera helix*
13 Maidenhair spleenwort, *Asplenium trichomanes*
14 Hart's tongue fern, *Phyllitis scolopendrium*
15 Ivy-leaved toadflax, *Cymbalaria muralis*
16 Common polypody, *Polypodium vulgare*
17 Starry saxifrage, *Saxifraga stellaris*
18 Royal fern, *Osmunda regalis*
19 Common quaking grass, *Briza media*
20 London pride, *Saxifraga umbrosa*

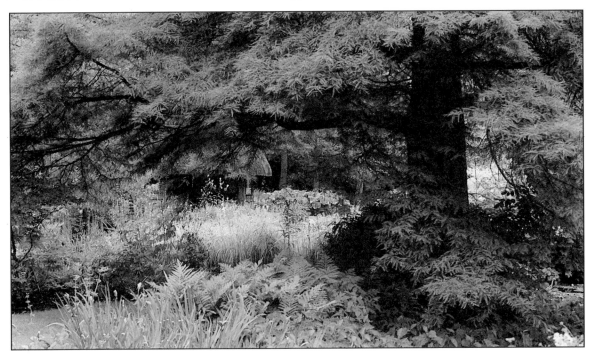

are deciduous, while most of those from Japan are evergreen. There are both kinds among the British species. In many fern species, the young fronds are tinted with attractive hues of copper or bronze, and even pink or magenta. Often the coloration may be more marked in a variety than in the type, and the shapes and characters of the fronds may differ also.

Nowadays it is wrong, and illegal in some countries, to uproot ferns from the wild, but many are to be found in nurserymen's lists. If you are unfamiliar with fern species but would like to start a fern garden, why not begin with the four easiest species, the lady, male, deer and hart's tongue ferns? The most majestic ferns are the male and lady ferns, both of which are strictly deciduous, except in mild winters or in very sheltered gardens. True evergreens are the ferns of the polystichum family, which prefer a slightly acid soil and must be kept moist at the roots at all times. See page 134 for cultivation of ferns.

Gravel areas often unexpectedly harbour some of the ferns we find growing wild on walls, and these ferns do not generally need shade or much moisture. For instance the pretty, yet tough, maidenhair spleenwort, *Asplenium trichomanes,* is to be found growing wild in very exposed situations. (I am growing this species on the ground in well-drained soil between paving stones.) The wall rue, *A. ruta-muraria,* will also grow on flat, stony, well-drained and limy soils. Even the handsome, much taller lady fern is sometimes to be found growing there, although it is mainly known to luxuriate in woods and on shady banks, even near water, on lime-rich soils. This fern has deeply divided fronds, some 45-90cm/18-38in long, and it is very variable. An attractive collection of lady fern varieties could perhaps be made.

Ferns which grow wild on walls can also be grown in rock gardens and, so long as they are covered by a shallow layer of soil, compost or leaf-mould, on stony banks, or even on heaps of rubble. (It might be one way of camouflaging the latter.) Two species suitable for this purpose are *Ceterach officinarum* and *Asplenium adiantum-nigrum.* Other

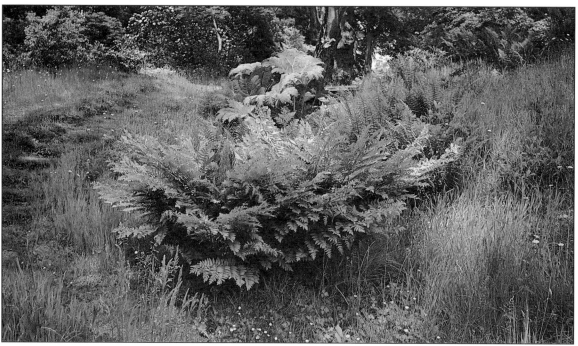

LEFT *The handsome male fern,* Dryopteris filix-mas, *will thrive almost anywhere. Like many native fern species it, too, has produced a great number of forms treasured by fern lovers. These differ, often greatly, in shape or size from the type. Although classed as deciduous, in a sheltered place or mild season it will remain almost ever-green. It can be grown informally, or in a border with other kinds of ferns and plants.*

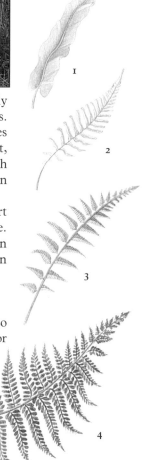

species are the bladder fern, *Cystopteris fragilis*, the common polypody, *Polypodium vulgare*, and the lovely hart's tongue, *Phyllitis scolopendrium*. This last species has many interesting varieties.

The hart's tongue will grow well in borders and in crevices on the level, but bear in mind that these are ferns that will wilt badly if they are in a too dry situation. They are much more handsome when they are grown in shade than when they are sub-jected to sun and drought. In my own garden some have appeared quite spontaneously on a north-facing hedge bank where they grow among the lush grass and hedgerow plants.

Should you wish to decorate an old wall, you can top it with the common polypody. Either make spaces, or find existing crevices, to fill with leaf-mould and plant young ferns. These have the best chance of survival. This little polypody, which grows on trees, is one of Europe's few epiphytic plants, but it also grows on rock faces, old walls and sometimes roofs, especially if these have become mossy. It can be planted on an old tree stump, and

will withstand drought. It grows a little differently from most of the other ferns and it is rhizomatous. When divided and transplanted, the rhizomes should not be completely covered by the soil, but, like flag irises, should be half in and half out, with the root portion anchored and the top part open to the air.

The polypody appears to prefer to stay apart from other ferns and to colonize its particular site. Give it a little area to itself so that its rhizomes can spread without competition. Division of plants can take place at any time of year.

Ornamental grasses

Those who hope to create a wild garden that is also a sanctuary for wildlife should find some space for

RIGHT 1 *The hart's tongue fern,* Phyllitis scolopendrium. 2 *The deer fern,* Blechnum spicant. 3 *The male fern,* Dryopteris filix-mas. 4 *The lady fern,* Athyrium filix-fermina.

grasses – as assorted a mixture of species as possible. Apart from the fact that almost all of them are decorative in some way, they offer cover and even nesting places to many creatures. Some species are host plants to both moths and butterflies (see also chapter on wildflower meadows, pages 56-67). One reason why it is helpful to retain some long grass throughout the winter is so that hibernating pupae are safe. Grass seed is highly nutritious and forms an important part of the diet of many birds and some mammals.

Borders of different tall grasses can be full of interest and beauty, but some of the loveliest effects come from those with long, arching stems that rise and lean out from a dense green cover.

One native grass which gives great pleasure for many months in my own garden is the tall, drooping woodland brome, *Bromus ramosus.*

Often to be found growing with it is the slender false or wood brome, *Brachypodium sylvaticum.* However, not all bromus grasses (many of which are meadow grasses) are welcome in gardens or on farmland. Others, mainly natives of the Mediterranean region, have become naturalized in places, such as *Bromus briziformis* which, cultivated, is used dried (and sometimes dyed) in flower arrangements.

The giant fescue, *Festuca gigantea,* is also found growing with bromus. The tall fescue, *F. arundinacea,* is another handsome species with varieties that appear to have become adapted to different types of soils and habitats. This species can reach

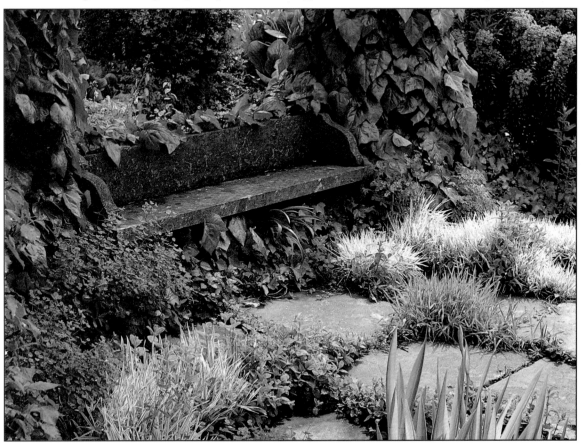

LEFT *Green plants are wonderfully restful and, in their way, reassuring. Most are furnished with living leaves at all times of the year, a solace for those who may be townlocked for days, even weeks on end. Varieties of native plants, variegated flag, grasses and ivy, flourish in this little paved yard and mingle with native spurges and the handsome exotic,* Euphorbia wulfenii.

1.5m/5ft, and those who want to grow it for height should take seed only from really tall specimens.

The wood or reed fescue, *F. altissima,* grows in woods, shady places and on watersides. It has wide, flat leaf blades which distinguish it from other fescue species.

The wood millet *Milium effusum,* an evergreen perennial, can grow to 1.2m/4ft and has ribbon-like leaves up to 30cm/12in long. Gardeners may be more familiar with the variety *M. aureum,* known to some as Bowles' golden grass.

Grasses to plant in drifts

On the very edge of a dense beech wood near my home, a misty drift of the wood melick, *Melica uniflora,* covers a steep bank where the light from above shines through the frail, arching stems. When it is not growing high on a wooded bank, it is seen at its prettiest reaching out from a shaded hedgerow or over a stream. It grows well on light or heavy soils. (*M.u. variegata,* striped green and cream, as well as an albino form which has white spikelets, are often grown in gardens.)

For those who favour golden grasses, there is a golden-leaved form of cat's tail, *Phleum pratense aureum,* also known as golden timothy. It is a good plant for informal positions in sunny or slightly shaded sites.

Presumably an escape from packets of seed fed to both cage and wild birds, the annual canary grass, *Phalaris canariensis,* a native of Mediterranean regions, is often to be found growing wild, mainly on wasteland. Another annual, *P. minor,* a species with a longer flower head, sometimes also appears in the wild. A much more vigorous species is the tall perennial often to be found growing wild near water, the reed canary grass, *P. arundinacea,* with its handsome purplish panicles. It has a variegated form, *P. a. picta,* known as gardener's garters, which has long been cultivated in gardens

SOME FLOWERING GRASSES
1 Upright brome, *Bromus erectus*
2 Madrid brome, *Bromus madritensis*
3 Reed sweet grass, *Glyceria maxima variegata*
4 Hare's tail, *Lagurus ovatus*
5 Giant fescue, *Festuca gigantea*

1   2   3   4   5

where it grows well in ordinary soil and in sun or shade.

Possibly the most endearing of all grasses are the quaking grasses, of which three species are to be found in Britain. The lesser or small *Briza minor*, like so many others really a native of the Mediterranean regions and so preferring a sunny situation, is now a common escape from gardens. It can also be grown in a meadow garden. The large quaking grass, *B. maxima*, is a good plant for dry banks. *B. media*, the common quaking or totter grass (to give it but two of its trivial names) is perennial, found on calcareous soils, but will grow in ordinary heavy or light soils and in dry or moist situations. The quivering pendulous shining spikelets are purple. *B. media* has two varieties, one with greener, one with yellower spikelets.

Even more widely cultivated, for flower decoration, is hare's tail, *Lagurus ovatus*, another Mediterranean plant that has become naturalized in certain areas. It is a good grass for dry and sandy sites as in the wild it is found on sand dunes.

Often to a seen in traditional gardens, where it is used as an edging plant or grown in clumps among flowering plants in borders, is the strangely named Yorkshire fog, *Holcus lanatus*, also known as velvet grass.

Called sweet or vanilla grass in North America, the rare and lovely *Hierochloe odorata* (it is scented with coumarin) is seldom to be found growing wild in Britain although it is native to both Britain and Europe. Known as Holy grass, in some parts of Europe it was a strewing herb placed at church doorways. The plicate sweet grasses, for example

6 Tall fescue, *Festuca arundinacea*
7 Quaking grass, *Briza media*
8 Wood mellick, *Melica uniflora*
9 Wood millet, *Milium effusum*
10 Velvet grass, *Holcus lanatus*

6   7   8   9   10

Glyceria pedicellata and *G. plicata,* with their graceful panicles of widely spaced spikelets, attract water fowl which feed on the seeds. They also grow in ditches and swampy places.

Sedges and rushes

The rushes and sedges may also play an important useful and decorative part in the wild garden. There are in all nearly one thousand species, most though not all of which prefer wet, acid soils.

The fluffy cotton grasses, *Eriophorum,* members of the Cyperaceae, like the sedges, and not true grasses, are found in peat bogs yet will grow in ordinary soil as well as on the margins of ponds.

Sow the seed where the plants are to grow. *E. angustifolium* is the common species, *E. latifolium* is the broad-leaved cotton grass and *E. vaginatum* is known as the hare's tail grass.

A few of the sedges and rushes have been cultivated in gardens, the favourite being the tall, pendulous sedge, *Carex pendula,* an inhabitant of damp woods and shady places. In gardens, it is usually seen growing on the margins of ponds but it need not be confined to this role.

In woodland gardens on damp, heavy soils, the pretty wood sedge, *Carex sylvatica,* will bring variety into the field layer. For wet, peaty soils try *C. rostrata,* the beaked or bottle sedge with its yellow-hued fruits.

Some of the genera will grow in dry situations and on chalky soils, for example the commonly found glaucous sedge, *Carex flacca,* the spring sedge, *C. caryophyllea,* and the dwarf sedge, *C. humulis.* These are just a few of those species attractive and interesting enough for the garden.

Except where there are fairly extensive water gardens, the rushes have not featured much in traditional gardens. Of those that have, the glaucous club rush, *Scirpus tabernaemontani,* is more likely to be represented by its variety, *S.t. zebrinus,* which has long tubular stems, distinctively banded green and white. The triangular club rush, *S. triquetrus,* which grows wild in muddy estuaries, has also been accepted as a garden plant.

One of the most attractive species is *Scirpus sylvaticus* the wood rush. This one has very broad green leaves, and a head of clustered green spikelets. The plant is a lover of wet, shady places. The true bulrush or club rush is *S. lacustris* (not to be confused with *Typha latifolia,* the reed mace and also sometimes called the bulrush). It has fat green stems or rushes 1-1.2m/3-4ft tall and clusters of chocolate brown flowers in August. One little evergreen species, the cosmopolitan *S. cernuus,* just under 30cm/12in high, is sometimes grown as a greenhouse pot plant.

Fine foliage

Many exotic foliage plants such as hosta, ligularia and rodgersia are grown in traditional English wild gardens. However, many native plants also have handsome leaves and are well worth growing for their foliage. The cuckoo pints, both *Arum italicum* and *A. maculatum,* have leaves which are handsomely sagittate. These are variable plants, some with plain apple-green leaves, others prettily spotted. In one, *A. italicum,* the leaves begin to appear in autumn, others in spring. They linger on into summer growing in thick groups while the young spikes of berries take the place of the arum flowers. They then die down.

The palmate leaves of the early flowering stinking hellebore, *Helleborus foetidus* (it really does not smell very unpleasant) are produced generously as are the thick clusters of green flowers. Together they give the plant a handsome mien. *Helleborus viridus,* the green hellebore, is equally handsome in or out of flower.

The gladdon, *Iris foetidissima,* has long, bold, deep green, spear-like leaves which stay evergreen all winter, a welcome touch. Although the flowers are drab, the plant produces pods of bright orange berries which add considerably to its decorative value in the dark days.

In woods and partial shade, the long leaf-laden stems of Solomon's seal, *Polygonatum multiflorum,* contrast well with shorter neighbouring plants, the leaves outliving the flowers, from which sometimes

ABOVE *Cuckoo pint, also called lords and ladies,* Arum maculatum, *is found in shady places in the wild, on banks and in woods. It has a spike of bright orange berries, much loved by birds.*

little black berries are produced. The leaves turn a golden yellow in the fall.

Daphne laureola, the spurge laurel, is an attractive little evergreen characteristic of beechwoods. It bears clusters of green, slightly scented flowers in early spring. The mezereon, *D. mezereum,* is rarely found wild nowadays but is often to be seen in cottage gardens where its scented flowers in early spring bring as much pleasure to the gardener as its red-purple berries bring to the birds.

The spurges or euphorbias are among the loveliest of all plants for the wild garden. The caper spurge, *Euphorbia lathyrus,* with grey-green leaves and stems, which often grows to 1m/3ft, has the presence of a shrub. It is an annual, although sometimes it behaves as a biennial. Once grown, it should seed itself.

There are many umbellifers with handsome foliage, such as angelica, sweet cicely, and fennel, described in the chapter on wild herbs, pages 96-101. In the chapter on water gardens, pages 102-113, further fine foliage plants are named.

BELOW *Most foliage plants are adaptable to different areas of a wild garden. The lush, exotic hosta or plantain lily, growing here in grass in the moist, humid atmosphere on the fringes of a water garden, will flourish under trees. The graceful Solomon's seal nearby, a woodland plant, will accept the slighter, dappled shade of shrubs instead of an overhead canopy of foliage.*

THE WILD HERB GARDEN

Through the centuries, herbs have been of great service to mankind, not only for cooking but as medicines, dyes, perfumes, salves and potpourris. I would urge those people about to create a wild garden to find space for as many species as possible for, practical uses apart, they are beautiful, fragrant and often irresistible to insect and bird life.

Among the wild herbs long naturalized are some of my favourite culinary ones, including chervil, caraway and parsley. The dainty caraway, *Carum carvi,* a biennial flowering in summer, is still rather rare in the wild, while parsley, *Petroselinum crispum,* is found, surprisingly perhaps, on limestone walls and rocks. The growth is never as lush as when grown in deep, well-manured soil in a vegetable garden, and the same is true of many species of wild plants brought into the garden: the good soil and lack of competition with other plants results in luxuriant growth.

Garden chervil, *Anthriscus cerefolium,* not to be confused with the native hedgerow or roadside species, rough chervil, *Chaerophyllum temulentum,* is an alien but well worth growing as the self-sown seedlings appear at a time when fresh green herbs are scarce, in late winter and early spring. It is an attractive, lady's lace type of flower, a daintier plant than 'wild chervil' or cow parsley, *Chaerophyllum sylvestre,* and better flavoured and more versatile. The seedlings will often appear at the sides of a path, which is often a useful place for herbs to grow, as well as a way of linking one part of the garden with another.

The thymes are a large and mixed race, notoriously difficult to classify and identify. There are probably about 100 species, all of the old world, and only a few of these occur naturally in Britain. My own attitude to this favourite pungent herb family, being a keener cook than botanist, is to ignore the confusion and just grow and use those that come to hand. Bees love them all.

Of the truly native British herbs, try the apple-aromatic chamomile, *Anthemis nobilis* (which can be used for lawns). The flowers of both double and single forms may be dried for a soothing tea.

It is not the purpose of this book to deal in depth with food from a wild herb garden, but there are times when a too generous crop of some plant or other might smother a species more cherished. If it is edible, then it is better eaten than thrown away!

Where to grow herbs in a wild garden

Traditionally, herbs are grown for convenience either in rows in the kitchen garden or in a herb plot or border near the house, a number of different species generally occupying the same plot. The gardener then tries to develop one type of soil to suit them all, although there is no horticultural reason for this measure. Growing wild, herbs will be found on many types of soil, and in sun or shade (whether dry or moist), or along the waterside. This means that most can happily be introduced into the less rigorous confines of the wild garden, and grow happily among other plants.

LEFT *A beautiful poppy with handsome glaucous leaves,* Papaver somniferum *has been described as 'a weed of cultivation'. An alien, it was probably first introduced in grain seed. The large, pot-shaped seed vessels contain thousands of black, oily seeds, provenance for wildlife.*

RIGHT *A display of sweet-scented herb leaves in a great variety of hue and texture. Many herb species – fennel, mint and marjoram, for instance – which are naturally green, produce golden, variegated, purple or bronze-leaved varieties. Most die down in winter but their seeding stems, a source of food for many creatures, should be left uncut until spring.*

In my own garden I have compromised, and have a long bank, on the site of an old hedge, which is entirely given up to herbs. The bank has been raised artificially, so that now, being much higher than the ground on either side and closely planted, it acts as a screen for the kitchen garden.

The bank itself offers several different habitats. It runs east to west, with one side in full sun, the other in full shade, and varying degrees of shelter and shade for species which occupy positions in between. Along its 20m/66ft length, the really dominant and would-be invasive species such as apple mint, tansy and soapwort have room to struggle among themselves for ascendancy, their contrasting foliage merging in a delightful harmony of woolly, shiny or lacy green. Between them and elsewhere, fennel, blue-flowered alkanet, marjoram, lemon balm and purslane increase in size and seed freely.

Among the umbellifers, a favourite is sweet cicely, *Myrrhis odorata,* a graceful and lovely plant for the wild garden, which tolerates most types of soil. The white umbels bloom in spring, followed by long seeds which can be eaten in salads when fresh, as can both leaves and roots.

The two burnets used as herbs grow side by side on the shaded slope of the bank. Salad or lesser burnet, *Poterium sanguisorba,* grows in dry, calcareous fields and has cucumber-flavoured leaves. Great burnet, *Sanguisorba officinalis,* usually grows in damper fields and will grow on heavy clay.

Excellent for clothing a bank and for holding the soil secure is tansy, *Tanacetum vulgare,* usually found wild on river banks, roadsides and in hedgerows. It has distinctive, fern-like foliage. The creeping rootstock enables it to cover ground quickly and effectively, so it may need restraining.

Various thymes have been planted at the foot of the bank, the carpeting species in sanded or shingled spaces between the paving stones on the sunny side, where trampling does not harm them.

Mediterranean sages, rosemary, hyssop and lavender keep firmly to their original planting sites, growing in girth as the years pass.

LEFT *For those who wish to gather herbs frequently, a path is essential, but it need not be conspicuous. A straight-sided path can be softened by yet more herbs growing at its edges and between the pavings. Thyme flowers bloom for weeks on end, but even after they have faded they leave dense mats of little, tough, pungently scented leaves which bear the pressure of treading.*

Certain annuals are left to fend for themselves: the grey-leaved poppy, *Papaver somniferum,* the seeds of which are eaten by humans and mice alike, and pot marigold, borage, feverfew and chervil.

The prostrate mint, pennyroyal, *Mentha pulegium,* is a perfect plant to cover ground or damp paving where there is also sand, and those who have ditches, damp or marshy ground should find space for the water mint, *Mentha aquatica,* a handsome plant with a delightful, characteristic scent, which is why it was once popular as a strewing herb. As it was harvested, so it was kept under control, for it can be invasive like most other mints

The cultivated angelica, *Angelica archangelica,* from central Europe, has found its way to some river banks. In a wild garden it will do best in shade in deep, moist loam, and it is a fine plant to grow near a pond. The native species, *A. sylvestris,* is also a handsome plant for a moist spot, but should not be eaten.

Alexanders, *Smyrnium olusatrum,* can be eaten, its thick stems peeled and cooked and eaten like asparagus. It used to be cultivated as a salad before the introduction of celery.

ABOVE *Once an esteemed culinary and medicinal herb, tansy,* Tanacetum vulgare, *is usually to be found growing luxuriantly on river banks. The fern-like leaves have a spicy, pungent scent.*

Rocky coasts seem to be the habitat of many of our most flavoursome plants, of which lovage or sea parsley, *Ligusticum scoticum*, gives a celery-like taste to soups. It grows in ordinary soil and, in my own experience, best where there is some humidity and where the roots can be kept fairly moist in dry weather.

The common valerian, *Valeriana officinalis*, is a graceful plant with flowers ranging from white to deep rose, and is happy in damp woods, ditches and all moist limy or chalky ground.

The calamint family, as their generic 'cala-mintha' implies, are beautiful, with their pungently scented leaves and little labiate flowers, and generally are found on dry, grassy banks, especially on lime or chalk. The lesser calamint, *Calamintha*

THE HERB BANK

Most cultivated and sweet herbs are native plants which for centuries have been grown alongside more treasured exotics. In a wild garden they look well grown on a bank, which can also form a lively and interesting boundary between one area and another, as well as providing a sunny and a more shaded site, sharply drained soil at the top and moister soil at ground level. The nectar-rich flowers of the herbs and later their seeds appeal to a variety of insects, birds and small mammals; butterflies, moths and bees are all frequent visitors. Unexpectedly perhaps, bees collect honey also from the globular blooms of chives and rocambole.

1 Curry plant, *Helichrysum angustifolium*
2 Thymes, *Thymus* sp.
3 Good King Henry, *Chenopodium bonus-henricus*
4 Everlasting onions, *Allium perutile*
5 Welsh onion, *Allium fistulosum*
6 Clary sage, *Salvia sclarea*
7 Chives, *Allium schoenoprasum*
8 Red sage, *Salvia officinalis* 'Purpurascens'
9 Egyptian onion, *Allium cepa* 'Proliferum'
10 Lavender, *Lavandula* sp.
11 Wormwood, *Artemisia absinthium*
12 Angelica, *Angelica archangelica*
13 Fennel, *Foeniculum vulgare*
14 Rocambole, *Allium scordoprasum*

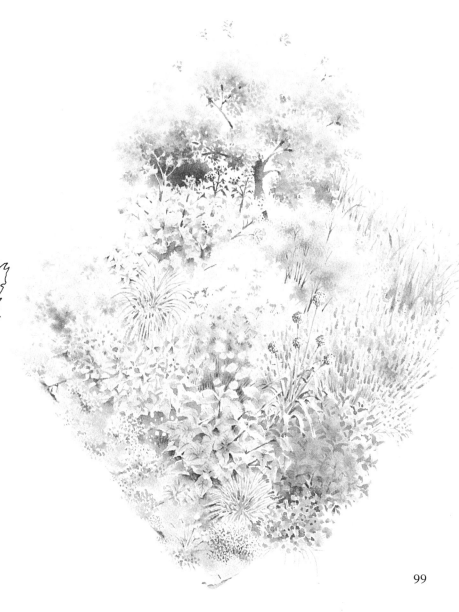

nepeta, has paler flowers on stalks. Said to be rare in Britain, it appeared from nowhere in my gravel drive. For a tall herb, grow the lovely wood calamint, *C. sylvatica,* with its large, lavender-coloured flowers blotched with purple.

Another tall, handsome herb is mugwort, *Artemisia vulgaris,* seen growing luxuriantly on roadsides and wastelands. It has narrow leaves, green above and white-green below. The name comes from 'midge-plant', for it was once believed that it would keep away these irritating insects. Its relative, wormwood, *A. absinthium,* was widely used to repel fleas, being strewn upon the floor or dried and bagged and placed among clothes. A beautiful plant, more aromatic and bitter than mugwort, it also grows on wasteground, especially by the sea. Whiter and woollier than the others is the aromatic *A. maritima.*

Herbs for bees, butterflies and birds

Always find room for those herbs which are particularly attractive to wildlife. Your garden will be alive with bees and butterflies and, later in the year, birds greedy for the seeds.

All thymes will attract bees. The common wild thyme, *Thymus drucei,* native to Britain and Europe, which is found growing through the short grass on dry banks and heaths, is sometimes called mother of thyme. The larger wild thyme, *T. pulegioides,* which has larger leaves and creeping stems, can be distinguished by the extra whorls of little flowers below the main head. It grows wild on calcareous soils, and has produced a great number of variants. The garden thyme, *Thymus vulgaris,* which seeds itself freely, is an upright, bushy plant originally from southern Europe (Spain to Italy).

Another bee plant indigenous to Britain is white horehound, *Marrubium vulgare.* Silvery and woolly, it grows best on poor soils. Even more popular, however, is the misty-leaved, bright blue-flowered borage, *Borago officinalis,* which makes really excellent honey. Found growing wild, it is a garden escape and, though ideal for a dry bank or other dry spot, it can be choosy.

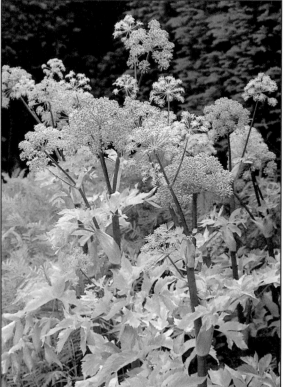

LEFT *Two species of angelica grow wild in Britain. Only this, the wild angelica,* Angelica sylvestris, *which favours moist, shady woods, is native. It is not edible. The other,* A. archangelica, *has, however, become naturalized. It is less colourful, has larger, round umbels and cut, fern-like leaves. For centuries it has been and still is used in confectionary and medicine. Both species are handsome enough to be grown in any garden, wild or cultivated.*

BELOW *Growing wild by rivers, canals and some road-sides, comfrey,* Symphytum officinale, *with white, purple or rose-coloured flowers, has long been a valued medicinal herb and was once used as a wound dressing. It is still used in cookery: the leaves, dipped in batter, fried and sugared, are delicious! The species has produced several varieties, all of which appear to be attractive to bees.*

A beekeeping acquaintance always grows bee balm, *Melissa officinalis.* near her hives, a beekeeper's tradition since it is believed that bees find their way home by its smell. This herb makes up for its lack of beauty by its refreshing lemon scent and the delight the bees take in it. There is a more showy, yellow variegated form, but the ugly-named bastard balm, *Melittis melissophyllum,* is the handsomer plant. This species has large flowers about 5cm/2in long, creamy-white with a long lip spotted purple. A perennial, it will grow in any soil, but gives the best account of itself in half-shade with its roots in deep loam. Try it as a woodland margin plant.

The mints flower in late summer, bringing a soft, lavender haze and attracting a great variety of insects. Many have been in cultivation for centuries and there should be a species to suit everyone.

The round-leaved mint, *Mentha rotundifolia,* is one of the best flavouring mints and appears to grow anywhere. Its leaves are indeed almost round, and grey and downy on the undersides. The lovely variegated form has a slightly different, very sweet fragrance, with leaves marked in white and pale cream, sometimes with the palest magenta tips.

The land at the end of my garden was once a cornfield, and while cornmint, *Mentha arvensis,* a strongly fragrant weed, has largely vanished from the countryside, it does still grow here.

A favourite of butterflies is marjoram, *Origanum vulgare,* which grows happily in a sunny hedgebank and seeds itself freely in calcareous soil. The flowers will vary considerably in colour, ranging from greenish white to a deep purple. The gold-leaved form, *O. aureum,* is as bright as any flower.

Chives, *Allium schoenoprasum,* have spread right across Europe from northern Asia. Sometimes found growing wild on limestone, they prefer a sunny place and, like most of the alliums, their pretty, purple globe flowers attract all sorts of insects. Where hedge garlic, *Alliaria petiolata,* is allowed to grow for the orange-tip butterfly, there will inevitably be a thick crop of seedlings which can be thinned for use in the kitchen.

Fennel, *Foeniculum vulgare,* one of the food plants of the beautiful and rare swallowtail butterfly, is often to be found growing wild on wasteland, roadsides or sea cliffs, in the sun. A native of southern Europe, there are green and bronze-leaved forms which, grown together, can make a handsome group, often reaching 1.8m/6ft in height.

Many herbs proffer large quantities of seed, so do not hurry to tidy plants, cutting them down once they have flowered. With the exotic lavender and rosemary growing near the house or in the butterfly border, you will be able to enjoy the antics of goldfinches, chaffinches and tits as they tightrope-walk the stalks to collect the oil-rich seeds. Such species as fennel, sweet cicely, parsley and chervil will be visited time and time again during the lean months until only the skeleton ribs of the umbels remain silhouetted against the winter sky.

ABOVE AND TOP *The bright-yellow composite flower of* Hieracium *and the orange of pot marigold – the first a native, the second an exotic species – prettily and naturally complement the vivid blue of borage, a close relative of comfrey.*

WATER GARDENS

One of the most engaging areas in my own garden is around a tiny, fibreglass pond, installed in the days when I was seeking to show the readers of a women's magazine how quick and easy it could be to make a water garden. Since its introduction, my husband and I have spent many hours on a seat beside it. We watch the newts, some of them beautifully crested, identify the occasional visiting dragon or damsel fly, note that both wasps and bees stand on lily pads to drink; we introduced tadpoles, later to be met as tiny frogs as we worked in the borders. We admire the floating water lilies and the marsh marigolds and savour the musky scent of meadow sweet. From the house we often see magpies and crows waddling in or hopping away, shaking their wet feathers, hurrying to a place in the sun to dry. Our next project is to make a larger pond, for a greater number of native plants.

A pond can be designed so that it offers suitable areas for special plants, deep in places for some, shallow at the edges for others. It can be made to spill over to provide a habitat for marsh plants. It can be fringed with a great variety of plants, with a flower for most seasons, or it can be simply surrounded with grass and a little shore to step on.

Pond plant life is at its best where there is open light for at least eight hours a day. Some plants, water lilies for instance, should grow in full sun if they are to flower well. Pond creatures that prefer shade will take cover under the lilies' leaves. Floating leaves help to prevent the excessive growth of algae by cutting off much of the light supply to the lower depths of the water, thus creating an essential balance of light and shade.

Although a natural woodland pool may have great charm, it is best to make a pond well away from overhanging trees because shade and fallen leaves combine to produce stagnant water. An accumulation of leaves at the bottom of a pool will result in gases being given off that have a deleterious effect on fish and other wildlife.

Pond preparation

Begin making a pond (see page 127) in early spring to give time for it to be filled and for the water to become weathered and warm and plant-furnished before pondlife becomes seasonally active. Get the waterplants in place before introducing fish, so that the latter need not be unduly disturbed.

For a small pond, it is recommended that plants are grown in containers. The plants can then easily be lifted out, thinned and replanted. These containers can be wicker baskets, or crates made from 2.5cm/1in square slats of timber or from specially manufactured mesh plastic. Alternatively, four bricks can be stood on the pond bottom to form a shallow box and the cavity filled with soil. Heavy soil is required, the best mixture being half well-rotted cow manure and half soil. For poor soils, in place of the manure use a slow acting organic fertilizer, such as bonemeal, in the proportion of a tablespoon to a two-gallon bucket of soil. Pack the enriched soil into the lower half of the plant holder and place the ordinary soil on top.

Rather than fill slatted or perforated plastic crates directly with loose soil, line them with turves. These are grass squares on which the grass has been allowed to rot, but not so much that the turves disintegrate. Plant and gently lower the filled crates into the water.

Oxygenating plants

Vital to the life of a pond, oxygenating plants very quickly and efficiently replace lost and consumed oxygen in the water. Few could be called decorative. One of the most common is the Canadian pondweed, *Elodea canadensis*, which has bluntish olive-green leaves that become tightly wrapped up during the winter months. *Elodea* can be invasive and is therefore best planted in a container and sunk into the water.

The water starworts, *Callitriches*, are useful tenants for a pond for, apart from being excellent

ABOVE *Native also to North America, the graceful water plantain,* Alisma plantago-aquatica, *growing wild beside ponds and ditches, was once highly valued as an antidote to rattlesnake bite.*

RIGHT *A water garden soon becomes an ideal environment for many little creatures, for where plants luxuriate there are secure hiding and breeding places. Some haunt the marginal plants, others stay close under floating leaves or in the safe mesh of waterweeds. When they leave the water as unlovely larvae, about to change into dragonflies and damselflies, they scale tall stems and hang there, jewel-like, until they are ready to take to the wing.*

oxygenators, their lush, interwoven growth holds many kinds of spawn safely and the young leaves are nibbled by fish.

There are also the tiny-flowered water milfoils, *Myriophyllum*, including the whorled and the spiked water milfoil. The alternate-flowered water milfoil, *Myriophyllum alterniflorum*, is found in lakes, slow streams and peaty water. One of the prettiest, a native and for long a favoured water garden plant is the water violet, *Hottonia palustris*, which makes a deep mat of submerged stems and foliage, but holds its lilac, yellow-eyed flowers in whorls some 25cm/10in above the surface of the water. One of my own favourites, although it can be invasive, is the water crowfoot or water buttercup, *Ranunculus aquatilis*, with flowers like a white celandine. This species is very variable.

Water weeds also help provide cover for young fish, which regrettably are often eaten by their elders, and for tadpoles, which suffer from several different predators.

Where the pond has a mud bottom, oxygenators are simply planted by tying a cutting of a plant to a smooth stone or pebble and lowering it into the water at the deepest part of the pond. Add one cutting approximately to each 30 sq. cm/12 sq. in of water surface. Or, plant the cutting in a container.

Most species are extremely rampant. They grow fast and need to be kept under control. This is best done by drawing a rake through the mass of stems, a few inches below the surface of the water and then tugging out as much as possible from the base of the plants.

Sometimes, on the other hand, an oxygenator does not thrive. It is not possible to say why. Obviously so much depends on local conditions as well as the size and content of the pond. For this reason it is usual, initially, to introduce at least four or five different species.

Deep water aquatic plants

When water lilies are to be grown, they should be started in at least 15cm/6in of water with their containers standing on bricks or breeze blocks. As

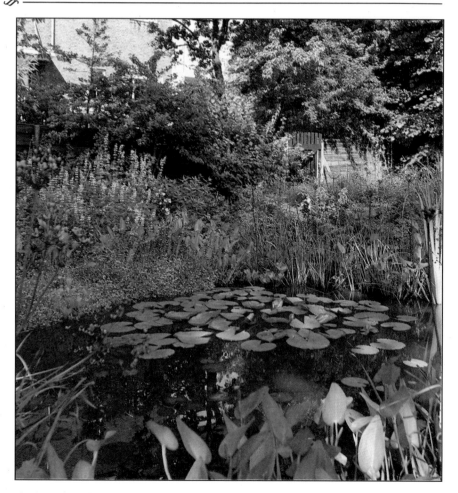

the leaves unfurl, the blocks should be removed at intervals so that the leaves float on the surface. Mature plants need a water depth of 30-45cm/12-18in. The white water lily, *Nymphaea alba*, needs sunshine for the flowers to develop fully. *N. pumila* is a much smaller species found in small lakes in Scotland, while the yellow water lily or brandy bottle, *Nuphar lutea*, and the smaller yellow-flowered *Nuphar pumila*, will tolerate some shade. Though unrelated to them, the charming fringed water lily, *Nymphoides peltata*, resembles a miniature yellow water lily. It is mostly seen in pools and ditches in southern England and tends to root well down into the mud.

ABOVE *A small garden or a part of a garden devoted to water will prove, after the initial effort, to be both labour saving and constantly full of interest. In addition to the handsome foliage of most aquatic plants, flower colour can be vivid and continuous, beginning in spring with, for instance, marsh marigolds, then following in summer with flowering rush, water plantain, forget-me-nots and yellow loosestrife, and on to purple lythrum and russet seedheads in autumn.*

Some other, less showy floating-leaved rooted plants include the broad-leaved pondweed, *Potamogeton natans*, and the bur-reeds, *Sparganium* sp. Both plants appreciate a soft rich pond bottom.

The arrowhead, *Sagittaria sagittifolia*, is a common plant of slow-flowing rivers. It actually sends up a series of three types of leaves: long, light green grass blades, followed by oval ones that lie flat on the surface, and later in the summer, arrow-shaped and emergent ones. This interesting plant appreciates clean water and appears to thrive with regular cutting back. Its leaves die down quickly after frost.

Those who have a large pond or slow stream may already be familiar with the vigorous reed sweet grass, *Glyceria maxima*, with tall stems bearing long branching panicles of spikelets. This particular species grows in deeper water than the other glyceria, as deep as 75cm/30in. Its roots will help prevent banks eroding at the waterside. A variegated form is also sometimes seen growing at garden pool sides.

Waterside or marginal plants

In gardening terms, aquatic, waterside or marginal as applied to water plants covers a range of species which in nature are found in quite different habitats. (The botanists' term is 'emergent' plants.) While some grow right down at the water's edge or even in the water itself, many others grow well above the water level, even high on top of the river bank. But even in this instance the plants benefit from the proximity of the water – the roots are constantly in contact with the moist soil, kept in this state by capillary action, and the plants also benefit from the high humidity.

In the garden, marginal plants can be slotted into different positions around your pond. Plant them either directly into the soil or in turves placed on specially installed shelves, or in containers placed on the shelves on on the pond bottom, raised if necessary to provide just the right shallow depth of water. Bricks, upturned crates or flower pots will do for this purpose. Cover any sharp edges to

prevent any possible perforation of the pond lining.

For a pond edge, the water forget-me-not, *Myosotis scorpioides* (sometimes called *M. palustris*), about 30cm/12in tall, has the brightest of blue flowers from spring to autumn. Given the opportunity, the plant will also paddle in the pond. Try it also in a marsh garden. Again true blue are two veronicas, the water speedwell, *Veronica anagallis, aquatica*, a tall plant flowering through the summer, and the brooklime, *V. beccabunga*, not quite so tall. These two will grow also in marshy conditions. Flowering in late summer is the pretty little skullcap, *Scutellaria galericulata*.

Sweet galingale, *Cyperus longus*, a sedge and a

ABOVE LEFT, RIGHT, *and* TOP
Most flowering waterside plants are free-flowering. The buttercup family (above right) is perhaps the brightest among our native species. There are also several beautiful exotics, mainly members of the balsam family, such as Impatiens capensis, *the orange balsam (above left). Another quite widespread species is the monkey flower,* Mimulus guttatus, *escaped from gardens (top). It can be seen growing wild by, even in, some rivers and canals, ditches and marshes.*

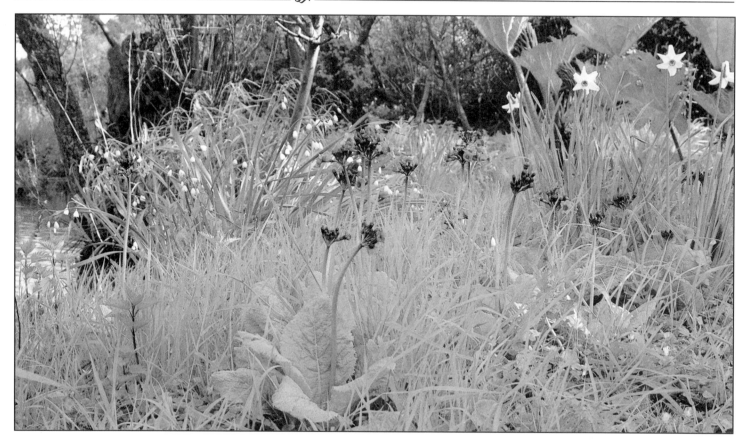

rush-like plant with attractive, irregular umbels of mahogany, forming a graceful spray in late summer, has pleasantly scented roots.

The marsh bird's-foot trefoil, *Lotus pedunculatus*, found in wet meadows and marshy places, has long been accepted by gardeners as a suitable plant for the edges of a wild pond. Sometimes known as marsh trefoil, but unrelated, is the bogbean, *Menyanthes trifoliata*, its leaves rather like those of the broad bean plant which, like its pretty flowers, it holds well above the water. It grows well in soil at the very edge of a pond, flowering from late spring to midsummer.

One of the most attractive marginal plants in my own tiny pond is the great water plantain, *Alisma plantago-aquatica*, which will only flower well if the water is shallow. The loosely branching stems of

ABOVE *and* LEFT *Lush waterside grass offers a perfect environment for meadow flowers, and if it has not been heavily weeded or constantly mown, or in an area newly turved with meadow grass, you can expect to find a good range of native plants. In time, some species may appear as if by magic. Depending upon the nature of the soil, for most seem to need some lime, you may find wild orchids of some species or another, or even marsh orchid. It is unwise ever to attempt to lift and transplant these particular plants. They resent disturbance and may die.*

A WATER GARDEN

A water garden is a wonderful place to linger by. Here, a little jetty and stepping stones enable one almost to stand in the water, as it were, all the better to peer into its depths. There is one important point to note. The stones, whatever they are made of (here, brick pillars capped with wood) should only be used on a cement base. Where the pond lining is of some form of plastic, the base of the stones and the pressure on them would in time damage the lining and cause the pond to leak. But, whatever its construction, the pond can be fringed with many lovely plants. In the water, some are completely submerged, producing essential oxygen. Others, like the water lilies, grow long stems so that leaves and flowers can float on the surface in the sun. Some paddle their roots in the water, while others sit happily at the edge.

1 Water lily, *Nymphaea alba*
2 Arrowhead, *Sagittaria sagittifolia*
3 Sweet galingale, *Cyperus longus*
4 Great spearwort, *Ranunculus lingua*
5 Meadowsweet, *Filipendula ulmaria*
6 Flowering rush, *Butomus umbellatus*
7 Monkey flower, *Mimulus guttata*
8 Bogbean, *Menyanthes trifoliata*
9 Hemp agrimony, *Eupatorium cannabinum*
10 *Dryopteris cristata*
11 Royal fern, *Osmunda regalis*
12 *Hosta fortunei*
13 Marsh marigold, *Caltha Palustris*
14 Yellow flag, *Iris Palustris*
15 Skunk cabbage, *Lysichitum americanum*
16 Ragged robin, *Lychnis flos-cuculi*
17 Purple loosestrife, *Lythrum salicaria*
18 Brooklime, *Veronica beccabunga*

little rosy flowers grow up to 1m/3ft tall. A smaller, less common species is *A. lanceolatum*.

Not a native, but well worth growing since it has been described as one of the handsomest aquatic plants in cultivation, is the sky-blue pickerel weed, *Portaderia cordata*, from North America. With large, glossy green leaves it flowers through summer into autumn. It grows best in water 15-30cm/6-12in deep. It is so accommodating that it can be propagated by division at almost any season, a point to bear in mind when visiting a friend whose pond is generously furnished with this plant.

Marsh gardens

An artificial marsh area is made by much the same method as a natural one, which is to allow water to overspill constantly at some point. Only very little water is needed to keep such an area moist without it becoming waterlogged. Natural marsh areas are, in fact, well drained and aerated. Use trickle irrigation, and experiment until you think that the volume is sufficient. Too little water can result in drought, and the death of water-loving plants, and too much can lead to an overfull pond and the drowning of the same plants.

I had a neighbour who kept an entire water and marsh garden moist simply by putting a hose pipe on a dairy tap with a faulty washer, which allowed a permanent drip. She planted the wet area with many kinds of water-loving exotics, dominant among which were the garden varieties of mimulus or musk. Species of this plant have become naturalized in Britain. Recently, in summer time, I saw a great drift of yellow *Mimulus guttatus*, the monkey flower from North America, growing in marshy grass, following a little stream which saturated an area in a steep field.

The floral colour in a marsh can be extended over many months. One of the earliest of our native water flowers to bloom, the marsh marigold, is followed a little later by the stately yellow flag iris and the ragged robin with his bright, seemingly tattered, rose-purple flowers. The cuckoo flower will grow among these.

Many aquatics recommended for other sites will grow well in marshy ground. For instance, the purple loosestrife, with its tall spikes of purple flowers and its not quite so tall yellow cousin, yellow loosestrife (which reminds me of an upright creeping jenny), which could grow at marsh edges. Meadowsweet will scent the air. From summer to autumn the great spearwort, an outsize buttercup some 1m/3ft tall, can contrast with one of the most beautiful of our wildflowers, the flowering rush, *Butomus umbellatus*, which blooms through most of the summer.

ABOVE *The graceful* Scirpus *is the true bulrush, a term often used mistakenly for the handsome reedmace, a much larger and more invasive plant suitable only for large ponds. There are many native species of* Scirpus, *most known more familiarly as club rushes, a reference to the shape of their inflorescences. They are easily grown, but in small ponds they need to be divided from time to time to restrain them.*

If the pond is made in a grassed area, the plants can be encouraged to merge into this in a natural manner. Grass does help to create a cool area around them, promoting essential humidity. It also provides safe cover for frogs and other little creatures which inhabit the pond area.

Some plants will gradually move into the grass as they seed, cuckoo flowers, marsh marigold, meadow rue, fleabane and meadowsweet for instance. Others such as fritillary and summer snowflake, bulbs of which can be bought, can be introduced further away from the pond.

Because marsh and many other water plants grow both damply and thickly, they offer good, shelter for a great many different invertebrates adapted to the lush amphibious conditions. For example, there are interesting marsh grasshoppers and spiders. Frogs and newts will breed in the pond, but outside the breeding season can be found hunting for insects in the marshy area. Grass snakes are attracted to marshy areas mainly for frogs, but of course the tangle of vegetation also houses mice and other prey, such as shrews and short-tailed voles.

ABOVE *The wild* Iris pseudacorus, *the* fleur de lys *of legend, one of the loveliest of our wild spring flowers, grows in wet fields and on marshy land as well as at the margins of ponds. It is popularly known as the yellow flag ('flagge' is the Middle English for sword, an allusion to the plant's leaf shape) to distinguish it from the sweet flag,* Acorus calamus, *which is not an iris but a member of the arum family.*

Bog gardens

A true bog is carpeted with bogmoss or sphagnum. It supports a special community of plants, some of which, because the static natural bog water is acid, are of the heather family. These, and other genera growing there as they decayed and decomposed over the centuries, helped to form the peat layer on which the bog lies. In Britain the bog plants include the insectivorous sundews, cranberry, bog asphodel, marsh andromeda, orchis and the rare Labrador tea. There are also grasses, sedges and ferns which have become specially adapted.

In the early days of wild gardens where money was no object and the achievement of a 'natural' feature in a garden a case for pride, a great deal of effort was put into making a bog, often in association with a rock garden, so that rare and beautiful plants could be grown. The modern gardener is usually less ambitious, mixing bog, marsh and marginal water plants together to create an attractive wetland area.

A pond can be made to overflow, or alternatively made in much the same way as a pond but providing means for the water to soak gradually away so that the area is drained. An example would be an excavation some 45cm/15in deep, lined, the plastic being perforated here and there to allow the water to escape. A layer of drainage material, shingle, pebbles or stone, some 8cm/3in deep should lie on the base. The soils should be well mixed with peat. Success will then depend upon never allowing the soil to dry out, yet also never allowing it to become waterlogged.

Many of the so-called bog plants on sale are exotics and in my own view most of them look very out of place in a wild setting, but this is a matter for the gardener. There is a wide choice.

Of our native bog plants, many have been grown in gardens, the grass of Parnassus for instance, the bog asphodel, *Narthecium ossifragrum*, recommended as 'suitable for naturalizing in boggy places' and the marsh helleborine, *Epipactis palustris*. There are large-leaved plants such as the butterbur, *Petasites hybridus*, suitable only really for those with large gardens, and our lovely royal fern, *Osmunda regalis*, for contrast, as well as some of the smallest and most endearing of flowers, the little butterworts, sometimes because of their shape and colour known as water violets. Surprisingly perhaps, these are insectivorous plants. They are, incidentally, easy to raise from seed.

A wildlife oasis

A healthy pond should be able to support a great many creatures. Whether these should include fish to keep down the numbers of annoying insects such as mosquitoes, midges and gnats is a matter of

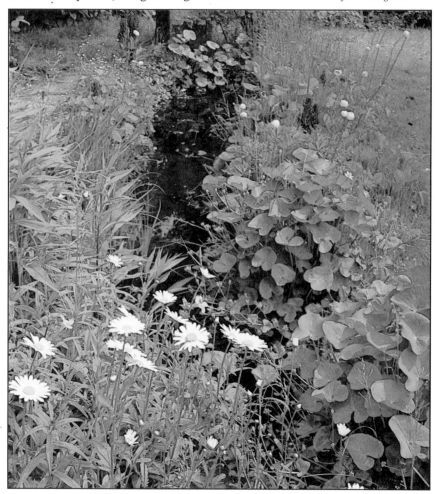

BELOW *One delightful way to establish a boundary, as well as to prepare one for a change from one part of the garden to another; a little canal separates the paved area near the house from the main garden. On its banks, on both sides, aquatic emergent or marginal plants, marsh marigold and* Mimulus *among them, mingle with meadow oxeye daisies and globe flowers, which enjoy the cool of the lush grass.*

ABOVE *Once common growing in watery bogs, the beautiful bogbean,* Menyanthes trifoliata, *a member of the gentian family, takes its trivial name from its leaves' likeness to the vegetable plant.*

LEFT *If you are fortunate enough to have a small stream, its sides can be planted with pond-side plants and other water lovers. In this rather sophisticated version of a wild garden, exotic primulas have been planted among ferns.*

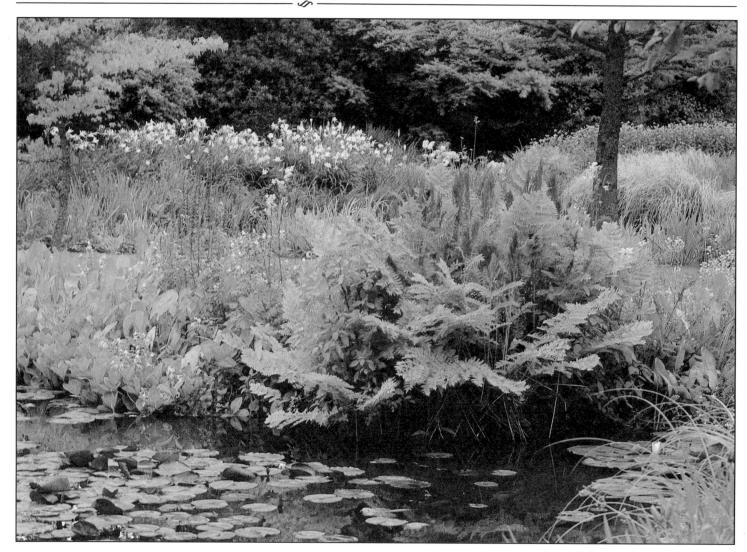

choice, for it is possible that these might perform their role just too effectively and eliminate other creatures we would like to see there. Although fish will prey on tadpoles, for instance, I have seen a goldfish attacked by the large dragonfly nymph. One way to ensure that as mixed a community as possible exists, is to see that there are shallow, weed-covered areas into which the smaller creatures can escape and hide. But bear in mind that in natural ponds all types do exist together.

Stocking a pond is a matter of trial and error. In my own pond, successive introductions of goldfish (aliens, incidentally) were lost to various unseen predators, and so now I just accept what nature sends – which I find exciting enough. However, for those who want to see fish in their pond, sticklebacks are a good choice. Minnow are also a possibility and tench are approved because they help to keep the water clear by cleaning the debris off the pond bottom; some of the other creatures,

ABOVE *Enjoying acid, boggy conditions, the royal fern,* Osmunda regalis, *furnishes a waterside for most of the year. Above its green pinnate fronds, it produces panicles of furry, fertile pinnules. In autumn and winter these, with the dying fronds, become a beautiful warm russet. The fern is almost cosmopolitan and is the only one of its genera native to Britain.*

such as water snails, will also perform this task. But before deciding which fish to stock, seek advice from local fish experts who will know which species are most likely to be ecologically at home.

Once there are fish in the pond, you can expect occasionally to be visited by their predators, perhaps a heron. Take precautions depending on circumstances. For example, if birds do become too much of a nuisance, secure a fine nylon string around the pond's edges, several inches off the ground, which will prevent them from wading in.

Let the insect population in the pond build up for a month or two before installing fish so that there is food waiting for them. As a rough guide to stocking the pond, allow one fish to every square metre of water surface.

If it is hoped to attract frogs and toads to the pond to breed, and especially if the pond has been stocked with the spawn of either of these creatures, make sure that it is possible for the young to leave the water. It is easy enough for the adults to jump in or out but not so easy for the tiny creatures to get out if the edge of the pond lies several inches above the water. One method is to have a landing stone or stones lying just under the water in one place or at several points according to the size of the pond. This is best situated where there also exists some cover, between two marginal plants for instance.

It is fascinating to learn how well so many creatures are hidden and protected by the water plants. Sitting immobile, a frog is hardly visible in the shadow under leaves which reach out over the pond edge, while in the depths of the water, it is often not until you lower a hand and sir the weeds that you can detect the life which abounds there.

RIGHT *One of the advantages of having water in your garden is the interesting wild-life it attracts, such as this beautiful damselfly. Both dragonflies and damselflies* *require water to breed. Their aquatic larva, known as a nymph, is extremely vora-cious and will feed on tad-poles as well as on small fishes.*

ABOVE *A 'jungle' in a town garden where water and water-loving plants dominate the scene. Such a place be-comes an oasis for wildlife, both local and visiting. The paths leading to the water and the safe wooden slats that bridge it, mean that there are many vantage points to stand and quietly become a part of the scene. In late summer, purple valerian, loosestrife, tansy and rushes provide pleasing colour.*

ROCK GARDENS

The natural effect of a wild rock garden can only be created with time and care, and it is not just a matter of introducing wild plants in between a random arrangement of rocks and stones. The natural features of a mountain landscape can be followed on a smaller scale, creating a series of ledges, overhangs and scree slopes. Alternatively, or incorporated into this scheme one can have on the level, a rock strewn area interspersed with shrubs, say junipers of different species. A stone pavement can add to the variety of rock garden planting with a whole range of different rock plants sprouting from between the crevices. For example, careful placement and alignment of the rocks is essential, which means that fissures and cracks should run in the same direction. Of the many crevice plants, species such as wall pennywort, *Umbilicus rupestris*, houseleek, *Sempervivum tectorum*, and ivy-leaved toadflax, *Cymbalaria rupestris* are useful plants to link the stones together.

Professional rock garden architects usually make the top of the rock garden flat, like a plateau, where dwarf shrubs such as tiny willows can be planted. Below this, according to the way the other stones are placed, there should be a series of plateaux, some in full sun, some in partial shade, some in full shade, depending upon their aspect and the shadow cast by the rock and stone.

At the lowest level the rock can continue outwards, perhaps merging with gravel, paving, grass or a path. Most rock plants will grow equally well on the flat, but here especially is a place for true sun lovers, for instance, thymes and rock roses such as the hoary rock rose, *Helianthemum canum,* or the semi-spreading common rock rose, *H. nummularium* which has many attractive garden varieties.

There are many examples of wild groupings that can be copied at home. For example, often on a hillside on a rock outcrop growing in shallow soil, you can find sparse rabbit-grazed turf with rock roses and wild thyme. This effect can be repeated in the garden with or without the grass and the rabbits. Another effective and easy cover is to plant some prostrate shrub, a juniper perhaps, so that it caps the rock, furnishing it softly. You can also create a rocky outcrop some distance away from the main rockery, and allow grass to grow almost to its base, and plant by it a prettily-shaped tree such as the dwarf birch, *Betula nana*.

Where a rock garden already exists, sometimes all that is necessary to create a more natural blending, is to alter some of the plants, replacing the hackneyed kinds such as aubrieta and yellow alyssum with less flamboyant but still colourful wildflowers such as harebell or moss campion.

Scree

Those gardeners who are striving for a really natural effect might consider making a scree which slopes gently down from the higher levels of the rock garden, spreading out as the slope lessens at the bottom. This can be made of two parts rock chippings to one part loam and one part peat or leafmould, should be 30cm/12in deep and should

ABOVE *The wild rock rose,* Helianthemum nummularium, *often found on limestone formations, is the source of many gorgeous garden varieties. As its generic name implies, it is a sun lover.*

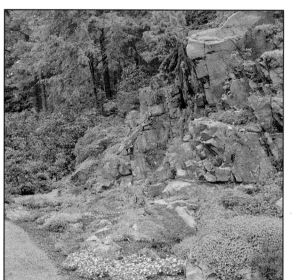

LEFT *Well-drained rock offers a home for many kinds of plants. Plateaux, crevices and cliff-like areas of the rock face provide a favourite habitat for a diverse number of species. Most like a good, open, light soil and sunshine but some prefer a rock's shadow or the shady or partially shady side of the rock. Some will seed or can be grown in a gravel or scree-like surface at ground level.*

RIGHT *The rocky slopes at the side of a steep, stepped path and its summit are overlaid with acid soil in which some of the less familiar wild plants can be grown.*

A WILD ROCK GARDEN

So many gardeners enthuse about rock gardens. Specialist nurseries have made it possible for them to collect beautiful species whose natural habitats are in faraway places on mountain sides and among rocky terrains. But some of the lovely native plants have always been given a place among the exotics. It is possible to make a rock garden which holds indigenous plants only, even creating a conservation area of rare rock plants. Some species that are rare in the wild will grow with exuberance where the ground suits them – the Cheddar pink, for example.

The rock garden here creates a harmony of rock and stony or gravelly areas, and such plants. There is a dry scree 'stream' bed, bridged at one end below a scree 'pool', and opening out into a larger 'scree' pool at the other. (For those gardeners who would actually prefer to see water here, this could be made into an artificial water course with a pond – the plants would have to be modified to suit.) At the top of the garden is a gravel area – which could be sanded instead.

1 *Thymus* sp., maiden pinks, *Dianthus deltoides*, thrift, *Armeria maritima*
2 Elder, *Sambucus nigra* 'Aurea'
3 Shrubby cinquefoil, *Potentilla fructicosa*
4 London pride, *Saxifraga umbrosa*
5 Mezereon, *Daphne mezereum*
6 Burnet rose, *Rosa pimpinellifolia*
7 Wall cotoneaster, *Cotoneaster horizontalis*
8 Holly, *Ilex aquifolium*
9 *Erica* sp.
10 *Juniperus horizontalis*
11 Creeping willow, *Salix repens*
12 Birches, *Betula* sp.
13 Tamarisk, *Tamarix gallica*
14 Mountain avens, *Dryas octopetala*
15 Roseroot, *Sedum rosea*, houseleek, *Sempervivum tectorum*, *Thymus* sp.
16 Ling, *Calluna vulgaris*
17 Gorse, *Ulex europaeus*
18 Barrenwort, *Epimedium alpinum*
19 Purple saxifrage, *Saxifraga oppositifolia*
20 Roseroot, *Sedum rosea*
21 Spring cinquefoil, *Potentilla tabernaemontani*
22 Field maple, *Acer campestre*
23 *Thymus* sp., stonecrops, *Sedum acre*, *S. album*
24 Mountain pansy, *Viola lutea*, spring gentian, *Gentiana verna*
25 Chalk milkwort, *Polygala calcarea*; autumn crocus, *Crocus nudiflorus*

preferably be situated on the sunnier side of the rockery. To make it more authentic and provide ideal conditions for alpine plants, occasional rocks should be sunk in the scree to allow a cool root-run, because the small stones that make up the scree can get extremely hot.

Most screes seen in well-tended gardens are furnished with beautiful species, though in Britain only a few of them are natives: the twinflower, *Linnaea borealis* for peaty soils, and of the lime lovers, the spring gentian, *Gentiana verna,* the alpine catchfly, *Lychnis alpina,* and the chalk milk-wort, *Polygala calcarea* are outstanding.

Limestone gardens

A new gardener can be forgiven for looking at a mass of bare stone in despair, incredulous perhaps that it could ever offer a home for such delicate-looking plants as so many rock plants appear to be. To visit a natural, flora-rich rock area is to appreciate more fully what it is that such plants ask of us. One such area, which remains for ever in the minds of those who know it, is that gaunt limestone pavement in Ireland's County Clare known as The Burren. There, within sight of the sea, there is an astounding collection of rock plants, many of which do not grow in the open but luxuriate low down in crevices between the giant rocks. One of the dominant plants there, and one of the alpine gardener's favourite, is the mountain avens, *Dryas octopetala.* Once it has taken its hold between the rocks, it grows in what one can only describe as carpets, with drapes of dark green leaves studded with yellow-centred flowers, which mature into beautiful fluffy seed heads.

In the crevices on a limestone rock garden, and so long as the root soil is well drained, you can grow *Alchemilla alpina,* which will seed freely; rose root, *Sedum rosea,* with its roots which when dried are rose-scented and both the Cheddar Pink, and its near relation the wild pink, *Dianthus plumarius,* the origin of the sweetly scented garden pink. Lower down, in a place where the roots will not dry out but where the site is open, the pasque flower,

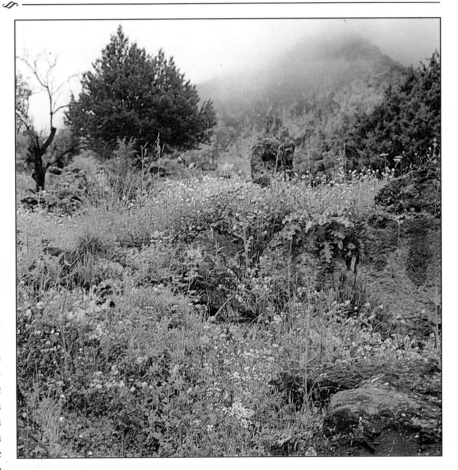

Pulsatilla vulgaris, might be coaxed to start a colony.

Where a prostrate plant is required, encourage the alpine milk vetch, *Astragulus alpinus,* to sprawl. This is a plant which resents being moved and so should be grown from seed. In my own garden, the showy blue gromwell, *Lithospermum purpuro-caeruleum* covers the soil gloriously but often a little too enthusiastically and has to be controlled.

Certainly, running water enhances any rock garden site, the spray providing the moisture many alpines like, providing that there is free soil drainage. The saxifrages thrive in this situation and form dense mats, cushions or simple rosettes, depending on the species. Commonest are the starry saxifrage, *Saxifraga stellaria*; the yellow bog

ABOVE *Yellow rock roses brighten and contrast with the pinks, white and green hues of their companions. Grown this way wild plants should seed freely, eventually filling fissures and holes in the rock with their own kind, which also will cascade or sprawl in the sunshine.*

saxifrage, *S. hirculus*; the lesser bulbous saxifrage, *S. cernus*; and the yellow mountain saxifrage, *S. aizoides*, for instance. The kinds known as mossy saxifrages are attractive at all times. *S. caespitosa* is an extremely variable species which forms dense cushions studded with starry white flowers.

London pride, *Saxifraga umbrosa*, familiar to many people, grows best in the shade or partial shade, and changes personality in sunshine! The light, foamy flowers look well growing with ferns. Also, for the shady side of a rock garden is Eve's cushion or Dovedale moss, *S. hypnoides*, whose spreading cushions remain colourful long after flowering is past.

In moist shade or partial shade, the May lily, *Maianthemum bifolium*, another mat-forming plant, will form attractive mats of its pairs of heart-shaped leaves.

Plants for acid soils

Here, plants of the heather family, both ericas and the low-growing shrubs (see Heath and heather gardens, pages 78-85) can be used as rock plants. Most will cascade prettily over the edge of a rock and even grow out from a crevice so long as the roots are not likely to dry out. Being evergreen and often varied in colour, and whether covered in new tips or old, or flowering stems, the plants are always decorative.

Where a soft grey carpet would look well, the native immortelle, cat's foot, *Antennaria dioica*, demands only a light, well-drained soil. It could be contrasted with the shining cranesbill, *Geranium lucidum*, which should soon seed itself. This plant needs a little more shade than the cat's foot.

One of my favourite rock plants comes from the seaside. I have happy memories of it draping cliffs in Devon and in Ireland. It is the little thrift or sea pink, *Armeria maritima*, which, so it seems to me, is prepared to grow anywhere it is planted so long as the gardener is liberal with sand. Apart from its attractive mode of growth, neat green cushions of tiny grass-like leaves, its globular flowers which ornament the plant from mid- to late summer are

especially attractive to bees. The species varies greatly in colour of its flowers – you may find them pale pink in one place, bright magenta-rose in another. This is a plant which will grow as well between paving stones as it does nestled down on the angles between a vertical and horizontal rock.

The enchanting harebell, *Campanula rotundifolia*, is most adaptable, and so long as it is not in the shade, it will settle down in acid, neutral or limy soils, and is most suitable for dry areas.

For a shady place, even under low-growing shrubs such as those that might top the rock, the naturalized barrenwort, *Epimedium alpinum*, will gradually fill the area, sending up new shoots from its creeping rhizomatous roots.

ABOVE *Herb robert, an annual geranium, becomes smothered with flowers through spring and summer. Seeding freely, it is an ideal plant for quickly covering an area of poor, stony soil.*

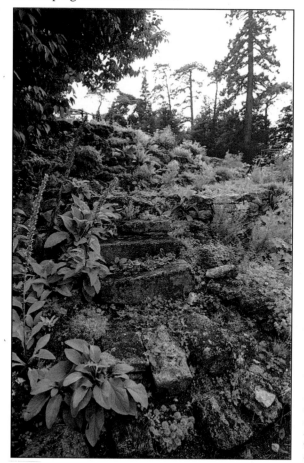

LEFT *The flat surface of a rock can quite quickly become naturally populated by plants. Often, in shade, mosses are the first to appear, sometimes thickly carpeting the stone. Seeds or fern spores falling or blown onto the moss germinate. Drifting soil and plant particles gradually and continually deposit enough humusy soil around the seedlings for them to become well-rooted even though the barren rock lies so near below.*

Gravel and stone gardens

Gravel can be used on its own with local stone. All the small stones collected from the soil where flower beds are made can be spread as a foundation for gravel. Some people like to lay gravel on a foundation of sand, 2-3cm/1in or so deep. In one little area my method was first to lay sand, then use whatever flat stones I had available (laying them quite closely), and finally I filled any spaces which were more than about an inch wide with gravel.

Once you have an area of gravel or laid stone, you soon discover that there are many wayside and wasteland plants which enjoy growing in a well-drained soil, sprawling in the sun on sun-warmed stones. There are, for instance, the bedstraws, those fragrant lacy ground covers of high summer (which, as we have seen, also attract some of the most handsome moths), the little pink lesser bind-weed which is sometimes seen sprawling along the edges of country lanes, toadflax, yarrow, herb robert, hawkweeds, teasels, mullein and campions, to mention a few. Groundsel and hairy bitter cress may not be so welcome, but can be hand-weeded.

Gravel is usually bought by the cubic metre and 1 cubic metre is usually sufficient to cover an area up to 30 sq. m/320 sq. ft with a layer 2-3cm/1in deep. A deeper layer will last longer, but if much walked on, gravel will usually need resurfacing every two or three years.

Plants which are not readily associated with rock or stone sometimes appear among gravel. In a little shady corner in my own garden a colony of dog violets has become established. The seed must have been brought in leafmould used as a mulch around some ferns growing in a nearby border. From a single specimen, the plants now cover an area of about 3m/10ft square. Elsewhere, unexpectedly and uncharacteristically, sweet violet and creeping jenny, both self-sown, thrive in gravel, in sun.

Broom does better on gravel and sand than elsewhere and thymes will grow well on shingle. Like the rock roses, thymes tolerate some treading.

The little pinks seem to fit in wherever they can be given gritty, well drained soil and sunshine. The

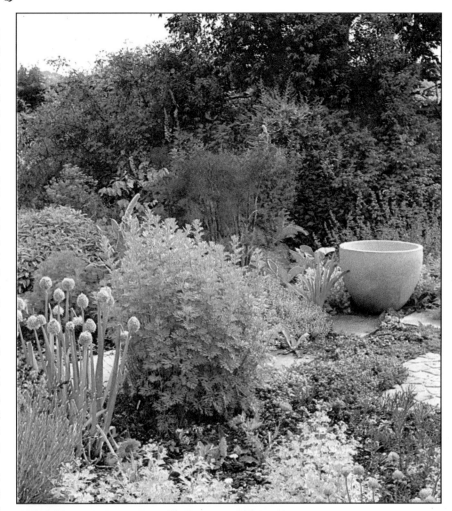

ABOVE *Well-drained and consequently comparatively warm, a gravel garden can hold a rich mixture of plants. The provision of low-carpeting plants ensures that the stones are well-covered.*

LEFT *There are some 25 European species of* Sempervivum, *many of which are treasured garden plants. In cultivation they hybridize readily with the British naturalized species, the houseleek,* S. tectorum.

sweetly scented Cheddar pink, and the maiden pink, *Dianthus peltoides,* will furnish stones with neat grey-green leaf tufts at such times as they are not in flower. Trailing St John's wort, *Hypericum humifusum,* described as a common but attractive garden weed, and the neat moss campion, *Silene acaulis* are two other examples of plants that sit comfortably on a gravelly base. The latter plant seldom flowers in the garden as freely as one wishes, but it does better on a well-drained gravel.

Plants for walls

When I think of plants for walls, I recall a narrow road winding through the hills in Ireland where for miles the bordering walls were rosy-topped with *Saxifraga umbrosa* in bloom. How odd, I thought, that this plant should be called *London* pride. The leafy rosettes made a dense cap and hung briefly over the edge, glistening under the film of ever-present mist. One is reminded that so many of the plants which will grow on rock gardens will also grow on walls so long as there is no danger of them drying out at the roots. Tufted, cushiony rock plants should grow well on wall tops or in crevices which are backed by good soil.

Some of them, like the saxifrage described, need to be planted on the shady rather than on the sunny side. Here also some of the little wall ferns can be grown. (See pages 89-90.)

On the other hand, there are many which will revel in the sunshine, the various stonecrops for instance, none of which are more glorious than the wall pepper, *Sedum acre.* Others include thick-leaved, English, white, rock and hairy stonecrops. A close relative of these is *Sempervivum tectorum,* the houseleek, sometimes to be seen growing on roofs. *Sedum reflexum,* or stone orpine, is not native but is to be found growing wild on old walls.

The alpine rock cress, *Arabis alpina,* from which many garden varieties have come, makes neat leaf rosettes, while the round-leaved cranesbill, *Geranium rotundifolium,* behaves like herb robert, *G. robertianum* (also good for walls) by presenting us with attractive leaf and stem colouring as it ages.

LEFT *A wall top, especially if it is at a convenient height both for working and viewing, is a good environment for most of the species known as rock plants. Where crevices or apertures between the stones are very small it may be best to sow seed or prick out tiny seedlings. In time, the plants will clothe the wall top and cascade prettily over the edges, like the* Dianthus *in the background.*

BELOW *Like most other stone-crops,* Sedum album *is seen at its best when it grows on walls which it drapes so attractively. This species prefers limestone rocks.*

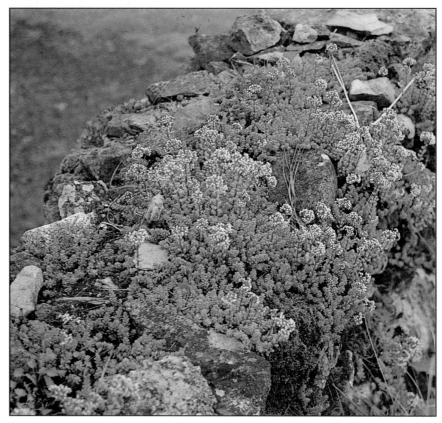

GARDEN AND PLANT CARE

This practical section is based directly on the author's own techniques and many of the illustrations originated on location in her own garden. The topics she covers are: how to assess your soil type and how to enrich soil by natural means; the role of mulching, both as a means of encouraging young plants to grow and as a way of suppressing weed growth; adding interest to your garden by altering contours – making banks and ponds, building a low dry-stone wall, varying path surfaces; collecting seeds and seed propagation – including the technique of scarification to encourage germination; other propagation techniques – layering, division and taking cuttings; sowing and raising plants for flower meadows; fern care and propagation; tree and hedgerow planting and enhancing existing hedgerows; the natural control of plants and pests.

THE SOIL

All types of soil will support some kind of flora. Where this is monotonous, it may be possible to introduce plants, even foreign plants, suited to that particular soil type. Rather than try to change the soil, remember that the most successful wild plant gardener will be the one who accepts the soil in his garden and finds plants to suit it (see also charts, pages 142-157, and page 159).

A great number of species accept a neutral, or neutral-to-slightly acid soil, which fortunately suits many gardens. There are a few species which seem happy to accept either a slightly acid or a slightly alkaline soil. The soil in a garden may vary and this can be used to advantage, to widen the range of species that can be grown.

TESTING SOIL

Determining basic acidity or alkalinity of soil is quite simple. Soil testing kits are inexpensive, and some chemists offer a service.

Take a trowelful of soil from several different parts of the garden. Keep these samples separate and clearly labelled, indicating the exact spot from where the sample was taken. The samples are then treated with the chemicals supplied and the resulting colours compared with those on a chart, to give the measure of acidity or alkalinity as a figure on the pH scale: 7.0 indicates a neutral soil; numbers higher than this indicate the degree of alkalinity, lower the degree of acidity. Generally, garden soils vary between pH 6.0 and 7.0.

SOIL ASSESSMENT

This method gives a good indication of the type of soil in your garden, and provides a guide to what you may grow. Take several trowelfuls of soil, one from each part of the garden, digging to a depth of 25cm/10in. Mix these thoroughly in a bucket, and then add a couple of tablespoons of the mixture to a jar of water. Shake this vigorously and leave to settle for half an hour. Organic matter will float to the surface, with the minerals settling in layers at the bottom.

Clay

Soil that has a high proportion of clay feels smooth and sticky when wet. Although it supports prolific plant growth, it is often hard to handle, being very heavy when wet, and sets hard in drought. It can also be very acid, badly aerated and poor to drain.

1 Organic matter
2 Clay
3 Sand
4 Gravel

Sand

Soil with a high sand content feels gritty when wet. Unlike clay, it does not bind together in a dry state. Often lacking organic matter, it tends to be infertile unless treated with compost or humus.

1 Organic matter
2 Clay
3 Sand
4 Gravel

Loam

Loamy soils contain plenty of organic matter, but vary from light to heavy, depending on the mineral contents. Loamy soil feels slightly gritty, and holds together when it dries. It is considered 'good soil', supporting rich plant growth.

1 Organic matter
2 Clay
3 Sand
4 Gravel

Chalk

Chalk soils are low in humus and are alkaline. With the incorporation of organic matter and the use of fertilizers, chalk will support a good growth of lime-tolerant plants.

1 Organic matter
2 Clay
3 Sand
4 Chalk and gravel

Humus-rich

Humusy soil will tend to be light, depending on the amount and type of mineral content. Woodland soil is rich in humus; so is soil to which liberal amounts of compost or leafmould have been added.

1 Organic matter
2 Clay
3 Sand
4 Gravel

ADDING HUMUS

If the local soil is poor, it is possible to make it acceptable to a wider range of plants by improving it with the addition of humus-rich materials. Humus is decayed organic material, something that is abundant in the wild. Animal manure, leaves, grass, peat, kitchen vegetable refuse and seaweed are all a source of humus.

One of the quickest and simplest means of providing soil with humus is to treat it with generous quantities of home-made compost. This is so easy to make, and the resulting organic substance, if properly made, should be almost as good as farmyard manure – and a lot cheaper.

Humus is not to be confused with fertilizer, which is an immediate source of food for plants. Plant foods are released slowly from humus by the action of bacteria. However, humus of all types and from all sources should be regarded as a way of treating soil to enable it to become rich and fecund rather than a soil enricher itself. It creates the right atmosphere and texture for the bacteria to multiply and so leads to a more useful soil.

Soils which drain too rapidly and constantly lose essential plant foods by leaching (particularly sandy or light soils) will be improved by the addition of humus which holds water and provides healthy soil bacteria.

On the other hand, heavy clay soils are sour and unworkable because they retain water and lack air. Here again humus does the trick, for it will lighten the soil by opening it up, providing more air spaces and improving its texture. Healthy soil is lively soil and, like all living things, needs air. Soil bacteria cannot live without it, which is why water-logged soil is such an unsatisfactory medium.

COMPOSTING

There are several methods for composting, but basically composts are made by mixing various soft-tissued vegetable materials together in a heap where the natural heating up of the heap and bacterial activity will transform the materials to a dark, sweet-smelling, crumbly, soil-like matter,

pleasant enough to handle. If a chemical accelerator is used, it will speed the decomposition so that it is possible to get two 'crops' a year from the compost heap, rather than a more probable one.

If the garden area is very small, or where a compost heap would be an eyesore, it is possible to make compost, albeit of lesser quality, in black plastic bags. The materials are treated in the same way as illustrated below, and the bag securely sealed, after which the surfaces are punctured to allow air to enter. These sacks should not lie in full sun or the heat generated will be too much for the bacteria to develop properly.

All leafy plant materials, soft hedge clippings,

The compost heap
BELOW *Two compost boxes are useful as one heap can be left to rot. Also, as the centre of the compost usually rots more quickly than the outside, the compost can be turned as it is moved to the second heap. Otherwise, the outside un-rotted portion can be set aside and used to start the next heap. The sides should be sufficiently open to allow the passage of air – they can be made of wood, wire, plastic or metal. It is convenient to have one side that can be opened or removed.*

LEFT *Cross-section through a well-made compost heap. Twiggy material is put at the base (not part of the compost) to allow air to enter from below, and prevent water collecting in time of heavy rains. Mesh can be used instead. Then, layers of vegetable material, 15-23cm/6-9in deep, are laid and covered with soil 5cm/2.5in deep, which helps weigh down the vegetable matter and speeds the movement of bacteria through the heap. In dry periods, water the heap well; keep it covered during rainy ones.*

lawn mowings, vegetable refuse (including peelings), fallen leaves and the top growth of such perennial 'weeds' as nettles, dock and dandelion can be used. Tough, hard or diseased matter should be burnt first and the ashes, purified by fire, can then be added to the heap.

MULCHING

Mulching is a method of covering the soil with a thick layer either of organic substances, such as compost, peat, leafmould, spent hops, grass mowings or chopped tree bark, or inorganic or other kinds of stone. Mulches play an important role by keeping the moisture in the soil down near the roots of the plant.

When organic mulches are used, they do in time disintegrate and become incorporated into the soil, thus enriching it, and making it more open and friable. Inorganic mulches will remain intact for a long time, but may eventually need renewing as they, too, will disappear into the soil.

Mulches have a secondary, important role in that they will suppress unwanted seedlings (for my own method, see page 138). But there are many other situations when mulches will prove useful. Ferns, shrubs and trees are likely to grow much better if after planting they are kept mulched with an organic substance until they are seen to be growing well. A mulched soil seldom freezes.

Proper composting breaks down the acidity of organic materials. Where fresh uncomposted materials, such as lawn mowings, are used as a mulch, these are likely to add a degree of acidity to the soil. The more they are used the more acid the soil will become – a good reason for using lawn mowings as a mulch around heathers, which is what I do. Elsewhere, a little liming from time to time will check the tendency to acidity.

LEAFMOULD

Leafmould is one of the best and most versatile mulches. It is also of great value when used in potting composts or soil mixtures. Those who hope to raise many of their own seedlings would be well advised to build up a supply for the year ahead.

Almost any kind of leaves can be used, but some – beech, oak and birch, for example – rot down more quickly than others. Leaves from evergreens and all similar tough leaves are not suitable as they take much longer to decompose. How quickly leaves decompose also depends on how much moisture and heat there is. Generally speaking, however, those leaves stacked one autumn should be ready for use a year later. To test if the pile is ready, check that no complete leaves remain. The leafmould should be flaky, easy to crumble between the fingers and hardly recognizable as leaves.

BELOW *After planting shrubs and tree seedlings, keep the ground around them mulched with chopped bark or other coarse mulch throughout the first two growing seasons. Fine mulches such as peat tend to absorb moisture and provide a rooting ground for wind-blown seeds.*

Mulching young plants

BELOW *When raising young woodland plants, it is particularly helpful to simulate the soil conditions found in a wood. A mulch of leafmould, dead leaves or chopped bark will help keep the roots moist and prevent competition from unwanted seedlings.*

Leafmould
RIGHT *Make a neat rectangular heap of leaves some 15cm/6in deep. Cover with a layer of soil deep enough to hide the surface of the leaves. Repeat the layers of leaves and soil until the heap is 60-90cm/24-36in high.*

soil layer

rotting leaves

ALTERING CONTOURS

Any garden can be given interest by changing contours here and there. This need not involve great earthworks, but just some modest 'landscaping': adding banks and terraces, making a small pond which will instantly attract wildlife, building a wall for plants to grow on, or simply letting a path meander round the garden.

MAKING A BANK

The quickest way to make a bank is to import soil or use that excavated when making a garden pond. The method we use, though much slower, makes a richer soil, suitable for ferns or herbs, for example. We begin with dumping hedge cuttings and all plant refuse that is not easily compostable. Since there is also a vegetable and a non-wild garden to be maintained, there are the inevitable barrowloads of spent stems. These are then covered by what lawn mowings can be spared, fallen fruit and leaves swept up from the drive which are not suitable for leafmould, the occasional load of brought in peat or soil. Like most else in a wild garden, such

banks need not be made in a hurry. My own have taken years, and one made this way is now some 9m/30ft long and 1m/3ft high in places. It is planted as an informal herb garden (see page 99), mostly with native or naturalized species.

Another mound, this time running from north to south, was made to serve two purposes: to screen the kitchen garden which had been situated fairly near the house; and to accommodate those calcyfuges we might wish to grow, placing those which needed it most on the sunny, south side.

For this purpose, quantities of both loose peat and peat blocks were brought in. Some of the latter were used as a 'wall' at ground level to stop

BELOW *Soak the blocks for an hour before they are laid. This not only makes them much heavier and therefore much easier to put into place, but it also helps them retain any moisture in the atmosphere. The more they swell the more effective the 'wall' will be. Once swollen, the blocks should stay this way except during a drought when they should be watered as often as possible preferably with soft rainwater, but not with limy or alkaline water.*

Using peat blocks for a terrace

BELOW *Do not leave any gaps between the blocks open to the drying air. Bank the peat or humusy-rich soil right up to the blocks. Once plants are established, the peat blocks should soon be disguised.*

An 'organic' bank

The bank shown here is made almost entirely from garden waste. The method, though slow, uses coppiced or pruned branches at the base, then layers of plant refuse, windfall fruit, leaves and soil or peat, as available, on top.

soil/peat top layer

plant and garden refuse

rotted apples in among branches

the loose peat packed behind them from washing away. Elsewhere on the mound, small areas of peat, held in curving walls of blocks, were made to hold shrubs and give them adequate rooting room. The peat here was later regularly covered with a mulch of lawn mowings.

As the years pass, the blocks gradually merge into the peaty soil they support. Moss, ferns and seedlings grow between and upon them attractively.

BUILDING A DRY-STONE WALL

Dry walls in which no bonding is used offer hollows and crevices as shelter for wildlife, and spaces for the roots of plants. They are not difficult to build, but certain rules apply. Some excavation will be needed to make a firm, level base.

Unlike bonded walls, dry-stone walls are normally 'battered', that is, they incline so that the top is slightly narrower than the base. A banked wall needs to incline more, to prevent it bulging.

Wherever possible, use regular-sized pieces of local stone that harmonizes with the garden as a whole. Rough stones, however, such as those put aside when they crop up in the garden, are seldom sufficiently even-sized. Grade the stones before you begin building, because different sizes are used variously in the construction.

Allow a little extra space between stones every so often, as a drainage hole and for adding plants as the wall is being built; this is the best planting method, because the roots can be covered with sufficient soil, more can be provided behind and below for them to spread into. As each course of stones is laid, spread a thin layer of slightly moist soil over it, both for plant roots and to help the next course to sit more securely.

A dry-stone retaining wall

1 *This wall was built around the base of an old tree in the author's garden. First a shallow trench was dug, just wider than the base of the wall to be built, and filled with small, unwanted stones.*

3 *Insert the longest stones as vertical ties here and there, or as anchors extending into the soil, to ensure stability. Have some plants to hand while building, and some good humusy-rich soil or compost for planting the wall as you go.*

horizontal anchor stone

vertical tie stone

humus or compost for planting up

2 *The largest stones were used for the lower courses. The second and subsequent courses were laid so that the stones covered the joins between the stones below. It is well worth taking time to find the right size of stone to keep the course level.*

4 *The wall a couple of seasons later. Plants sprawl up the tree, and over the bank to trail down the wall.*

gap to encourage wildlife

MAKING A GARDEN POND

Concrete is seen to have too many disadvantages for use as a pond lining nowadays. The options are either a flexible sheeting material which will mould itself to the shape excavated, or a rigid, pre-moulded container, placed into a hole dug to its exact dimensions. The latter is largely a question of trial and error; start by marking out the circumference as accurately as possible, using string to guide you.

The heavier the plastic sheeting the better; butyl or artificial rubber with a nylon fabric base is probably best. It can be bought by the square metre, and the quantity required is the maximum length of the pool times the maximum width, times twice the maximum depth. This material will stretch enough to mould itself closely to the pond's contours. Take care that no stones or projecting roots remain to puncture the sheet; it is best to line the hole with peat or sand first. The sheet should then be stretched over the hole and weighted down around the edges; folds and tucks will hardly show if the liner is dark. Water trickled gently into the centre of the sheeting will push the sheet down, eventually pressing it closely against the base and sides. Smooth out any wrinkles as the water pressure reveals them.

WINTER CARE OF THE POND

Remove all leaves from the pond, certainly before early spring when frogs and toads visit the pond to breed. Better still, stretch small-gauge plastic netting tautly over the surface of the pond to catch and hold the leaves and other debris.

In winter, if the surface ices over, damaging gases build up, especially if there are any leaves in the water. These gases may kill wildlife, so the ice must be punctured or melted to allow them to escape. Never break ice forcibly, as the shock waves produced may damage fish and other creatures.

Preformed pond

1 Fibreglass ponds come in various shapes and sizes, priced (not cheaply) according to size and complexity. The overall depth will vary considerably.

2 The hole dug for this type of pond must be an exact fit, for the fibreglass must be supported in all places, and the rim must be level with the ground so that when the pond is filled, the water does not appear to slope! Watch particularly the angle of slope of the sides, the depth of the shelves and the levels on the bottom. It is best to dig out too much soil and then fill in.

Plastic sheeting

Unlike the preformed pond lining, flexible sheeting gives you a free hand in design of the pond. Do not make the slopes too steep, which might cause the plastic to slip at the sides. Leave shallow shelves all round, at a depth of 20cm/8in or so for marginal plants.

The pond edges

For both types of pond, the best way of finishing off the sides is to surround them with pavings. This will hide the rim or the edges of the sheeting while holding it firmly in place.

water lilies in position

butyl or rubber sheeting

marginal plants

sand or peat layer

heavy, rich soil at bottom

PATH DESIGN AND CONSTRUCTION

Where your wild garden pathways need a more substantial surface, you should consider carefully the form and materials that will blend in best. Harsh concrete or coloured pavings will upset the natural effect of the scene. Straight lines should be avoided; any permanent surface should curve gently. By keeping the path narrow, but bearing in mind the kind of traffic that will use it (wheelbarrows, tricycles, etc.), you should be able to keep it a discreet feature of the garden. This could be helped by using several different surfaces, and not continuing any one of them for any great length (see plans on pages 31, 73 and 116). The surface could perhaps change according to the character of the different parts of the garden that the path links. Carpeting or mat-forming plants are useful as a link between one type of surface and another, and help make the transition gradual.

The path along the length of my herb bank, where I need to walk in all weathers, is a mixture of pale grey paving slabs set well apart, with the space between each well-gravelled and planted with creeping thymes and pennyroyal – one species, or variety, per space. These plants have gradually formed leafy mats, which can be trodden on, and they trail prettily over the edges of the stones, softening their appearance.

An unusual surface that would suit a sitting area by a pond, or in a cool shady fern garden, or wooded area, is made from short lengths of wood – elm or other hardwood – bedded in gravel. This helps keep the wood well-drained and prevents slipperiness. A path through a damp area, or perhaps adjacent to a lawn or meadow area, could be gravelled, using thin poles of alder or birch as edging to contain the stones. On a slope the path could be terraced, using the poles, almost buried, across the path to edge the steps.

Stepping stones, set in grass or across a pond or marshy area, are useful and look attractive. If set in grass, they should be level with the ground. If set in a pond, they will need to be well-founded on piers of brick or stone.

A gravel path
Poles embedded both along and across a sloping gravel path help contain the gravel.

A log path
1 *An informal path constructed with pieces of sawn log about 20cm/8in thick.*
2 *They should be set in coarse sand or gravel with a base of larger stones or hardcore. The gaps between the stones and the base will ensure good drainage.*

Pavings and gravel with interplanting
Gravel planted with fragrant herbs that withstand crushing and soften the edges of the hard paving stones. A hardcore base is essential; the stones would sit even more securely set in light cement.

A stepping-stone path for a pond or marshy area
Stepping stones across a natural or cement-based pond provide easier access for cleaning. The piers, which can be brick or stone, should be firmly set in strong cement. Make sure that the stones do not appear more than a few inches above the optimum water level.

PLANT CULTIVATION

Earlier in this book I suggested that the successful wild gardener is one who adopts a different philosophy from those who intensively cultivate and tidy their gardens. Nowhere is this more true than in the matter of seeding plants.

SEED COLLECTION AND STORAGE

In traditional gardening practice, once herbaceous plants have finished flowering, most of their number are soon tidied by the removal of spent stems. In the wild, these stems remain so that the seed may ripen properly and then be dispersed in whatever manner is characteristic of the plant. This is a sequence which should also be allowed in the wild garden. Obviously it cannot be possible that all seed produced by a plant develops into another plant and it is quite likely that by allowing your plants to seed themselves there will be sufficient seedlings produced to suit your demands. Should too many grow then hand-weeding is called for. On the other hand, if you wish to establish quickly a colony of one kind of plant, it would be best to collect the seed and sow it more carefully so that each little seedling can be saved. Perhaps the plants you would like do not grow in your garden yet and you wish to collect some from the wild. On page 160 is a list of those native species from which seed should never be taken in the wild. Although the list is long, there are many others

Poppy seed heads
If you wish to save poppy seed, cut the seed stems as soon as they are ripe, otherwise some animal will be there before you to eat the oily seeds. Hold them upright for transport. When ripe, seeds fall readily when the stem is shaken.

which you can propagate with confidence.

My own method is to collect the seed stems, slipping them into a plastic bag or box so that no seed is wasted on the journey home, then to spread them out in a dry place for two weeks or so to ripen thoroughly. Since the plant was itself ready to shed its seed, I follow its example and sow seed in autumn in a nursery bed, where it can be subjected to weather in a natural manner.

If you do want to store seed, it should be in dry, cool conditions to maintain its viability: a plastic container in a refrigerator at about 2°C is ideal. Place a small packet of silica gel in the container to remove any moisture from the air and so prevent mould developing.

Stratifying berries
Berries and hard-coated seeds can be softened and so induced to germinate by stratifying them. They should be laid on sand, covered with more sand and left to over-winter outdoors.

Self-seeding parsley
This method is used in my own garden for parsley, which is always lush and plentiful. Allow some plants to flower and form seed. When the stems turn yellow, uproot and lay them along the ground. The dropped seed is then protected by the stems which are left until seedlings are visible.

Drying seed stems
Where seed vessels are small and numerous, lay the ripe stems well spaced apart on newspaper in a dry place away from draughts. When the stems are dry, shake out the seed.

PROPAGATION

The traditional methods of plant propagation – seed sowing, plant division, cuttings and layering – may be used just as effectively for wild plants. Seeds, however, do not all germinate at the same rate or under the same conditions, and gardeners who are used to the prompt and easy response of well-bred cultivars are likely to be put off by the frequently delayed behaviour of some wild plant seed. Germination of some once common plants, such as cowslips, remains unpredictable, which must be baffling to those who know how abundantly this plant once grew.

It is most likely that there are substances in the soil which act on some seeds to soften their outer coats. It may be that germination is long delayed if these substances are absent at the time of sowing.

SEED SOWING

The basic method of seed sowing is extremely simple. The seed is broadcast on soil made ready by first clearing, forking and finally raking to get a fine tilth. Once the seed is cast, gently rake the surface to cover it. The ground can then be lightly trodden to anchor the seeds and to dissuade birds from using the fine tilth as a dust bath.

Spacing seeds
A simple method for ensuring that seeds do not cluster too thickly so they are wasted. Empty a few seeds into a folded slip of paper and gently flick them, using a pencil tip or other pointed object, into their required position.

The other method is to sow the seeds in good seed compost in containers or in a specially prepared seed or nursery bed. Once the seedlings have grown large enough to handle easily, they can be lifted, carefully separated and individually transplanted, so that they are well-spaced. Then, as they grow large enough, they can be planted out in their permanent positions.

HASTENING GERMINATION

In the wild, most seeds lie on the soil surface where they are subjected to rough treatment. They become frozen, soaked by rain, and blown back and forth. Thus it often helps germination if these conditions are simulated by artificial means, particularly for those seeds which are sown undercover. Some tough seed coats can be nicked with a sharp knife so that moisture can enter and start the seed swelling. Other seed, such as that of most members of the pea family as well as meadow cranesbill and

Avoiding taproot damage
Plants with fibrous root systems are easy to transplant, but particular care must be taken with taproots because if their growing points are damaged, growth will cease. Avoid this by sowing the seed in small soil or peat pots which break down in the soil and are planted direct into the ground. The developing root need suffer no check in growing if the pot is planted out before the root tip protrudes through it. The units must be kept moist. Peat pots in particular become very tough if they dry out.

Watering seedlings
To avoid seedlings being disturbed or knocked over by a flow of water, use a plant spray. An alternative method for seedlings in containers or peat pots, is to stand the container or pots in a vessel of water for half an hour or so.

Stratification of seed
1 *The seed is placed on a layer of sand over a base of drainage material. More sand covers the seed to fill the pot.*
2 *The flower pots are left outside over the winter for the weathering process. Here they are half-buried and protected from rain by cloches.*

Helianthemum, should be rubbed between two sheets of coarse sandpaper to scarify their coats so that moisture can again enter and the seed swell. Other treatments include heat, refrigeration in sealed bags, or stratification.

Germination of many kinds of berries and hard-coated seeds can be speeded up by stratification (see illustration). Use separate flower pots for each type of seed – I prefer to use earthenware pots, though this is not essential. A layer of suitable drainage material – shingle or broken flower pot crocks, for instance – is laid at the bottom, for it is important that water should not linger and cause the seed to rot. Over this, spread a layer of sand, half filling the pot. Space the large seeds, or sprinkle smaller kinds, on the surface of the sand. Cover with more sand. More than one layer of seeds can be made, but one is usually easier to deal with. Stand the pots in a cold place outdoors, either half-buried in open ground or placed in a frame or box

of sand. To prevent mice from raiding the pots, secure fine mesh wire netting over the pots or the box, and cover with a cloche or piece of clear plastic. If this is done in mid-autumn, the seeds will be ready for sowing in compost in peat pots in early spring.

A quicker alternative to stratification for some seeds or berries, is to mix them with damp sand and place inside a plastic bag in a refrigerator, generally for one or two months before they are sown. There are some plants, usually alpines, which are said to respond after just 24 hours cold storage, and it is certainly useful to experiment.

Seed from berries can be sown directly, but as a rule germination does not take place until the second year after sowing. When the berries are ripe, the seeds are removed and sown at once in containers in a 50:50 mixture of moist peat and sharp grit, at a depth of just a little deeper than the seed's own thickness. The soil should never be allowed to dry out, and after the seeds have received one winter's natural 'vernalization', they are left to grow in these containers until the following winter when they can be transplanted into individual pots or planted in rows in the open ground. It is a good way to raise hedging plants.

NURSERY BEDS

We are warned by seed merchants that seed simply cast into rough grass or onto unprepared ground is most likely to be wasted. The method that is particularly suited to wildflowers for a meadow area is to propagate the seedlings in a nursery bed, and then to let them mature there before transplanting to the meadow area.

The bed is better drained and warmer if it is raised a little above ground level, 8-10cm/3-4in will do. Keep it narrow, 1-1.2m/3-4ft, so that you can reach the centre from one side or another without treading on the soil. After preparing the soil by forking and raking, some gardeners add a top layer of specially prepared seed compost, about 2.5cm/1in deep. This is helpful but not essential, and it serves to give the seedlings a good start.

Nursery bed
A special nursery bed is well worth making and maintaining. Keep it filled most of the time. Here the seed is sown directly into a patch of good soil. Later, the crowded seedlings are carefully lifted and transplanted into rows spaced a few inches apart each way. There they stay until they touch or are ready to go into their permanent places.

1 Oxeye daisy
2 Knapweed
3 Meadow clary

LAYERING

The illustration shows one method of layering heather. Another one, which can be used for most other members of the Ericaceae while the plants are dormant, is as follows. Spread out the stem or stems of low-growing types, or bend down those of more upright plants until some part of the stem other than the tip touches the soil. If necessary, use a strong twig, forked or bent hairpin-wise, to straddle the stem and pin it in place. Heap a mixture of peat and sand over the stem at the point where it touches the soil so that it is well covered.

When layering dianthus, make a horizontal cut on the underside of each stem at the point where it touches the soil. Do not sever the stem. Place a little heap of sand and soil mixture under the cut stem and push the cut portion into it so that the cut opens. Place more soil over the stem to hold it down. The roots should form in a few weeks. Heather takes longer – six months or so – the more shrubby the plant, the longer it takes to root. To transplant, after the layer has formed roots, detach it from the parent plant with secateurs. Then lift it from the soil carefully and replant.

Layering heathers

1 *Test to determine how far the heather stem will reach when spread out comfortably. At this point, scoop out a slight depression around the plant. Make sure that you do not dig so deeply that roots are damaged.*

2 *If several stems are to be layered, take each singly and space them well apart so that none are crossed. Bend the stem a little so that it touches the soil at the bottom of the depression. Anchor it in place with a large stone.*

TAKING CUTTINGS

Some plants take root easily in water – for example willow and dogwood – though you could also experiment with others. If a good example of either is available, such as a dogwood with particularly brilliant coloured bark, follow the method shown below. The cutting should be left to stand outdoors, sheltered from the wind. See that the level of water in the vessel does not drop to less than 15cm/6in from the bottom of the stem. The speed of root production varies with the time of year, but may take two to three months in spring.

When a good mass of roots has been formed, a mixture of sand and potting compost can be added to the container as shown. When you can see the roots growing out to the edges of the compost, the root ball can be lifted out and transplanted in a larger pot. Once the roots have filled this, it can be planted in the open ground.

Taking a willow cutting

1 *Stand the cutting in a wide-mouthed jar or container placed inside a bucket so that the stem is supported and held steady. Fill the jar with rainwater, immersing about 10cm/4in of the stem.*

2 *When a root mass has formed, pour sand into the container to settle in a 3cm/1½in layer at the bottom. In a few days, add a layer of potting compost and gradually build up the layers until the roots are covered. Transplant into a proper flower pot.*

Using forks to divide plants

I Some plants are easily pulled apart by hand, but old, usually tough specimens need more force. The usual method is to use two forks. Here a border fork is used with a small handfork.

2 Find the centre of the plant or some part into which a border fork will go easily. Take another fork, place the two back-to-back and wrench them apart, bringing the separated halves of the plant with them. Divide these further in the same manner.

PLANT DIVISION

An excellent way of obtaining more plants of the same kind is by taking a well-grown specimen, lifting it with as large a root mass as possible, and then separating, or dividing, it into many smaller, vigorous, well-rooted pieces. This technique is also useful for checking the spread of plants, for example herbs, that are beginning to occupy too much space. Suitable subjects are fibrous-rooted perennials and small, bushy shrubs. Very compact or tough roots – some ferns, for instance – can be cut with a sharp knife while others are best pulled apart in some way, by hand or with the aid of garden forks (see illustration). Discard obviously aged and spent portions. Rhizomatous plants may also be divided, the most healthy-looking or youngest rhizomes being pulled off from the mass. Do not replant these deeply: most of the top half of the rhizome should be above the soil surface.

Division should be carried out in autumn, even in a mild winter, when the plants are dormant or in spring, before they have started into growth.

INTRODUCING POT-GROWN MEADOW FLOWERS INTO TURF

Bulb planters (originally designed for planting bulbs into lawns or rough grass) provide an easy way of introducing pot-grown plants into existing grass. The seed is first sown in seed trays in the normal way, and pricked out into Jiffy pots when at first or second true leaf stage. Use a soil-based compost rather than a peat compost, to ensure that shrinkage does not occur when pots are planted out. Plants should be grown on in the pots until roots begin to show at the bottom.

Pressing the bulb planter into the turf, a core of soil is removed as the planter is taken out. The Jiffy pot with the plant, which should be the same size as the bulb planter, is given a thorough soaking before being inserted into the hole. Press gently around the edge with the heel of your boot. Do not replace any turf, but add a little soil around the plant if necessary to keep the ground level.

Water the plant well if rain does not follow within seven days. It is best to introduce pot-grown plants into turf either in early spring or in autumn, though summer plantings can be successful if water is available.

Bulb planters are not advised in stony soil, but work well in most garden soils. The advantage of planting pot-grown plants is that they will often flower within a year of planting.

Bulb planter
This device was designed for planting bulbs in grass. By pushing the corer into the soil, a plug of soil is removed as the corer is withdrawn. The bulb is placed in the hole as shown, and the plug of soil tipped out of the corer (use a stick to push if the soil is sticky clay), replaced over the bulb and firmed in. The method is also successful for planting pot-grown plants.

wooden handle

metal cross bar

metal corer

plug of soil

bulb

SOWING WILDFLOWER SEED IN LAWNS

An alternative to introducing pot-grown plants into turf (see page 133) is to sow seed. Scattering seed onto the turf itself, however, is a waste of time. It is essential to 'scarify' the turf first, in order to make bare batches of soil into which the seed can be sown. The turf is ripped out with a rake exposing the soil and at the same time dead grass and unwanted plants should be removed. It is easier if the grass has not been long established so that there are gaps in the sward. The poorer the soil, the more chance of successful germination, but this depends also on soil type and seasonal conditions. If the soil is at all rich and the weather wet, grasses will soon swamp the seedlings, unless controlled in some way. If the seed is sown in autumn, the gaps are less likely to close over quickly, though in the right conditions, seed can also be sown in spring. Choosing species to suit your soil type is very important (see page 159). It is worth sowing seed of 20 species and hope for perhaps half of them to germinate and grow.

A NEW FLOWER LAWN FROM SEED

You should not be put off by the idea of starting a flower meadow from scratch. The secret of success is ground preparation, and a low-fertile, clean soil

Introducing species-rich turves into lawns
A method that has met with success among some conservation bodies, and could be tried whenever the opportunity arises, is to take whole turves from threatened meadows (perhaps where roads are being widened or made), or by kind permission of the owner. The benefit of this method is that a community of plants and insects can be transplanted (and perhaps saved), thus spreading and increasing their stock.

Scarification
This is the technique of ripping patches of turf from lawn or meadow with a rake to expose bare soil. It is essential that the meadow flower seed makes good contact with the soil in order to germinate.

with no drainage problems. Avoid topsoil altogether. The site should preferably be sunny, as few meadow species will tolerate shade.

In order to clear the site sufficiently of all unwanted perennials (docks, thistles etc.), it may well be necessary to use a herbicide. After spraying, it is a good idea to leave the site, say for a couple of months during the summer to clear any weeds that grow over this period before the meadow flower and grass mixture is sown.

The best time for sowing, again, is early autumn. Mid-spring is the alternative, though some species will then not germinate until the following year. (For examples of seed mixes for soil types, see page 159. See also pages 142-3 and 145.) Even distribution of seed is vital. Because seed varies so much in size, it is important that it is well-mixed. Adding sand or fine sawdust to it to increase the bulk helps spread the seed more evenly, and the light colour helps you see where seed has been spread. Over a small surface, lightly rake the soil and tread the seed in well. Over a larger surface use a roller to keep the surface firm.

Sowing grasses and planting wildflowers
The method shown below is a combination of sown meadow grasses and pot-grown meadow flowers. The grass seed is sown in circular drills, and pot plants (a bulb planter could be used, see page 133) interplanted in the gaps the following spring.

circular drill

pot plant

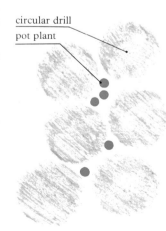

PLANTING AND CARING FOR FERNS

In Victorian times, it was fashionable to grow ferns in a purpose-built place made much like a rockery, or sometimes even on a steep, rocky slope attached to the north wall of a house. Usually this was done to ensure that the site was well drained, and this is important. Although some ferns need moisture, they do not grow well in sour, wet soil. The better the soil the more luxuriantly the ferns will grow, although some species do well in little soil on walls. The method traditionally used is good.

Make a compost of 2-parts fibrous turf, 1-part half-rotted leafmould and 1-part coarse silver (i.e. horticultural) sand. Builders' sand, unless washed, may contain harmful substances. Make planting holes at least twice as wide and deep as the root ball of the fern. After planting and watering in, mulch the soil surface with either leafmould or home-made compost, or failing that, with a mixture of peat and soil. As the years go by, keep the soil surface well mulched, preferably with leafmould, to help retain the soil moisture. In a dry season, water the ferns from time to time. Try not to splash the fronds in hot, dry weather and certainly not if the sun shines on them or they may become spotted or marked in some way. Dusty ferns can be gently hosed in the evenings in summer, but as a rule rain showers keep them clean and unmarked.

The faded fronds should be left on deciduous ferns, for they help to protect the crown of the plant; an important point, especially in districts or seasons where the winter is hard.

PROPAGATING FERNS

Ferns that form several crowns as they age can be lifted and divided, pulled or even cut apart, in early spring. Those which are rhizomatous are best propagated by detaching rooted pieces from the parent, and immediately planting these in the ground. The method is more reliable if the pieces are layered into small pots of soil sunk in the ground next to the parent plant so that their rhizomes can grow before they are severed from the parent. This can be done at almost any time of year.

root ball

enlargement of frond showing spore clusters

Planting ferns
When planting a fern make the hole at least twice as wide and as deep as its root ball, in order that a good amount of the soil mixture can be placed below as well as around the roots. Water well. Mulch the surface after planting and keep it mulched.

Fern spores
Fern spores, arranged in small round clusters, or sori, are found on the under surface of fertile fronds. These must be ripe for propagation to be successful. The fronds which bear them should be examined frequently so that the spores can be taken as soon as they are ready, and before they have a chance to disperse.

Experts are agreed that the best way to raise a stock of ferns is from spores, a delicate process needing patience. The spore-cases are ripe when they are a light-brown colour. Collect a few pieces from a fertile frond, place them in an envelope and allow to dry for 48 hours or so in a warm place.

When the spores are released, they will be found as a fine dust – brown, yellow or green, according to species – in the bottom of the envelope.

Mix a compost of equal parts of sand, peat and leafmould, place in a crocked pot and sterilize by pouring boiling water over. Allow to drain and cool. Scatter the spore dust into the pot and cover with a glass sheet or enclose in a plastic bag. Stand in a warm place out of direct sunlight, and do not allow to dry out.

Germination and fertilization may take several weeks, even a few months, depending on species. The first sign will be a greenish tinge to the compost. Later the first fronds will begin to show, and these can be pricked off into individual pots as soon as they are large enough to be handled. The pots must be kept moist continually.

TREE PLANTING

Whether planting individual trees, or laying out a small copse, the wild gardener would do better to choose tree seedlings, either grown himself from seed or bought from nurseries, rather than buy pricy standard trees, which will look inappropriate in an informal setting. Two-year old saplings cost a fraction of the price of standard trees. Normally they will not need staking, and within two or three years should have overtaken the standards.

If you are establishing a small copse, the poorer the soil the better as the seedlings will not be smothered by competitors, such as couch grass, *Agropyron repens*, which often happens if trees are planted in topsoil. It is essential that all plants that might compete with the seedlings are eliminated, and though this can be done by using herbicide to prepare the ground first, my own method is to use a newspaper mulch (see page 138). If the ground is already clear, mulches such as chopped bark will prevent germination of the wealth of dormant weed seeds disturbed in the planting.

The method I use for planting trees in grass is as follows. A roughly rectangular area is cut with the spade and a deep turf lifted. The soil at the bottom of the hole is forked and well-broken. Some good, humusy soil is then laid over it, and the plant's roots placed on this. A cane or stake, both as a marker and support, may be set in place at the same time. Soil is then taken from the underside of the lifted turf (or turves) and used to cover the roots. The plant is firmed into position and the remains of the turves turned over (tucking any long grass under) and placed around the plant.

CARE OF SHRUBS AND TREES

The danger period for shrubs and trees is the first few months after planting. Make sure that they are never allowed to dry out, and water daily if the weather is hot, and when drying winds blow. Spray the foliage with clean water, rainwater preferably. An initial heavy watering followed by the application of a thick mulch will keep the roots from drying out over a long period.

After periods of heavy wind, examine young trees and shrubs to make sure that they have not been rocked. If this happens, a hollow area may form round their roots which will fill with water

Staking a tree in a very exposed position
Where strong winds prevail it is prudent to stake newly planted trees. Where there are adequate windbreaks one stake should be sufficient. Otherwise a tripod of stakes can prove most effective. Inspect ties regularly to ensure that they are not weakening nor so tight that they cut into the tree bark.

Planting a tree using a stake

stick to indicate soil level

1 *Make the planting hole wider than the tree's root spread and/or deeper than the root ball. Pile the excavated soil on a plastic sheet nearby. Into this, mix compost, leaf soil or peat and general garden fertilizer. Insert stake.*

2 *Place the stem near the stake. To ensure that the tree's roots will be at the same depth as they were growing at before transplanting, place a stick across the hole.*

3 *A clearly visible soil-level mark will be seen on the stem a little above the roots. Cover these with the new soil, firming it thoroughly so that no air pockets exist. Water the area thoroughly.*

4 *Fasten the tree to the stake using a tree tie.*

and induce rotting. Hold the plant upright again and tread the soil, firming it around the roots and the stem base once again. If the tree is in a particularly exposed situation, it may need staking.

PLANTING A WILD HEDGEROW

Hedgerows bordering lanes and fields have been in sharp decline in recent years, and their loss has meant a severe decrease in the stock of wild plants and wildlife that enjoyed the hedgerow habitat. A hedge of native plant species as a feature of the wild garden is an important aid to conservation.

Hedges are best planted in the autumn. Clear a strip of ground some 1.2m/4ft wide, and dig the soil deeply before incorporating plenty of organic matter. Using a garden line or length of string down the centre of the prepared ground, plant two-year-old seedlings (obtainable from nurseries). Do not alternate them singly but plant in runs of threes or fives of a kind. Mix the species so that they set one another off. You could follow this sequence: hawthorn, field maple, holly, blackthorn, hornbeam, privet – then repeat it. The mixture can be

as varied as there are plants available; my own ancient hedge has guelder rose, hazel, willow, buckthorn, beech, oak and elm.

ADDING PLANTS TO A HEDGE

This method can be used for repairing a gappy hedge, enlivening a single-species hedge, or introducing climbers into a newly established hedge.

Grow the seedlings to be introduced in plastic or fibre pots. It is much easier to establish a pot than to dig out a large planting hole in the base of the hedge. Crack or split plastic pots at the bottom so that when the root is ready, it can grow out into the soil. Remove some soil at the spot where the seedling is to grow, so that the pot stands secure, half-buried. Keep the seedling well-watered, remembering that the cracked pot will lose water quickly.

Filling a gap in an old hedge
Have a seedling ready in a plastic or fibre pot, and dig a hole where the plant is to grow in the hedgerow. Leave the plant in the half-buried pot, which is split apart at the bottom so that the roots of the seedling can grow into the soil below. The pot can be removed later, or covered with soil.

Planting a hedgerow

1 *The two-year-old seedlings placed closely together, about 50cm/20in apart. After planting, the ground must be well-mulched to keep roots moist and suppress weeds.*

2 *Once the seedlings are established, it is advisable to cut some species back hard in the spring after planting to encourage bushy basal growth. Evergreen species should merely be tipped, so if the hedge is very mixed, it may be necessary to prune some plants and not others. Beech, hornbeam, holly and yew are best left uncut for two years. Use secateurs rather than shears in the early years.*

3 *After four or five years, the hedge will be ready for clipping into shape, or for traditional 'laying'. However, precise clipping and shaping will not be desirable for the wild garden, neither will it suit any climbers growing in the hedge.*

PLANT AND PEST CONTROL

In the wild garden, we need to avoid using chemical sprays to control plants, although there are times, for example when clearing larger areas of poor undergrowth, when selective weedkillers are necessary, and, indeed, are recommended by some conservation bodies. In this latter case, once the area has been cut down or mown, those species that cannot be successfully hand-pulled or cut out may be treated with a gel-based non-selective systemic contact herbicide such as glyphosate. Once the planting is underway or the garden established, all herbicides should be avoided.

MULCHING AS A WEED INHIBITOR

One of the simplest inhibitors of weed growth is a heavy mulch of some kind. This will not only keep down other seedlings in the soil around a planted patch, but will maintain moisture at the plant's roots (see mulching, page 124). This method will take longer than an application of herbicide, but it is effective, less unsightly and is beneficial to the soil, as long as organic materials are used. (Black plastic or purpose-made plastic mulch sheets can be used, but, unless they are covered with thin soil to disguise them, they look unsightly and are not recommended for the wild garden.)

In my own garden, where space for a little copse is being cleared in rough grassland, the following method is being used successfully. Whenever a plant, such as a small tree seedling, is added to the scheme (see page 136), several overlapping sheets of newspaper are laid on the ground around the plant, and the grass, together with other unwanted plants, pressed down as flat as possible under the paper. This is then covered and weighted with some organic material. As this mulch is laid down at each planting, gradually all the space between the introduced plants is covered, and the ground will eventually be ready for field layer plants.

Unplanted areas or spaces between rows of plants (such as in the nursery bed) can also be treated this way, to suppress new weed growth. The vegetation underneath the newspaper is so deprived of light that it gradually rots and eventually both paper and covering are drawn into the soil. The time this takes depends on the vitality and

Newspaper mulch as a weed suppressor

1 *Overlapping double or triple sheets of newspaper should be laid around a shrub, tree seedling or any other plant, leaving it free but closely covering all growth around it. If necessary, weight down the papers as they are being laid.*

2 *The grass and weeds are pressed flat under the paper, which is then weighted and covered with a layer at least 5cm/2½in deep of some organic material such as lawn mowings, chopped bark, peat (moistened to prevent it from blowing away), chopped spent bracken, fallen leaves, compost, or whatever comes to hand.*

population of the soil: if many worms are present, it may take a couple of months only. So far, the only plants that have managed to penetrate this newspaper and mulch cover have been a very few thistles, which are easy enough to pull up as they appear. If unwanted grasses appear, the process will be repeated so that a thicker mat is formed.

It is worth noting that in many countries there are certain plants which are listed as being undesirable to plant or for which planting is prohibited. Some may have become too invasive, some may be host plants of pests of important agricultural or horticultural plants.

In the United States and in some other countries, the common berberis has been eradicated and its cultivation prohibited because the plant acts as an intermediate host for black rust, a fungus which attacks wheat. Other species of berberis do not appear to be attacked by this fungus. In the UK, cultivation of the beautiful ragwort is discouraged.

COPPICING

Coppicing is the term used when a tree is grown as a 'stool' rather than as a trunk, the stool throwing out many young growths from ground level which can be cut and used as poles etc. In the first instance the main trunk is cut; buds are then produced at or just above ground level. Subsequently the thicket of young growths is cut back almost to ground level. Coppicing is done on a

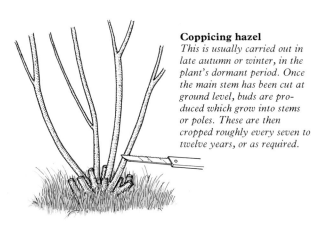

Coppicing hazel
This is usually carried out in late autumn or winter, in the plant's dormant period. Once the main stem has been cut at ground level, buds are produced which grow into stems or poles. These are then cropped roughly every seven to twelve years, or as required.

Pruning buddleia
Once, goldfinches nested among the old seedy tips of the buddleias in my own garden, so now only half of them are pruned, the other half left till the following year. Although not essential, pruning in spring encourages good, strong, flowering stems which produce heavy racemes of flowers for butterflies and others. Simply cut back last year's flowering stems back to a good pair of fat buds.

regular cycle, ranging from about seven to twelve years, depending on the size of timber required. Hazels were once widely coppiced because their poles were required for horticultural and agricultural purposes. Coppicing is a good method of keeping down those species which as full-grown, seed-bearing trees might become invasive.

POLLARDING

This is done to restrict the growth of large, deciduous trees. The tree is severed at about 2m/6ft 6in from ground level. New growth sprouts from this point. Pollarded trees most often include willow, wych elm and lime.

CONTROLLING NETTLES

When nettles are growing vigorously it is difficult to lift the massed net of thick, thong-like ochre coloured roots from the soil. A tip from Gertrude Jekyll is useful for those who do not wish to use herbicides. Simply thrash the plants down with a stick whenever they have grown tall. If this is done three times during the year, the roots will become weakened and they will loosen their hold on the soil. They can then easily be forked out. Remember that butterflies will only lay their eggs on young, soft nettle growth, so nettles should be cut back in late summer to promote this new growth, ready for late broods. Use shears and a rake for this. Do not waste the stalks – remember that they are good material for the compost heap.

CONTROLLING BRAMBLES

The various brambles around my own garden are easily controlled as they are cut back when the farmer cuts the hedges each year. However, birds still feed from their fruits and spread the seed, so bramble seedlings abound as they will do where the blackberry grows locally. It is important that the bramble seedlings are pulled up when young, so search regularly for them. They soon develop long, anchoring roots and their young stems also root at their tips, thus further entrenching them.

Plants allowed to grow as naturally as possible, instead of being trained against a flat surface or along wires as is customary when cultivated varieties are grown, can be restricted in size if old stems are cut down to ground level in the autumn. But if the plant is grown mainly for the benefit of wildlife, pruning can be delayed until spring, so that it affords good cover during winter, but be sure to do this before the nesting season begins.

PEST CONTROL

It is well known that ladybirds and their larvae are useful in combatting some garden pests: they feed voraciously on aphids and their relatives. Lacewing and hoverfly also have larvae that feed on aphids, and one way to encourage these insects is to have a ready supply of nectar and pollen for the adults – they in any case make attractive insect visitors. For hoverflies, grow flat open flowers, especially those of the families Compositae and Umbelliferae.

One of the secrets of a healthy garden is a large range of plants and habitats. Planting native flowers, shrubs and trees will encourage a rich insect life. The more niches available for nesting birds, the greater the chance there is of encouraging these birds to stay and feed over a season and not just pass through your garden. Thrushes will tackle your surplus snail population and blue tits and great tits will keep buds and foliage clear of greenfly and small caterpillars.

There really is no need to use pesticides in a wild garden. If the plants are well diversified, and

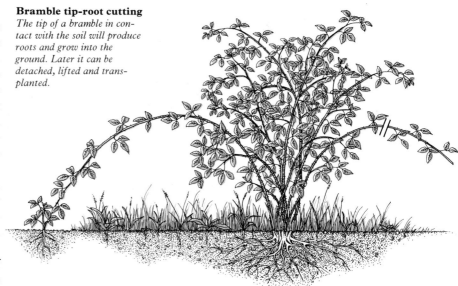

Bramble tip-root cutting
The tip of a bramble in contact with the soil will produce roots and grow into the ground. Later it can be detached, lifted and transplanted.

no one species of a kind massed together, there should be enough predators in the form of insects, and the odd toad and bird visitor, to deal with an aphid epidemic or a plague of caterpillars.

Yet sometimes, usually because of forces beyond control, some creatures increase so rapidly that they become a nuisance. The so-called 'garden pests' are in this category and it is not always the absence of predators that explains their great numbers. Sometimes, as in the case of the cabbage white butterfly, whose caterpillars eat brassica crops, it is more to do with the fact that in a garden (or on a farm) their host plants are concentrated in greater numbers than they would be in the wild. Or, in the case of hybrid roses, the plant's growth is softer and more succulent than that of a wild species and so more attractive to insects and animals.

The introduction of ash trees is our garden had an unexpected result. Although the bullfinches were welcome for their beauty, we regretted that they destroyed so much blossom. But once the ash bore seeds, the birds turned their attention to the 'keys'. Thus the once denuded trees are again as beautiful as they should be.

APPENDICES

A selective plant guide appears on pages 142-159, beginning with charts that give fuller information on many of the native species featured in the chapters in *Planting successful wild gardens*: meadow flowers and meadow grasses; bulbs suitable for planting in lawns or longer grass; trees, shrubs, climbers and field layer plants for woodland gardens; heathers together with other heath plants suitable for acid soils; ferns, grasses and sedges, and 'green' herbaceous plants; wild herbs; plants for ponds and pond margins; plants for walls, rocks and gravel. There are check lists of native plants for growing in special situations – sun, shade, ground cover, climbers, trailers, acid/alkaline tolerant – and a section on meadow flower and grass mixtures for different soil types, plus the 62 specially protected plant species, and nectar and berry-bearing plants to attract wildlife.

MEADOW FLOWERS

A selection of colourful wildflowers, suitable for a variety of soil and moisture conditions. They will enhance an existing lawn, or form the basis of a spring or summer meadow area in the garden. All these species can be obtained from specialist seed merchants (see page 168). For a guide to flower and grass seed mixtures for three soil types, see page 159.

SL = Spring lawn   FL = Flower lawn
M = Summer meadow

	Habit H = height	Flowers Nos = months 1-12	Propagation	Suitability for SL, FL, M	Cultivation
Achillea millefolium Yarrow	Downy, aromatic, perennial; H 10-70cm.	White rose-forms; 6-9.	Seed.	FL, SL, or best in M.	Grows on most soils except the most acid. Tolerates some shade.
Bellis perennis Daisy	Low perennial with a rosette of basal leaves; H 3-20cm.	White or pink with yellow centres; 3-10.	Seed. Avoid cultivated double forms.	Best in FL (where it is often a 'weed') or in SL.	All soils and moisture conditions. Will tolerate some shade.
Cardamine pratensis Cuckoo flower	Graceful perennial with pinnate leaves; H 15-60cm.	Lilac or white; 4-6.	Seed or as pot grown plants.	Only suitable for wet areas in FL, SL, or M.	Does best in damp meadows, by ponds or streams on most soil types.
Centaurea nigra Common knapweed	Downy perennial with stiff ribbed stems; H 15-90cm.	Pale purple-red to dark purple; 6-9.	Seed, or as pot grown plant.	Because of its stature best in M.	Will grow on all but the most acid soils. Suitable for all moisture conditions.
Centaurea scabiosa Greater knapweed	Handsome perennial with stiff grooved stems and pinnately lobed bristly leaves; H 30-90cm.	Red-purple; 7-9.	Seed or as pot grown plants. Germination often slow.	Suitable only for M. Very vigorous with tendency to shade other plants.	Prefers dry calcareous soils, but will also grow on basic clays. Excellent on chalk or limestone.
Chrysanthemum leucanthemum Oxeye daisy	Large daisy, a perennial with small glossy green leaves; H 20-70cm.	White with yellow centres; 6-8.	Seed. Germination usually 90% plus.	Essential for all meadows and easy to grow.	On all but the most acid clays or sands. Tolerates a wide range of moisture.
Daucus carota Wild carrot	Hairy biennial with stiff solid stems; umbellifer; H 30-100cm.	White; 6-8.	Seed. Sow in autumn.	M. Cut late if this is to survive.	Has a preference for dry calcareous soils.
Galium verum Lady's bedstraw	Sprawling perennial; smells of new-mown hay; H 15-100cm.	Bright yellow; 7-9.	Seed.	Can survive in mown lawns, but best in M.	In grassland on all but the most acid soils. Will grow in hedgebanks. A scrambler.
Geranium pratense Meadow crane's-bill	Handsome stout perennial; stems often reddish; H 30-80cm.	Violet blue; 6-9.	Seed (scarcity) or as pot grown plants.	M. Often takes at least 4 years from seed to flower.	Suitable for all but the most acid soils. Likes damp soils, good in a border.
Hypochaeris radicata Cat's-ear	Erect tufted perennial with round-toothed leaves in basal rosette; H 20-60cm.	Bright yellow, grey violet beneath; 6-9.	Easy from seed or as pot grown plant.	Common as 'weed' on many lawns, but also good for M.	Will grow in all soils and moisture conditions. Tolerant of same shade.
Jasione montana Sheep's-bit	Scabious-like biennial of variable form; H 5-30cm.	Blue; 5-8.	Seed or as pot grown plants.	FL or SL.	Light, sandy or gravelly soils on non-calcareous substrates.
Leontodon hispidus Rough hawkbit	Dandelion-like roughly hairy perennial; H 10-60cm.	Yellow, orange or reddish beneath; 6-9.	Seed or as pot grown plants.	FL, SL or M.	Prefers neutral or calcareous soils, moist or dry.
Lotus corniculatus Common birdsfoot-trefoil	Prostrate perennial with trifoliate leaves, highly variable; H 10-70cm.	Yellow often streaked with red; 6-9.	Seed. Scarification enhances germination.	Strains suitable for FL, SL and M. Beware vigorous agricultural strains.	A highly variable species which will grow on all but the most acid soils. Suitable for all moisture conditions.

	Habit H = height	Flowers Nos = months 1-12	Propagation	Suitability for SL, FL, M	Cultivation
Lychnis flos-cuculi Ragged robin	Slender perennial with pointed leaves; H 30-75cm.	Rose-red, rarely white; 5-7.	Seed or as pot grown plants. Seed very small.	SL or M. Damp areas only.	Damp or wet soils. Good for edges of ponds, marshes, stream banks.
Malva moschata Musk mallow	Graceful hairy perennial; H 30-85cm.	Rose-pink, also a white form; 7-8.	Seed or as pot grown plants.	M or shady ride in wood.	On most moderately fertile soils. Tolerates shade.
Medicago lupulina Black medick	Low prostrate downy annual; H 5-30cm.	Yellow; 4-8.	Seed.	Does well in FL. Also suitable for SL and M.	All soils and will grow in dry places. Often short-lived but replaces itself by seeding.
Ononis repens Common restharrow	Creeping downy, woody, perennial, soft spines; H 30-60cm.	Pink; 6-9.	Seed. Scarification enhances germination. Also as pot grown plants.	SL or M.	Prefers calcareous soils and dislikes wet places.
Ononis spinosa Spiny restharrow	Darker green than previous species with erect stems; H 30-60cm.	Pink; 6-9.	Seed (scarcity) or pot grown plants.	A 'must' for the M.	Good for rough places on neutral, basic or calcareous soils.
Plantago media Hoary plantain	Grey downy perennial with flat rosette of leaves; H 5-20cm.	White with purple stamens; 5-8.	Seed or as pot grown plants.	Best in FL or SL but will survive in open M.	Forms a rosette on neutral or basic soils, either dry or damp. Will tolerate some shade.
Poterium sanguisorba Salad burnet	Perennial smelling of cucumber when crushed; H 5-60cm.	Green-purple tinged; 5-8.	Seed or as pot grown plants.	A 'must' for the M.	Only grows on neutral or calcareous soils. Good on chalk.
Primula veris Cowslip	Perennial with crinkly downy-haired basal leaves; H 10-30cm.	Deep yellow or buff with orange spots; 4-5.	Seed or as pot grown plants. Seeds only germinate after winter cold treatment.	FL, SL, or M. A 'must' for most gardens.	Likes damp to wet calcareous soils, but will also grow in alluvial and clay soils. Does well on the chalk.
Prunella vulgaris Self-heal	Short creeping downy perennial; H 5-30cm.	Violet to pink; 6-9.	Seed.	FL, SL or M.	Prefers basic or neutral soils under a wide range of moisture and light conditions.
Ranunculus acris Meadow buttercup	Hairy perennial with deeply cut palmate leaves; H 15-100cm.	Bright yellow, glossy; 5-7.	Seed or as pot grown plants.	SL or better in M.	Best in damp grassland on neutral or calcareous soils.
Ranunculus bubosus Bulbous buttercup	Hairy perennial with marked swollen base to stem; H 15-45cm.	Bright yellow underside shiny; 4-6.	Seed or as pot grown plants.	Common 'weed' of many lawns, but good for M.	Dry soils, with a marked preference for calcareous or neutral.
Rhinanthus minor Yellow rattle	Variable annual (semi-parasite), with 4-angled stems; H 10-40cm.	Yellow; 5-8.	Seed. Must be sown in autumn with a grass mixture for successful germination.	M. The seeds shake out then re-establish each year.	Thrives in most soil and moisture conditions.
Rumex acetosa Common sorrel	Perennial with long-stalked, arrow-shaped leaves; H 30-100cm.	Flowers small reddish; 5-6.	Seed.	SL, or M. Leaves good in salads.	Will grow on most soils. Prefers moist soils. Shade tolerant.
Trifolium dubium Lesser trefoil	Low annual, often goes purplish; H 5-25cm.	Yellow turning brown; 5-10.	Seed.	Excellent in mown lawns and survives by seeding.	Grows best in open vegetation on all soil types. Completes life-cycle quickly.
Trifolium pratense Red clover	Slightly downy perennial; H 10-60cm.	Pink-purple; 5-9.	Seed. Scarification enhances germination.	SL, or M.	Tolerates all but the most acid soils. Avoid vigorous cultivars.
Veronica chamaedrys Germander speedwell	Weak hairy perennial; H 10-40cm.	Bright blue with white eye; 3-7.	Seed. Germination usually low and erratic.	FL, SL or M.	Will grow in most soils and will tolerate shade, e.g. suitable for woodland paths.

BULBS AND MEADOW GRASSES

Closely mown lawns give one no idea of how beautiful grasses can be when allowed
to flower nor how attractive they are to many forms of wildlife. It is so easy to
add to existing kinds by sowing seed. In short grass in spring or autumn,
little drifts of bulbous plants, bought from bulb merchants, will provide
a succession of enchanting flowers.

	Habit H = height	Foliage	Flowers Nos = months 1-12	Natural habitat	Cultivation
BULBS AND CORMS					
Allium oleraceum Field garlic	Fleshy perennial, arises from white or brown bulb; H 30-60cm.	Fleshy and solid with rough margins.	Bell-shaped, green. tinged with red in loose umbels; 7-8.	Rare, field borders.	Well-drained soil in sunny position.
Allium ursinum Ramsons	Garlic-scented perennial; H 10-30cm.	Usually 2, flat and reversed narrowing to a stalk.	White in a flat umbel; 4-6.	Common in moist woods.	Will grow in grass in shade.
Colchicum autumnale Meadow saffron	Variable perennial which produces flowers in the autumn and leaves the following spring; H 20-25cm.	Bright green; 3-8, large and lanceolate.	Rosy-mauve, rarely white, crocus-like with long orange anthers; 8-10.	In damp meadows and woods.	Prefers damp, neutral or basic soils; good by pond.
Fritillaria meleagris Fritillary	Very variable perennial; H 20-50cm.	Grass-like, 4-5 about the middle of the stem.	Solitary, usually dull purple chequered dark and pale; 4-5.	Damp meadows.	In short turf, in moist conditions.
Galanthus nivalis Snowdrop	Very variable perennial; H 10-20cm.	Grey-green, linear, usually 2.	White, streaked green; drooping; 1-3.	Possibly naturalized, in damp woods and shady river banks.	Grows well in short grass.
Leucojum aestivum Summer snowflake	Perennial; H 60cm.	Mid-green; linear.	Pure white, green-tipped in clusters of 4-8; 4-5.	Local in wet meadows and withy beds.	Easily grown in ordinary soil.
Leucojum vernum Spring snowflake	Perennial; H 20cm.	Yellow-green; linear.	White with green-tipped petals; solitary; fragrant; 2-3.	Rare, in moist shady places.	In rich soil in open position.
Muscari racemosum Grape hyacinth	Perennial; H 20cm	Long, narrow and limp.	Dark-blue tipped with white; small; egg-shaped; in dense raceme: musk-like scent; 4-5.	In sandy dry grass-land.	In short grass.
Narcissus majalis Pheasant's eye	Distinctive perennial; H 25-45cm.	Erect, smooth.	Outer petals white; eye-like corona, short with red rim; fragrant; 3-5.	Possibly naturalized; a feature of meadows in the South of France.	Almost anywhere in or out of grass.
Narcissus pseudo-narcissus Wild daffodil	Very variable species, parent of many garden varieties; H 20-35cm.	Erect, glaucous.	Bright yellow, somewhat drooping trumpet, petals paler; scented; 3-4.	Damp meadows, riversides, lakesides.	In fairly moist soil.
Ornithogallum umbellatum Star-of-Bethlehem	Perennial; H 30cm.	Dark green; limp.	Satiny white within; striped green outside; in flowered corymb; 5-6.	In grassy places mainly in East Anglia.	Good for grassy woodland borders.
Scilla autumnalis Autumn squill	Perennial producing leaves; H 15cm.	Narrow, grooved.	Red-purple in short raceme; 7-9.	Dry pastures usually near the sea.	Open grassland.

	Habit H = height	Foliage	Flower head Nos = months 1-12	Natural habitat	Cultivation
Scilla non-scriptus Blue bell	Variable perennial, arises from long, white bulb; H 25-45cm.	Linear, concave.	Mostly blue on racemes of 1 to 12 flowers, drooping; 4-6.	Abundant in woods, hedgerows and meadows adjoining woods.	In fairly moist soil, partial shade.
Scilla verna Spring squill	Perennial which produces leaves before the flowers; H 5-20cm.	Very narrow and grass-like.	Blue- star-like; on 6-12 flowered raceme; 4-5.	Coastal pastures.	Very difficult to cultivate, try short grass and sandy soil.
MEADOW GRASSES					
Agrostis canina Brown bent	Tufted perennial spreading by rhizomes or stolons forming a dense turf; H 10-60cm.	Narrow and flattened.	Purple-brown, contracted at first but spreading later.	Damp and dry grassland and heaths.	Best on more acid soil; useful in a mixture, never alone.
Agrostis tenuis Fine bent	Tufted perennial forming a loose or dense tuft; H to 20cm.	Flat and fine.	Purple; on loose and spreading flower heads.	Acid soils	Useful for dry acid soils but will also grow on clays and sands.
Alopecurus pratensis Meadow foxtail	Loosely tufted perennial, rarely forming dense patches; H 30-90cm.	Roughish; upper sheaths inflated.	Grey-purple; on long cylindrical flower head.	Common in meadows and by roadsides.	For low-lying moist to wet areas on clay and alluvial soils.
Anthoxanthum odoratum Sweet vernal grass	Slender tufted perennial; rarely forms a turf; H 20-50cm.	Flat.	Purplish, on slightly branched, egg-shaped flower head.	Common in grassland and in woods.	Suitable for a wide range of soils; a 'must' for most mixtures.
Briza minor Lesser quaking grass	Annual, never forms dense tufts in mixtures; H 10-40cm.	Broad, rough, finely pointed.	Loose and open flower head, nods in the wind.	Prefers calcareous soil in the South; on arable or waste land.	Sometimes difficult to grow from seed, often better pot grown.
Festuca ovina Sheep's fescue	Densely tufted perennial; very variable; H 10-50cm.	Stiff and narrow, almost hair-like, often waxy-green.	Greenish or purplish; small and variable.	Drier grassland on chalk and limestone.	Suited to poor, well-drained soil; withstands close-cutting.
Festuca rubra Red fescue	Slightly hairy perennial, usually short, creeping; very variable; H 10-60cm.	Inrolled, wire-like and pointed.	Usually with a purplish tinge; variable.	Widespread in all grassy places.	Varieties for all soil conditions; cultivars are too vigorous.
Festuca tenuifolia Fine-leaved sheep's fescue	Densely tufted perennial; tough and wiry; H 10-50cm.	Bright green to dark green.	Yellow-green or green-purplish on erect flower head.	On dry and damp acid soils with sand, peat or gravel.	Useful for 'difficult' situations; fairly drought-resistant.
Helictotrichon pubescens Downy oat-grass	An attractive loose-tufted perennial; not vigorous; H 30-70cm.	Flat and downy.	Green-purple; branched and spreading.	In rough grass and on dunes.	On damp calcareous soils in milder situations.
Holcus lanatus Yorkshire fog	Grey, softly downy perennial with tough creeping rhizomes; H 20-60cm.	Grey-green; downy; narrowed to fine point.	Whitish then pale-pink to purple; on downy flower head.	Widespread.	Too vigorous for lawns but good for meadows; shade-tolerant.
Hordeum secalinum Meadow barley	Tufted perennial; H 10-50cm.	Grey-green or green.	Green then fawn; forms dense spike.	In meadows and pastures.	Does best in heavy soils; worth including for its inflorescence.
Poa pratensis Smooth meadow-grass	Stiff stocky creeping perennial; forms compact turf or tufts; H 15-80cm.	Green or slightly bluish or greyish; blunt-tipped.	Purplish; flower head often tri-angular in outline.	Drier grassy places.	On well-drained soil; will tolerate some shade.
Poa trivalis Rough meadow-grass	Loosely tufted perennial with creeping stolons, vigorous; H 20-60cm.	Pale and flat.	Green, purplish or reddish; in erect, dense panicles.	In moist and often shaded grassy places.	Useful for damp soils, green in winter.
Trisetum flavescens Yellow oat-grass	Pale, slender loosely tufted perennial with few basal leaves; H 20-50cm.	Narrow and flat.	Shining yellow; on spreading flower head.	In grassy places on chalk and limestone.	Best on calcareous soils, drought resistant; not highly competitive.

145

TREES AND WOODLAND PLANTS

These trees and shrubs can be bought as mature plants, in which case they may take
two or three years to become properly established. Those grown more cheaply
from seed mature surprisingly quickly and soon outpace the others.
The field layer flowering species can be bought as plants,
roots or seed from garden centres and specialists.

	Habit Height = H; Spread = S	Foliage	Flowers	Fruit	Cultivation
TREES					
Acer campestre Field maple	Round-headed; H 6-9m; S 5.3m.	Deeply divided; turns clear yellow, occasionally red.	Green; in erect clusters.	Downy keys turn crimson then brown.	Calcareous clays and loams; good hedging plant.
Betula pendula Silver birch	Slender and graceful; bark white; H 15-18m; S 2.5-3.5m.	Triangular in alternate pairs.	Pale-green female catkins, purple-brown male catkins.	Small, winged seed.	Will grow in poor, acid soil; very hardy; many varieties.
Carpinus betulus Hornbeam	Rounded crown, unspreading branches; bark fluted grey; H 15-21m; S 3-4.5m.	Ovate with marked veins; changes from yellow to gold to a rusty hue; often retained through winter.	Catkins.	Three-lobed green and leafy bracts, each with hard, rigid nut.	Rich loam and clay, good for hedging as retains leaves throughout winter; very hardy.
Crataegus monogyna Hawthorn	Densely branched and thorny; H 7.5-9m; S 3m.	Dark and glossy.	White, sometimes fading to pink; in corymbs, scented.	Small, crimson haws attract birds.	Ordinary soil in sun; makes dense growth. Comes into leaf early.
Ilex aquifolium Holly	Narrow-crowned, conical; pale grey bark; H 5.5-7.5m; S 2-3m.	Evergreen with sharp spines; waxy on top, matt below.	White; tiny; male and female born on separate trees.	Bright red berries in autumn and winter; borne by female tree.	Well-drained loam; variegated forms very slow to grow.
Malus pumila Crab apple	Shrub-like tree, rounded with widely spreading branches when young; vigorous; H 7.5-9m; S 4.5-7.5m.	Pointed tips; alternate	White, tinted pink or crimson.	Small yellow apples, striped red.	Well-drained soil enriched with well-rotted compost or manure.
Prunus avium Wild cherry	Pyramidial habit with up-spreading branches; reddish-brown bark; H 9-12m; S 6-9m.	Drooping, bronzey-brown in spring, pale-green to crimson in autumn.	White; cup-shaped; borne in stalkless umbels.	Bright dark-red.	Well-drained soil; not as demanding of lime as other *Prunus* sp.
Sorbus aria Whitebeam	Compact pyramidial with few upswept branches; H 9-15m; S 3-5m.	Ovoid; white undersides; turns yellow then orange.	White; in loose clusters.	Round scarlet fruits.	Well-drained soil; sunny position.
Sorbus aucuparia Mountain ash	Narrow-crowned conical; H 12.5-18m; S 2.5-3.5m.	Pinnate; turns yellow then orange.	White in wide clusters.	Bright orange-red berries; very attractive to birds.	Well-drained loamy soil; sunny position; hardy and easy to grow.
SHRUBS					
Cornus sanguinea Dogwood	Erect shrub; slender red twigs are conspicuous in winter; H 2-4m; S 2-2.5m.	Green and pointed, turning dark red-purple.	White; in small clusters; attracts flies, beetles.	Purplish-black in large, loose clusters; attractive to birds.	Alkaline or neutral soils; very hardy.
Coryllus avellana Hazel	Forms dense thicket of erect stems; H 3.5-6m; S 4.5m.	Large; heart-shaped; downy beneath.	Handsome male catkins appear early in the year.	Clusters of nuts or cobs encased in a green-toothed husk.	Well-drained soil; sheltered, sunny site; interesting varieties.
Prunus spinosa Blackthorn	Dense, finely-branched, spiny black shoots, hence common name; H 2.5-3m; S 2-3m.	Bright green; small.	White, starry blossom appears early in year long before foliage.	Bluish-black fruit (sloes) with bloom, like small plums.	Alkaline-neutral clay and loam; suits more exposed situations.

	Habit Height = H; Spread = S	Foliage	Flowers Nos = months 1-12	Fruit	Cultivation
Rhamnus catharticus Purging buckthorn	Many-branched and thorny; H 4-6m; S 2-3m.	Yellow-green, with glabrous shoots.	Yellow-green; small; sweetly scented.	Berries first green then black in clusters.	Limy soils; partial shade.
Rosa canina Dog rose	Stout with arching stems bearing prickles; H 2-3m; S 1.5-2m.	Pinnate, sometimes downy beneath.	Soft-pink with golden stamens.	Large, ovoid to round crimson hips; attractive to birds.	Long-lived, hardy and very variable species.
Sambucus nigra Elder	Takes on a small tree-like form when given light and space; H up to 9m; S 3.5-4.5m.	Pinnate with 5-7 leaflets; foul-smelling.	Creamy-white; in cymes; heavy sweet smell.	Purplish-black berries, in large, loose clusters; attractive to birds.	Very vigorous in fertile garden soil. Keep well-pruned. Many beautiful varieties.
Viburnum opulus Guelder rose	Upright, bushy; H 3-4.5m; S up to 4.5m.	Maple-like, turning a flaming red.	White; flat-topped; with outer ring of much larger flowers.	Translucent red berries often persist well after leaves fall.	Damp soil and shade; used in hedgerows; attractive varieties.
CLIMBERS					
Clematis vitalba Old man's beard	Vigorous and woody; H up to 12m.	Pinnate and opposite.	Creamy-white; in panicles; slightly fragrant; 7-9.	Woolly greyish-white whorls of feathered styles.	Grows naturally on calcareous soils.
Lonicera periclymenum Honeysuckle	Strong and woody; H 3-6m.	Oval; paler beneath.	Pale-yellow flushed with purple; tubular; attractive to moths; 6-8.	Red; in close clusters; attractive to birds.	Humus-rich soil in shade; against tree or arch.
Rosa arvensis Field rose	Shrub with long green or purplish trailing stems; H 1.5-3m.	Pinnate.	White; usually solitary or small corymbs; 7-8.	Red hips, ovoid or oblong.	Grows well in shade; parent of Ayrshire roses.
Tamus communis Black bryony	Grows over hedges, bushes, etc.; twining stems; H to 4m.	Broad and heart-shaped.	Yellow-green, turning yellow; tiny; 5-8.	Scarlet, poisonous berries.	Prefers alkaline soils; vigorous climber for partial shade.
FIELD LAYER					
Anemone nemorosa Wood anemone	Slender, horizontal root-stock; forms drifts in woodland; H 7.5-15cm.	Trifoliate; deeply-lobed and coarsely toothed.	White, often with pink or purple tinge; 4-5.	None.	Planted in groups under trees; effective under early-flowering shrubs and trees; very variable.
Convallaria majalis Lily-of-the-valley	Creeping rootstock; H 15-20cm.	Broad, oblong or elliptical.	White; bell-like in raceme; richly fragrant; 5-6.	None.	Needs humus-rich soil and moisture at roots; does well in light shade.
Digitalis purpurea Foxglove	Biennial; H 50-150cm.	Broad oblong leaves form radical rosette in first year from which tall flower spike arises.	Purple, pink or white, often spotted within; 6-9.	None.	Moist soil in partial shade.
Myosotis sylvatica Wood forget-me-not	Perennial or biennial in cultivation; H 30-60cm.	Oblong.	Sky-blue or pale-blue with yellow eye; in long racemes; 5-6.	None.	Best in sun so long as soil is moist; will tolerate slight shade.
Primula vulgaris Primrose	Low perennial; H 15-30cm.	Crinkly, in rosette; grows longer after flowering.	Sulphur-yellow; on long stalks; 3-5.	None.	Fertile soil that does not dry out.
Vinca major Periwinkle	Spreading sub-shrub; H 15-30cm.	Evergreen, oval.	Blue-purple; 3-7.	None.	Good trailing plant for moist shady places.
Viola riviniana Common dog violet	H 8-20cm.	Toothed; heart-shaped.	Blue-violet with creamy spur; 4-6.	None.	Fertile soil; partial shade.

...l habitat	Cultivation
...gs.	Peaty soil with adequate moisture; preferably in sun or partial shade.
...n on stony ...nd mountains.	Well-drained, light, lime-free peaty soil in woodland borders.
...moors and ...d borders.	On acid peaty soil in open position. Water during dry spells.
...distributed on ...heaths.	Well-drained soil; does best in sand and gravel.
...in Co. Mayo ...Galway.	Good for woodland fringes; needs protection from cold winds and drought.
...n on drier ...nd moors.	Well-drained deep peaty cool moist (never water-logged) soil.
...ths in W	Needs shelter from strong winds; suits most soils; does best in warm wet climate.
...n on boggy	Cool moist peaty soil or leafy loam.
...gs in mild ...ns.	Vigorous; will tolerate ordinary garden soil. Easily grown, pollution-tolerant.
...n dry heathy ...nd.	Light well-drained soil in sun.
...gs.	Moist peaty soil or lime-free loam.

	Habit H = height; S = spread	Foliage	Flowers Nos = months 1-12	Natural habitat	Cultivation
Linnaea borealis Twinflower	Trailing, sub-shrubby, evergreen perennial; H 5-8cm; S to 60cm.	Rounded or small, ovate, slightly hairy.	Pink, trumpet-shaped, pendulous on slender stems; fragrant; 6-8.	Shady northern coniferous forest and rocky places.	Shade; cool peaty or leafy soil.
Moneses uniflora One-flowered wintergreen (St. Olaf's candlestick)	Single species of its genera, dwarf perennial; H 8-15cm.	Radical, vaguely spoon-shaped, leathery and toothed.	Fragrant, waxy-white, or pink, solitary and drooping; 6-7.	Open moist mossy places in coniferous forest in N. hemisphere.	Edge of woodland in light peaty soil, or in partial shade in rock gardens.
Myrica gale Bog myrtle	Small tufted deciduous, resinous shrub with reddish-brown twigs; fragrant; H 60-120cm.	Oblanceolate, dark glossy green above, paler or downy underneath.	Males on orange stalkless catkins; females small, closely packed and resinous; 4-5.	Bogs, fens and wet acid soils.	Only grows well on acid loam or peat soils.
Pyrola media Intermediate wintergreen	Slender, creeping, dwarf, hardy, glabrous perennial; H 10cm.	Ovate, in a rosette on long stems.	White tinged red in many-flowered racemes on 10cm long stem; 6-8.	Woods, especially pine, and moors.	As for *Moneses*.
Pyrola minor Common wintergreen.	As above, but smaller in all parts.	Roundish.	Waxy white tinged with rose in many-flowered racemes.	Moors, woods and dunes.	As above.
Trientalis europaea Chickweed wintergreen	Perennial with erect stem, creeping rhizome. Only 2 species – NW America and Europe; H 10cm.	Shining rigid, mostly broad lanceolate 5-7 in a whorl at top of stem or below the flowers.	White or pale pink, few on long stem, 6-7.	High moors and coniferous woods.	Light, rich soil, plenty of leafmould; shady site.
Ulex europaeus Common gorse	Thick-set, spiny evergreen bush with long spines 2-10cm; H 06.2.4m.	Three-foliate on young seedlings only, later modified as rigid furrowed spines.	Yellow, pea-like with an almond-coconut fragrance; 4-6.	Common on heaths.	Most floriferous on poor or well-drained garden soil in full sun. Avoid root disturbance.
Ulex gallii Dwarf gorse	Densely spiny shrub, spines 0.5-2.5cm, young shoots hairy; H 45-100cm.	As above; spines often curved.	As above but smaller; 7-8.	On heaths and moors.	Not quite as hardy as *U. minor*.
Ulex minor Lesser gorse	Dwarf shrub of dense habit growing taller in cultivation. Young shoots downy; H 30-60cm.	Shorter spines than *U. gallii*.	Pale yellow, smaller than *U. gallii*; 7-8.	Local on heaths and moors.	As *U. Europaeus* above.
Vaccinium myrtillus Bilberry, blaeberry, whortleberry	Deciduous dwarf shrub with angled green twigs; H 15-45cm; S 30-45cm.	Bright green, oval, turning dull purple and gold; pointed, downy on veins beneath.	Pink, almost round, attractively lobed; 4-7.	Common on heaths and moors.	Moist rock or heather garden; acid soils, more tolerant of exposure and shade than *Calluna*.
Vaccinium oxycoccus Small cranberry	Creeping, straggling evergreen shrub with wiry ascending stems.	Dark green above, glaucous below, sparse and alternate.	Pink, usually solitary or 2-4 urn-shaped; 6-8.	In bogs with sphagnum moss.	Moist rock or heather garden; acid soil.
Vaccinium uliginosum Bog bilberry	Deciduous, stiff, much-branched low broad bush with glabrous young shoots.	Blue-green waxy round, glaucous beneath.	Pink, usually solitary or 2-4 urn-shaped; 5-7.	Wet moors.	As above.
Viola lactea Pale heath violet	Leafy-stemmed perennial; H 5-12cm.	Long-stalked, narrowly ovate or lanceolate rounded at base; minutely hairy.	Fairly large, pale milky blue with long yellow-green spur on leafy stem; 5-6.	Heaths.	Rich acid soil.
Wahlenbergia hederacea Ivy-leaved bellflower	Slender, trailing perennial or annual with thread-like stems.	Small, almost orbicular, vaguely ivy-shaped.	Long, pale blue, bell-shaped; 7-8.	Damp pockets of heath, moor and peat bogs.	Moist, peaty places.

FERNS AND FOLIAGE PLANTS

Because, for some years, flower arrangers have been interested in growing
and gathering leaves and grasses as much as they have been in blooms,
most nurseries and garden centres offer a fine range of green flowers, ferns, plants
with handsome foliage and grasses in great variety. At the same time,
many of the species listed here can be raised from seeds.

	Habit H = height	Foliage	Flowerhead Nos = months 1-12	Natural habitat	Cultivation
FERNS					
Asplenium trichomanes Maidenhair spleenwort	Small and delicate forming dense tufts; H to 20cm.	Long, with oval or oblong leaflets narrowing at base.	None.	Moist, moss-covered cliffs, rocks and walls.	Lime-loving; well-drained site.
Athyrum filix-femina Lady fern	Large, showy, lacy-cut; H 15-150cm.	Fresh green; fronds divided into lesser fronds.	None.	Damp woods, rocks, hedge banks.	Leafy soil or loamy peat; moist; in semi-shade.
Blechnum spicant Hard fern	Extremely variable, ever-green, sturdy; grows in a tuft; H to 50cm.	Dark green, lanceolate; barren fronds shorter and narrower than fertile fronds.	None.	On heaths and moors, among rocks and in woods; on acid soil.	Ideal for moist shady nooks; dislikes lime.
Dryopteris filix-mas Male fern	Extremely hardy and very variable; almost evergreen; H 60-120cm.	Broad fronds with pinnae; 10-15cm long.	None.	Wooded and rocky areas.	Prefers a light sandy loam to stiff clay; prefers shade.
Phyllitis scolopendrium Hartstongue	Tufted evergreen; H 45-60cm.	Undivided, strap-shaped, wavy.	None.	On rocks and hedge-banks.	Leafy well-drained soil.
Polypodium dryopteris Oak fern	Graceful with creeping rootstock; H 15-30cm.	Emerald green.	None.	Damp woods and rocky screes.	Peaty soil, well-drained.
Polypodium vulgare Common polypody	Small vigorous evergreen; mat-forming; H 15-35cm.	Broad, green, deep-cut, wavy, oblong-lanceolate fronds, sometimes lustrous-golden above.	None.	In woods elevated on trees, stumps, moist banks and walls.	Most luxuriant in almost any position except marsh; will take sun and drought.
Polystichum aculeatum Hard shield fern	Variable, bold, handsome tufted with long-stalked fronds; H to 1.2m.	Broad, leathery, ovate-lanceolate.	None.	Hedge banks, wood margins and thickets.	Best in shade; should be watered freely.
GRASSES & SEDGES					
Briza maxima Pearl grass	Annual; forms small tuft of erect smooth stems; H 38-50cm.	Bright green, narrow and pointed with rough upper-sides.	Panicle nodding with about 8 large, green, ovate spikelets.	Naturalized in Channel Islands; common around the Mediterranean.	Well-drained soil in sunny position.
Briza media Quaking grass	Slow-creeping rhizomatous perennial with erect, slender smooth stems; H 23-45cm.	Light green, flat and tapering with rough margins.	Panicle 15cm long, small purple-brown heart-shaped spikelets.	On sunny well-drained calcareous grassland.	As above.
Carex pendula Drooping sedge	Graceful tufted perennial; H 90-150cm.	Pale glossy, green, broad.	Very long, drooping spikes.	Damp woods and shady places.	Suitable for watersides also.
Eriophorum polystachion Common cotton grass	Perennial untufted sedge; H 15-60cm.	Grooved, grass-like, triquetrous.	Brown-green; terminal drooping cymes.	Bogs.	Suitable for pool margins and boggy places.
Festuca arundinacea Tall fescue	Grows as large coarse tussocks; H to 1.5m.	Long, flat, coarse with hairy sheaths.	Graceful panicle with opposite branches.	Dry grassy places on clay.	Any meadow garden.
Glyceria maxima Plicate sweet grass	Stout, smooth-stemmed grass with creeping roots; H 1-2.4m.	Flat with sharp edges.	Panicle terminal; fluffy, white, ovoid; many-flowered.	Margins of fresh and brackish water.	Useful for waterside gardens, also on moist soil.

	Habit H = height	Foliage	Flowerhead Nos = months 1-12	Natural habitat	Cultivation
Lagurus ovatus Hare's tail grass	One of the handsomest of British grasses – a distinctive tufted annual or biennial; H 30cm.	Grey-green, hairy, narrow linear, shorter than stem.	Panicle terminal; fluffy, white, ovoid, many-flowered.	On sand dunes, dry places in Channel Islands; naturalized in S. England.	On well-drained loam in sunny position.
Melica uniflora Wood melick	Common, graceful, slender-stemmed perennial; H 30-45cm.	Limp, flat and downy, pointed leaf sheath often hairy.	Open panicle with branches of purplish-brown, egg-shaped spikelets.	Woods and shady hedge banks, especially on calcareous soils.	In leafy soil.
Phalaris canariensis Canary grass	Tufted annual; H 25-90cm.	Flat.	Large green and white plumes.	Naturalized from Mediterranean.	Ordinary soil; full sun.
GREEN HERBACEOUS PLANTS					
Alchemilla vulgaris Lady's mantle	Hardy perennial with short, stout, black rootstock; H 16-46cm.	Hairy above, green beneath; numerous, wide, and kidney-shaped on long stalks.	Yellow-green; in foamy racemes or panicles; 6-8.	Grassland.	Ordinary soil well-drained.
Arum italicum Cuckoo pint	A variable plant similar to *A. maculatum* (below); H 25-70cm.	More triangular than *A. maculatum* with creamy, patterned veins; on long stalks.	Light-green drooping spathe with yellow-orange spadix; 5-6.	Woodland.	Sheltered shaded site.
Arum maculstum Cuckoo pint	Tuberous perennial with handsome foliage; H 25-40cm.	Dark-green often spotted purplish-black; large, bluntly arrow-shaped leaves in spring.	Arum-like, green spathe, often with purple margin and veining; 4-5.	Hedgerows and woods.	Any rich, moist, partially shaded site.
Daphne laureola Spurge laurel	Smooth erect evergreen shrub; H 60-90cm.	Dark-green, glossy, leathery, broad-lanceolate.	Green, small, fragrant, in racemes of of 5-10; 3-4.	In woods on chalk and limestone.	In limy soil in partial shade.
Eryngium maritimum Sea holly	Very glaucous, spiny, umbelliferous perennial; H 30-45cm.	Leathery, white glaucous; basal, heart-shaped, upper stem-clasping palmately lobed.	Powder blue and mauve, globular; surrounded by broad, spiny bracts; 7-8.	On sand and short turf by the sea.	Gravel gardens in light sandy soil and sunny position.
Euphorbia lathyrus Caper spurge	Handsome, glaucous, waxy, erect, annual or biennial; H 90cm.	Lower leaves lanceolate, upper ones broad.	Small yellow-green on long-stalked umbels.	In woods on chalk and limestone.	Self-seeds freely.
Helleborus foetidus Stinking hellebore	Leafy, glaborous evergreen sub-shrub.	Dark shining green; leathery; palmate with 7-10 lanceolate toothed segments.	Yellow-green; cup-shaped; crowded panicles of bracts and flowers; 3-5.	In woods and scrub on chalk and limestone in the South and West.	Ordinary soil, deep but well-drained, in shade.
Helleborus viridis Green hellebore	Glaborous, deciduous.	Dull green above, paler with prominent veins beneath; 7-11 segments on long stem.	Bright green; cup-shaped; scentless; few flowers on each stem; 3-5.	In woods on chalk and limestone in the South.	As above.
Iris foetidissima Gladdon	Hardy perennial, grows in thick tufts; H 50cm.	Dark evergreen; glossy; acrid and highly foetid when crushed.	Slate grey-purple in lateral clusters: small; short-lived; 6.	In dry woods, thickets and hedge banks on dry calcareous soils.	In shade in rich humus.
Petasites fragrans Winter heliotrope	Naturalized perennial with deep rhizomes.	Very large, cordate, coming just after flowers emerge.	White or pale lilac, vanilla-scented, 6-8 heads per stem; 1-2.	Banks and roadsides.	Effective by watersides. Good on banks; can become invasive so should be isolated.
Polygonatum multiflorum Solomon's seal	Graceful hardy perennial with round, arching stems; H 60-120cm.	Oblong; alternate; stem-clasping.	Greenish-white; in small hanging clusters; 5-6.	In woods.	Ideal for naturalizing in woods and shady borders.

WILD HERBS

Herbs are among the easiest of all plants to grow. Most settle down as happily in a
garden environment as in their natural habitats. None seems to be rare.
Most are easily raised from seed and have been propagated this way for centuries.
Alternatively, you can often find plants on sale, or beg one or two from
a kind gardener who is willing to share them.

	Habit H = height	Foliage	Flowers Nos = months 1-12	Natural habitat	Cultivation
Allium schoenoprasum Chives	Hardy, tufted perennial; narrow bulb covered with crimson sheath; H 8-30cm.	Hollow, cylindrical, glaucous green; fine-pointed.	Rosy-violet, rose in a dense umbel; 6-7.	Rare in the wild; on limestone cliffs.	Ordinary soil in sun or semi-shade.
Angelica archangelica Angelica	Statuesque hardy biennial with a stout hollow stem; aromatic; H 2m.	Bright green compound with terminal leaflet in 3 parts, 0.6-1m wide.	White or green in large compound umbels; 7-8.	Naturalized on some river banks, wet woods and damp grass.	In deep moist soil, in sun or partial shade; keep moist.
Anthemis nobilis Chamomile	Procumbent aromatic perennial; H to 25cm.	Finely-cut 2 pinnate linear; a little downy.	Daisy-like rays, white disc, yellow solitary; 6-7.	Sandy soil; grassy and heathy places.	Tolerant of acid soils and some shade.
Anthriscus cerefolium Garden chervil	Free-seeding hardy annual; with furrowed, pubescent stalks; H 60cm.	2 pinnately-cut, delicate; anise-scented.	White in small slightly radiate umbels; 5-6.	Naturalized in some waste places.	Ordinary soil in dappled shade.
Artemisia absinthium Common wormwood	Herbaceous perennial with a woody rootstock; H 1m.	2 or 3 pinnate, silky both sides; bitter-scented.	Downy, yellow; globose; borne in slender leafy panicles 40-45cm long; 7-8.	Waste ground, road-sides and coastal.	Well-drained soil in sunny position.
Artemisia maritima Sea wormwood	Downy sub-shrub with woody, branched root-stock and herbaceous stems; H 40-60cm.	Pinnate, covered with white down.	Tiny yellow or red, in leafy panicles; 8-9.	Sandy seashores and seasides.	Ordinary soil.
Borago officinalis Borage	Naturalized, stout, roughly hairy annual; H 30-60cm.	Large, ovate, young leaves taste and smell of cucumber.	Panicles of bright blue, star-shaped, drooping; 6-9.	Waste places in the South.	In ordinary dryish soil in sunny position.
Calamintha nepeta Lesser catmint	Branched, downy grey, tufted perennial; H 20-30cm.	Small and hairy, pungently scented.	Pale lilac in loose whorls on leafy stem; 7-8.	Rare; mainly in S. England.	Light soil, in sunny position; will grow on gravel.
Carum carvi Caraway	Biennial with strong tap-root and hollow furrowed and branched stem; H 30-60cm.	2-pinnate, narrow, deeply-cut, much-divided and feathery.	Irregular white umbel and outer flowers; 6-7.	Naturalized but rare.	Ordinary, well-drained soil in full sun.
Foeniculum vulgare Fennel	Short-lived but free-seeding perennial with stout erect stems; H 90-150cm.	3-4 pinnate with very fine segments; beautifully feathery.	Yellow in large umbels; 8-10.	Sea cliffs, waste-ground, motorway verges.	Any type of well-drained soil in sunny open position.
Hypericum androsaemum Tutsan	A medicinal sub-shrub with angled or winged shoots; H 1m.	Broad-oval, pale beneath, resinous.	Yellow in terminal cymes of 3-9; 6-9.	Grass in damp hedge-rows, thickets and ditches.	Almost any soil and situation.
Ligusticum scoticum Lovage	Glabrous perennial with stiff, ribbed, purple stems; H 22-45cm.	Pinnate, bright-green, leathery, glossy; smelling of celery.	12-20 rayed umbels of white or tinged pink flowers; 6-7.	On rocky coast of the North East and Scotland.	Will grow in any ordinary soil.
Marrubium vulgare White horehound	Hoary or woolly perennial with short stout rootstock; H 35-45cm.	Ovate, wrinkled with rounded teeth, in opposite pairs at right angles to each other.	Off-white crowded in axillary whorls; 7-10.	On downs and chalk cliffs.	Well-drained sunny position.

	Habit H = height	Foliage	Flowers Nos = months 1-12	Natural habitat	Cultivation
Melissa officinalis Balm	Hardy perennial with erect branched stems; H 30-60cm.	Lemon-scented when bruised; yellow-green, oval, pointed.	White, small and narrow, in whorls on leafy stem; 6-10.	Naturalized; native to Central and South Europe.	Well-drained soil in full sun.
Mentha arvensis Corn mint	Perennial with sprawling leafy stems; H 7-45cm.	Oval, pointed and toothed.	Small, lilac, in tight axillary whorls; 6.	In arable fields and grassland.	Ordinary soil in sun.
Mentha pulegium Pennyroyal	Prostrate, much-branched perennial; H 5-25cm.	Long-stalked, small, oval; scented.	Pale purple in dense, well-spaced whorls; 7-8.	Damp, sandy places.	Light soil with sand added.
Mentha rotundifolia Round-leaved mint	Stout, erect, hairy perennial; taller than most other mints.	Strongly-scented round-ovate, hairy and wrinkled above.	Purple-white in dense conical-cylindrical spikes; 8-9.	In damp and watery places.	Ordinary soil; sun or shade but prefers cool soil.
Mentha spicata Spearmint	Erect perennial with creeping rootstock; H 30-60cm.	Ovate-lanceolate almost sessile; strong mint smell when crushed.	Lilac flowers in whorls on a narrow, loose, interrupted spike; 8-9.	Naturalized, usually as a garden escape.	Best in fairly moist soil in partial shade.
Myrrhis odorata Sweet cicely	Hairy perennial with hollow, furrowed stem; H 1.5m.	Pale green, finely divided or 3-pinnate, smelling of liquorice and aniseed.	White compound umbel with only outer flowers fertile; 5-6.	In grass and hedge-rows in N. England and Scotland.	Thrives in almost all soils.
Nepeta cataria Catmint	Single species of its genus; erect, hoary, leafy-stemmed perennial; H 30-60cm.	Heart-shaped, deeply lobed at base, white and hairy beneath.	White with dark pink spots; in dense, many-flowered whorls forming broad heads; 7-11.	Open hedge banks roadsides.	Ordinary soil.
Origanum vulgare Marjoram	Strongly aromatic perennial with softly hairy crimson stems; H to 60cm.	Oval, blunt, slightly toothed.	Dark purple buds opening to pale purple, in loose corymbs; 7-8.	Common on calcareous soils.	Well-drained soil in sunny position.
Papaver somniferum Opium poppy	Glaucous, erect annual; very variable; H 45-120cm.	Large (8-12cm) with wavy margins.	Lilac with purple blotch at base; 6-9.	Widespread, naturalized weed of cultivation.	Any soil type in sunny position.
Poterium sanguisorba Salad burnet	Perennial; H 45cm.	Pinnate leaflets in pairs; smell of cucumber when crushed.	Unisexual, green, tiny and petal-less. 5-8.	Grassy places on chalk and limestone.	Well-drained soil in sunny position.
Rumex acetosa Sorrel	Succulent perennial; H 15-60cm.	Arrow-shaped, long stalked, alternate.	Female in greenish erect panicle; male in dense 4-8 flowered clusters; 5-7.	Dry pastures.	Ordinary soil.
Tanacetum vulgare Tansy	Stiff stout aromatic perennial with grooved stems; H to 60cm.	Pinnate with numerous leaflets, deeply toothed.	Golden-yellow; button-like; many in stout corymbs; 8-9.	Riversides, grassy verges, waste places and hedge banks.	Ordinary soil; can be invasive.
Thymus drucei Mother of thyme	Extremely variable prostrate mat-forming faintly aromatic perennial; H 5cm.	Oval, very small.	Reddish-purple in roundish heads on erect stems; 6-8.	Dry grassland, heaths and dunes.	Well-drained soil; sunny position.
Thymus pulegiodes Large wild thyme	Spreading, bushy sub-shrub with mostly ascending shoots; H 10-30cm.	Very variable in shape.	Purple, mauve, white or crimson; stems 4-sided; 7-9.	Calcareous dry soils.	Light, well-drained soil on sunny site.
Valeriana officinalis Common valerian	Hardy perennial, with grooved stems; H 1.5m.	Pinnate, the lower stalked, the leaflets toothed.	Pale pink, darker in bud; small; in numerous corymbs.	Common in ditches, damp woods.	Ordinary soil.

habitat	Cultivation
of ponds.	Shallow water and loamy soil.
gin and ater on silt; limestone.	In water up to 30cm deep.
and ditches; on clay.	Pond margin.
laces;	Pond margin.
tches and wet very local.	Water depth up to 45cm; can be invasive.
aces by nd streams;	Pond margin; apt to be invasive.
streamsides t ground;	Easily grown in ordinary soil; tolerates some shade; pond margin.
dows and	Moist soil and partial shade.
s and ponds.	Will grow in water at least 30cm deep.
in wet fields shes.	Pond margin; needs full sun to flower.
anks.	Pond margin.
erbage by onds and fens.	Watersides and moist places.
nks, ditches, commons.	Pond margin; moist soil.

	Habit H = height	Foliage	Flowers Nos = months 1-12	Natural habitat	Cultivation
Mentha aquatica Water mint	Hairy, often purplish perennial with stiff stems; H 22-60cm.	Oval, serrated, becoming smaller at top of stem.	Lilac or reddish in a dense, terminal head, rounded in 2-3 whorls; 7-9.	Damp meadows and river banks.	Moist soil.
Menyanthes trifoliata Bogbean	Distinctive aquatic perennial with procumbent stem and dense mat of roots; H 25cm.	Olive green, smooth, trifoliate.	White, pink in reverse fimbriate, in conspicuous spikes; fragrant; 7-9.	Common in watery bogs.	Will grow in or out of water in a moist site.
Mimulus guttata Monkey flower	Attractive hollow-stemmed perennial; H 10-60cm.	Ovate or oblong, toothed, opposite.	Yellow with 2 dark-red marks at mouth; 6-9.	Naturalized by shallow streams.	Moist soil.
Myosotis scorpioides Water forget-me-not	Creeping perennial; H 15-30cm.	Bright glossy green, oblong	Cobalt blue with yellow eyes; often in paired racemes; 4-7.	Ditches, streams and pond margins.	Likes a heavy fertile loam, waterlogged or to depth of 7cm; in full sun.
Narthecium ossifragum Bog asphodel	Short creeping perennial; H 15-30cm.	Often orange-green, small, sword-shaped.	Yellow with orange anthers; star-like; in a continuous raceme; 7-8.	Bogs and wet heaths.	Boggy, acid soil.
Nuphar pumilum Least yellow water lily	Aquatic perennial.	Oval.	Yellow; has wide gaps between petals; 7-8.	Highland lakes.	For large ponds only.
Nymphaea alba White water lily	Aquatic perennial with thick fleshy rootstock.	Red when young; smooth and heart-shaped.	White with yellow stamens, floating; 6-8.	In ponds, canals and slow streams.	In a fertile loam, 20-30cm deep, in full sun.
Nymphoides peltata Fringed water lily	Long-branching, stemmed aquatic perennial.	Almost orbicular; purple below.	Yellow, 5-lobed in umbels; buds submerged but rise up before opening; 7-9.	Ponds and slow streams.	Can become invasive unless controlled.
Osmunda regalis Royal fern	Graceful and striking perennial with erect fronds, coloured in autumn; H to 180cm.	Pale green; 2-pinnate; long and broad.	Fertile pinnules form an attractive velvety panicle; 6-8.	Lake sides	Moist peat, naturalized in turfy loam.
Pontederia cordata Pickerel weed	Compact aquatic perennial with rigid stems; H 45-75cm.	Bright glossy-green often with maroon patches; heart-shaped and thick.	Sky-blue or white with yellow eye, closely set in terminal spike; 8-9.	Native to N. America.	Pond margin; in loam at edge of pool to depth of 30cm; full sun.
Ranunculus aquatilis Water crowfoot	Variable aquatic perennial; stems trailing or creeping.	2 sets: small and floating and submerged, variously cut.	White buttercup-like, solitary on stem, often in masses; 5-6.	Ponds and streams.	Can be invasive.
Ranunculus lingua Greater spearwort	Hollow-stemmed perennial with densely fibrous roots; H 60-90cm.	Very large; lanceolate; half-stem clasping.	Yellow, twice as large as meadow buttercup; 7-9.	Marshes, ditches and fens.	For damp places; good marginal.
Sagittaria sagittifolia Arrowhead	Aquatic perennial with stoloniferous swollen rootstock; H 60-90cm.	3 sets of leaves: earliest submerged, then spear-like; later aerial arrow-shaped, on long stalks.	White petals with dark centre, in whorls of 3-5 on long stalk; 7-8.	In mud by streams and ponds.	Wet loamy soil.
Scutellaria galericulata Common skullcap	Slender-stemmed perennial; H 15-45cm.	Tinged purple on underside; variable shape, oblong to ovate, and cordate; crenately toothed.	Bright-blue with white markings within; in pairs in leaf axils; 6-9.	Edges of ponds and streams.	Good marginal plant for all types of water garden.

ROCK PLANTS

Many a gardener spends a lifetime in search of the rarest rock plants. As one would expect, some are found in specialist nurseries, but others are discovered in out of the way places, on market stalls in small towns or villages, or on 'Gardens Open' days. Many are easily raised from seed, that offered by garden seedsmen as well as by wildflower firms.

	Habit H = height	Foliage	Flowers Nos = months 1-12	Natural habitat	Cultivation
Alchemilla alpina Alpine lady's mantle	Low-growing perennial; H 20-30cm.	Handsome green-grey, divided into 5-9 segments; silvery hairs on underside.	Yellow-green, tiny, without petals; borne in corymbs; 6-9.	Grassy and rocky crevices on mountains.	Moist but well-drained soil.
Antennaria dioica Cat's foot	Short neat perennial; forms a dense creeping mat; H 6-30cm.	Spoon-shaped; woolly-white beneath.	Male white and spreading, female, pink and erect; borne on different plants: 5-6.	Heaths, dry pastures and mountain slopes.	Light, well-drained soil in sunny position.
Arabis albida	Mat-forming perennial; H 7-15cm.	Oblong, toothed.	White, large and fragrant; 2-6.	Limestone cliffs and old garden walls.	Well-drained soil in partial shade. Too invasive for smaller rock gardens; best on wall.
Campanula rotundifolia Harebell	Slender creeping perennial; H 15-50cm.	Small and heart-shaped; basal leaves wither early.	Slate-blue to blue- purple; bell-shaped and nodding; 6-9.	Dry grassland.	Light, well-drained soil; open position.
Corydalis lutea Yellow corydalis	Tufted perennial; H 15-20cm.	Fern-like; slightly glaucous.	Rich yellow in short spikes; 4-11.	In hilly districts and as garden escape on walls.	Best on walls and between paving stones.
Cymbalaria muralis Ivy-leaved toadflax	Trailing perennial; H 5-10cm.	Ivy-shaped; long-stalked.	Short-spurred, snapdragon-like; lilac, with yellow honey-guide on lower lip; 4-10.	Shady rocks and woods; prefers lime- stone; garden escape on walls.	Ordinary soil in some sun; good trailing plant.
Dianthus deltoides Maiden pink	Sprawling, thin perennial; H 15-30cm.	Narrow; mid to deep green, often with a red or purplish flush.	Pink, notched; freckled; blue stamens; 6-8.	Dry grassy banks and hills.	Well-drained sunny site; many garden varieties.
Dryas octopetala Mountain avens	Creeping woody perennial; forms extensive mats; H 15-30cm.	Shiny; mid to deep green; downy-white beneath.	White with many gold stamens; anemone-like; 5-6.	Rocky limestone ledges.	Well-drained sunny site; prefers limestone. Do not disturb roots.
Gentiana verna Spring gentian	Perennial; forms a small rosette; H 7.5cm.	Small; oval.	Usually intense blue, but variable from white to violet; 4-6.	Limestone turf.	Well-drained soil containing leafmould and lime.
Geranium lucidum Shining cranesbill	Slender annual with red translucent stems; H 10-30cm.	Shiny; palmately lobed; often colouring prettily from green to red.	Pink, small and neat, with narrow petals; 5-8.	Hedge banks and walls; common on acid soils.	Well-drained soil; light shade.
Geranium robertianum Herb robert	Much-branched, hairy, strong-smelling annual; H 15-38cm.	Round-ovate, 3-5 lobed; often turning to red as plant ages.	Crimson to pink. There is also a white form; 5-10.	Light-shade on walls, rocks and shingle.	Easy to grow.
Helianthemum apenninum Hoary rock rose	Compact spreading shrub with erect stems; H up to 50cm.	Shoots and leaves covered with a thick down.	Small white flowers borne in racemes; 5-6.	Sea cliffs in SW England.	Sunny banks.
Helianthemum nummularium Rock rose	Low, open, often pros- trate semi-shrubby plant. Many garden varieties; H 10-15cm.	Narrow, oblong; green above, downy beneath.	Yellow, 5-petalled; 5-9.	Grassy places on chalk and limestone.	Well-drained soil in a sunny position.

	Habit H = height	Foliage	Flowers Nos = months 1-12	Natural habitat	Cultivation
Lithospermum purpurocaeruleum Blue gromwell	Perennial, with creeping, erect flower stems; H 22-38cm.	Dark green lanceolate, with narrowed base.	Red at first becoming deep blue; in leafy twin racemes; 5-7.	Rare; thickets on chalk and limestone.	Apt to become invasive.
Maianthemum bifolium May lily	Perennial with slender creeping rootstock; mat-forming; H 10-20cm.	Two, thickly-veined, shiny and heart-shaped.	Fragrant, white with prominent stamens in a 12-30 flowered raceme; 5-6.	Woodland; very rare in the wild.	Ideal ground cover for cool, moist (not wet) places.
Myosotis alpestris Alpine forget-me-not	Small and variable tufted hardy perennial; H 5-20cm.	Hoary, green; oblong-lanceolate with pointed tips.	Fragrant, azure-blue with yellow eyes; in small corymbs; 7-8.	Rare; from European mountains.	Well-drained soil that retains some moisture.
Polygala vulgaris Common milkwort	Prostrate or erect, freely branching perennial; H 5-7.5cm.	Small, glabrous, lanceolate.	Bright blue, pale blue, pink or white, in terminal short racemes; 5-9.	Rough pastures and banks on chalk and limestone.	Full sun in well-drained soil.
Potentilla tabernaemontani Spring cinquefoil	Prostrate, bristly evergreen perennial; mat-forming; H 5-7.5cm.	Basal, stalked and palmate.	Yellow, on ascending, slender stalks; 4-5, and often again in summer.	Dry chalk and limestone rocks and grass.	Full sun in well-drained soil.
Primula farinosa Birdseye primrose	Small perennial; rosette of leaves; H 10-15cm.	Pale green; narrow and oblanceolate.	Lilac-pink with yellow eye; in umbel; 5-6.	Banks and slopes on limestone outcrops in north.	On soil enriched with peat or leaf mould.
Pulsatilla vulgaris Pasque flower	Variable tufted perennial with thick black fibrous rootstock; H 15cm.	Feathery, deeply divided and hairy.	Rich violet with golden anthers, silky outside; 4-5.	Chalk and limestone slopes.	Open sites and well-drained soil.
Saxifraga aizoides Yellow mountain saxifrage	Loosely tufted perennial, short and mat; H 5-15cm.	Thick and lanceolate.	Orange or yellow, often spotted red; on leafy stems; 6-8.	Moisture-loving on wet rocks and gravelly rills on mountains, by the sea.	Well-drained soil with lime and plenty of grit.
Saxifraga hypnoides Mossy saxifrage	Very variable low perennial, forming moss-like cushions; H 10-15cm.	Short, palmately lobed, with bulbils in axils.	White with nodding pink-tipped buds; very variable; 5-6.	Rocky screes; high grassy hillsides.	Well-drained soil; plant away from direct sun. Many garden forms.
Saxifraga oppositifolia Purple saxifrage	Small perennial with numerous densely leafy trailing stems; H 2-15cm.	Very small and hard, un-stalked, mainly opposite.	Large, purple; sessile or nearly so; 5-6.	Granite or limestone rocks.	Cool, slightly moist, some sun; use limestone grit mulch.
Saxifraga stellaris Starry saxifrage	Attractive perennial with rosettes of leaves; H 10-15cm.	Sub-sessile; toothed; leathery, of various shapes.	White, starlike; on branching stems; 6-8.	Wet places on mountains.	Good for margins of rock pool or stream sides.
Saxifraga umbrosa London pride	Perennial; forms neat rosette; H 30cm.	Mid-dark green; thick and leathery.	Pink; star-shaped, in loose panicles; 5.	Mountains, woods and gorges.	Best in partial shade.
Sedum acre Wall pepper	Mat-forming glabrous evergreen; H 2.5-10cm.	Yellow-green; bluntly conical; acrid taste.	Yellow; borne in flattened heads; 6-7.	Limestone rocks, walls and roofs.	Suitable for walls and for ground cover over stones.
Sedum album White stonecrop	Mat-forming glabrous evergreen; H3.5-15cm.	Oblong; cylindrical; alternate.	White; borne profusely in loose clusters; 7.	Limestone rocks and walls.	As above.
Sempervivum tectorum Houseleek	Perennial; forms fleshy rosettes; H 5-7cm.	Green with marron tips.	Rose-purple; numerous; 7.	Introduced from Pyrenees and Alps; naturalized on walls; roofs.	Well-drained soil, sunny position.
Umbilicus rupestris Wall pennywort	Fleshy tuberous-rooted perennial; H 5-7cm on dry wall; 30cm in moist shade.	Disc-like with a dimple in the centre; in an open rosette.	Green-white with red dots, in a simple spike; 6-8.	Rock crevices, walls and hedge banks on acid soils.	Rock or wall garden in peaty soil.

PLANTS TO ATTRACT WILDLIFE

Nectar plants for bees and butterflies
(*nos refer to flowering months*)
Balm, *Melissa officinalis*, 5-7
Bellflowers, *Campanula* sp., 6-8
Blackthorn, *Prunus spinosa*, 3-5
Bugle, *Ajuga reptans*, 5-7
Clovers, *Trifolium* sp., 5-9
Columbine, *Aquilegia vulgaris*, 5-7
Cowslip, *Primula veris*, 4-5
Crab apple blossom, *Malus pumila*, 5
Daisy, *Bellis perennis*, 3-10
Gorse, *Ulex europaeus*, 3-5
Groundsels, *Senecio* sp., 1-12
Heathers, *Erica* sp., 4-8
Knapweeds, *Centaurea* sp., 7-9
Ling, *Calluna vulgaris*, 8-9
Marjoram, *Origanum vulgare*, 7-9
Meadow saffron, *Colchicum autumnale*, 9-10
Mints, *Mentha* sp.,
Mulleins, *Verbascum* sp., 6-9
Purple loosestrife, *Lythrum salicaria*, 8-9
Soapwort, *Saponaria officinalis*, 8-10
Thrift, *Armeria maritima*, 4-9
Thymes, *Thymus* sp., 6-8
Toadflax, *Linaria* sp., 5-10
Willowherbs, *Epilobium* sp., 6-9
Willows, *Salix* sp., 3-5
Yarrow, *Achillea millefolium*, 6-8

Fruit- and seed-producers, for birds and others
Birches, *Betula* sp. (seeds)
Black bryony, *Tamus communis* (berries)
Buckthorn, *Rhamnus cathartica* (berries)
Cherries, *Prunus* sp. (fruits)
Chickweeds, *Stellaria* sp. (seeds)
Elderberry, *Sambucus nigra* (fruits)
Forget-me-nots, *Myosotis* sp. (seeds)
Garlic mustard, *Alliaria petiolata* (seeds)
Guelder rose, *Viburnum* sp. (berries)
Hawthorns, *Crataegus* sp. (haws)
Hazel, *Corylus avellana* (nuts)
Holly, *Ilex aquifolium* (berries)
Honeysuckles, *Lonicera* sp. (berries)
Ivy, *Hedera helix* (berries)
Mezereon, *Daphne mezèreum* (berries)
Mountain ash, *Sorbus aucuparia* (berries)
Pines, *Pinus* sp. (seeds)
Privet, *Ligustrum vulgaris* (berries)
Strawberry tree, *Arbutus unedo* (fruits)
Teasel, *Dipsacus fullonum* (seeds)
Thistles, *Carduus, Cirsium, Onopordon* sp. (seeds)
Tutsan, *Hyericum androsaemum* (berry-like fruits)
White bryony, *Bryonia dioica* (berries)
Wild arums, *Arum* sp. (berries)
Woody nightshade, *Solanum dulcamara* (berries)
Yew, *Taxus baccata* (berries)

PLANTS FOR SPECIAL SITUATIONS

Plants for ground cover
1. Herbaceous
Bugle, *Ajuga reptans*
Creeping jenny, *Lysimachia nummularia*
Ground ivy, *Glecoma hederacea*
Lady's mantle, *Alchemilla vulgaris*
Lily-of-the-valley, *Convallaria majalis*
Pennyroyal, *Mentha pulegium*
Speedwells, *Veronica* sp.
Stonecrops, *Sedum* sp.
Woodruff, *Asperula odorata*
Yellow archangel, *Galeobdolon luteum*
2. Shrubs
Bear berry, *Arctostaphylos uva-ursi*
Bilberry, *Vaccinium myrtillus*
Cow berry, *Vaccinum vitis-idaea*
Crowberry, *Empetrum nigrum*
Heather, most *Erica* sp.
Ivy, *Hedera* in great variety
Juniper, *Juniper communis montana*
Ling, *Calluna vulgaris*
Mountain avens, *Dryas octopetala*
Periwinkle, *Vinca* in variety
Rock rose, *Helianthemum* sp.
Thyme, *Thymus* sp.

Trees and shrubs tolerant of both extreme acidity and alkalinity
Alder buckthorn, *Frangula alnus*
Aspen, *Populus tremula*
Barberry, *Berberis vulgaris*
Beech, *Fagus sylvatica*
Birch, downy, *Betula pubescens*
Birch, silver, *Betula pendula*
Beech, *Fagus sylvatica*
Elderberry, *Sambucus nigra*
Guelder rose, *Viburnum opulus*
Hawthorn, *Crataegus monogyna*
Holly, *Ilex aquifolium*
Juniper, *Juniperus communis*
Oak, *Quercus robur*
Poplar, grey, *Populus canescens*
Poplar, white, *Populus alba*
Privet, *Ligustrum vulgaris*
Scots pine, *Pinus sylvestris*
Whitebeam, *Sorbus intermedia*
Willow, grey, *Salix cinerea*
Willow, pussy, *Salix caprea*
Yew, *Taxus baccata*

Plants for shady places
Alkanet, *Pentaglottis sempervirens*
Columbine, *Aquilegia vulgaris*
Comfrey, *Symphytum officinalis*
Cyclamen, *Cyclamen neapolitanum*
Foxglove, *Digitalis purpurea*
Green hellebore, *Helleborus viridis*
Jacob's ladder, *Polemonium coeruleum*
Lungwort, *Pulmonaria officinalis*
Monkshood, *Aconitum anglicum*
Masterwort, *Astrantia major*
Nettle-leaved bellflower, *Campanula trachelium*
Pearly everlasting, *Anaphalis margaritacea*
Solomon's seal, *Polygonatum multiflorum*
Spotted dead nettle, *Lamium maculatum*
Streaked cranesbill, *Geranium versicolor*
Spurge laurel, *Daphne laureola*
Wood forget-me-not, *Myosotis sylvatica*
Wood sorrel, *Oxalis acetosella*
Wood violet, *Viola reichenbachiana*

Plants for sunny places
Chicory, *Cichorium intybus*
Corn marigold, *Chrysanthemum segetum*
Fumitory, *Fumitaria* sp.
Germander speedwell, *Veronica chamaedrys*

WILDFLOWER AND MEADOW GRASS SEED MIXTURES

Herb robert,
   Geranium robertianum
Lady's bedstraw, *Galium verum*
Mullein, *Verbascum* sp.
Pinks, *Dianthus* sp.
Poppies, *Papaver* sp.
Pyrenean cranesbill,
   Geranium pyrenaicum
Rock roses, *Helianthemum* sp.
Scarlet pimpernel,
   Anagallis arvensis
Scottish thistle,
   Onopordon acanthium
Sea holly, *Eryngium maritimum*
Toadflax, *Linaria vulgaris*
Viper's bugloss, *Echium vulgare*
Wild mignonette, *Reseda lutea*
Yellow horned poppy,
   Glaucium flavum

Climbers and trailers
Bindweeds, *Calystegia* sp.
Black bryony, *Tamus communis*
Everlasting pea,
   Lathyrus latifolius
Field rose, *Rosa arvensis*
Honeysuckle,
   Lonicera periclymenum
Hop, *Humulus lupulus*
Ivy, *Hedera helix*
Lesser bindweed,
   Convulvulus arvensis
Old man's beard,
   Clematis vitalba
Periwinkles, *Vinca* sp.
Trailing azalea,
   Loisleuria procumbens
White bryony, *Bryonia dioica*
Woody nightshade,
   Solanum dulcamara

Wildflowers and grasses for clay soils
% GRASS SPECIES
40.0 *Festuca rubra* ssp. *communta*, red fescue
35.0 *Festuca rubra* ssp. *rubra*, red fescue
3.0 *Hordeum secalinum*, meadow barley;
EACH *Trisetum flavescens*, golden oat grass
2.0 *Anthoxanthum odoratum*, sweet vernal grass;
EACH *Briza media*, quaking grass

% WILDFLOWERS
2.0 *Rhinanthus minor*, yellow rattle
1.5 *Anthyllis vulneraria*,
EACH kidney vetch;
   Primula veris, cowslip
1.0 *Galium verum*,
EACH lady's bedstraw;
   Chrysanthemum leucanthemum, oxeye daisy;
   Malva moschata, musk mallow;
   Medicago lupulina, black medick;
   Plantago media, hoary plantain;
   Prunella vulgaris, self-heal;
   Stachys officinalis, betony
0.5 *Achillea millefolium*,
EACH yarrow;
   Leontodon autumnale, greater hawkbit;
   Leontodon hispidus, greater hawkbit;
   Linaria vulgaris, toadflax;
   Ranunculus repens, creeping buttercup;
   Saxifraga granulata, meadow saxifrage

Wildflowers and grasses for loam and alluvial soils
% GRASS SPECIES
25.0 *Festuca rubra* ssp. *commuta*,
EACH red fescue;
   Festuca rubra ssp, *rubra*, red fescue
10.0 *Alopecurus pratensis*,
EACH meadow foxtail;
   Cynosurus cristatus, crested dogstail;
   Poa pratensis, smooth meadow grass
5.0 *Agrostis tenuis*, fine bent

% WILDFLOWERS
2.0 *Sanguisorba minor*, salad burnet
1.5 *Agrimonia eupatoria*,
EACH agrimony;
   Ranunculus acris, meadow buttercup;
   Rhinanthus minor, yellow rattle
1.0 *Centaurea nigra*,
EACH black knapweed;
   Echium vulgare, viper's bugloss;
   Knautia arvensis, field scabious;
   Plantago lanceolata, ribwort plantain;
0.5 *Daucus carota*, wild carrot;
EACH *Leucanthemum vulgare*, oxeye daisy;
   Linaria vulgaris, toadflax;
   Lychnis flos-cuculi, ragged robin;
   Primula veris, cowslip;
   Rumex acetosa, common sorrel;
   Sanguisorba officinalis, great burnet;
   Silene alba, white campion;
   Tragopon pratense, goatsbeard

Wildflowers and grasses for chalk and limestone
% GRASS SPECIES
35.0 *Festuca rubra* ssp. *commuta*
23.0 *Festuca rubra* ssp. *rubra*
20.0 *Cyanosurus cristatus*
5.0 *Trisetum flavescens*
2.0 *Briza media*,

% WILDFLOWERS
1.0 *Primula veris*, cowslip
EACH *Anthyllis vulneraria*, kidney vetch;
   Campanula glomerata, clustered bellflower;
   Filipendula vulgaris, dropwort;
   Chrysanthemum leucanthemum, oxeye daisy;
   Plantago media, hoary plantain;
   Prunella vulgaris, self-heal;
   Reseda lutea, wild mignonette;
   Scabiosa columbaria, small scabious
0.5 *Blackstonia perfoliata*,
EACH yellow wort;
   Campanula rotundifolia, harebell;
   Galium verum, lady's bedstraw;
   Hieracium pilosella, mouse-ear hawkweed,
   Helianthemum nummularium, common rock rose;
   Hippocrepis comosa, horseshoe vetch;
   Leontodon hispidus, greater hawkbit;
   Linaria vulgaris, toadflax;
   Medicago lupulina, black medick;
   Origanum vulgare, marjoram

PROTECTED PLANTS

The following 62 wild plants found in the United Kingdom are specially protected by the Wildlife and Countryside Act 1981; removal of any part of these plants is an offence.

Adder's-tongue spearwort,
Ranunculus ophioglossifolius
Alpine catchfly, *Lychnis alpina*
Alpine gentian, *Gentiana nivalis*
Alpine sow-thistle,
Cicerbita alpina
Alpine woodsia, *Woodsia alpina*
Bedstraw broomrape,
Orobanche caryophyllacea
Blue heath, *Phyllodoce caerulea*
Brown galingale, *Cyperus fuscus*
Cheddar pink,
Dianthus gratianopolitanus
Childing pink,
Petrorhagia nanteuilli
Diapensia, *Diapensia lapponica*
Dickie's bladder fern,
Cystopteris dickieana
Downy woundwort,
Stachys germanica
Drooping saxifrage,
Saxifraga cernua
Early spider-orchid,
Ophrys sphegodes
Fen orchid, *Liparis loeselii*
Fen violet, *Viola persicifolia*
Field cow-wheat,
Melampyrum arvense
Field eryngo, *Eryngium campestre*
Field wormwood,
Artemisia campestris
Ghost orchid, *Epipogium aphyllum*
Great yellow-rattle,
Rhinanthus serotinus
Jersey cudweed,
Gnaphalium luteoalbum
Killarney fern,
Trichomanes speciosum
Lady's slipper,
Cypripedium calceolus
Late spider-orchid,
Ophrys fuciflora
Least lettuce, *Lactuca saligna*
Limestone woundwort,
Stachys alpina
Lizard orchid,
Himantoglossum hircinum
Military orchid, *Orchis militaris*
Monkey orchid, *Orchis simia*

Norwegian sandwort,
Arenaria norvegica
Oblong woodsia,
Woodsia ilvensis
Oxtongue broomrape,
Orobanche loricata
Perennial knawel,
Scleranthus perennis
Plymouth pear, *Pyrus cordata*
Purple spurge, *Euphorbia peplis*
Red helleborine,
Cephalanthera rubra
Ribbon-leaved water-plantain,
Alisma gramineum
Rock cinquefoil,
Potentilla rupestris
Rock sea-lavender,
Limonium paradoxum and
L. recurvum (two rare species)
Rough marsh-mallow,
Althaea hirsuta
Round-headed leek,
Allium sphaerocephalon
Sea knotgrass,
Polygonum maritimum
Sickle-leaved hare's ear,
Bupleurum falcatum
Small alison, *Alyssum alyssoides*
Small hare's-ear,
Bupleurum baldense
Snowdon lily, *Lloydia serotina*
Spiked speedwell,
Veronica spicata
Spring gentian, *Gentiana verna*
Starfruit, *Damasonium alisma*
Starved wood-sedge,
Carex depauperata
Teesdale sandwort,
Minuartia stricta
Thistle broomrape,
Orobanche reticulata
Triangular club-rush,
Scirpus triquetrus
Tufted saxifrage,
Saxifraga cespitosa
Water germander,
Teucrium scordium
Whorled solomon's seal,
Polygonatum verticillatum
Wild cotoneaster,
Cotoneaster integerrimus
Wild gladiolus,
Gladiolus illyricus
Wood calamint,
Calamintha sylvatica

GLOSSARY

Acid Term applied to soils with a pH lower than 7.0.

Acuminate Term applied to a leaf which tapers to a long, narrow point.

Alkaline Term applied to soils with a pH higher than 7.0, normally with a comparatively high lime content.

Alpine A plant that grows naturally on mountain slopes; a plant suitable for a rock garden.

Annual A plant that germinates, grows, flowers, seeds and dies within the space of 12 months.

Anther The terminal part of a stamen containing the pollen.

Aquatic Term applied to a plant of any genera living mainly in water.

Axil The upper angle formed by the union of the leaf and the stem.

Axis The part of a plant around which the organs are developed.

Bedding plant Any flowering annual used for seasonal display in the traditional garden.

Biennial A plant that germinates, grows, flowers, seeds and dies within two years.

Bog Wet land of an acid nature but not so wet that plants are constantly under water, nor so dry that the roots dry out.

Broadcast To sow or scatter seeds over an area of soil instead of in marked rows or drills.

Bulb A storage organ with fleshy scales or a swollen leaf base containing food for a resting period.

Bulbils Small bulbs that grow on some plants and can be detached and grown into full-sized bulbs.

Calcareous Term applied to soil containing chalk or lime.

Calcifuge A lime-hating plant that will not grow well if there is lime in the soil.

Chalk Calcium carbonate, chemically identical with limestone; chalk is used as hydrated lime to counteract high acid content of soils; a chalk soil has a high pH.

Clay Term applied to a soil mixture of very fine sand and alumina which is moisture-retentive, heavy and sticky but usually fertile if treated.

Composite Term applied to a plant in which the flowerhead consists of separate florets.

Compost The product of rotted vegetable matter; also used to describe a soil mixture used for seed sowing.

Conifer A tree bearing cones.

Corm A storage organ comprising a thickened underground stem.

Corymb A flat head of stalked flowers ranged at different levels.

Crown Top of the rootstock from which new shoots orginate.

Cultivar Cultivated *variety* (q.v.) either bred purposely or developing spontaneously, but incapable of exact reproduction by seeds.

Deciduous Term applied to a plant that drops its leaves in winter.

Dentate Term applied to a leaf with toothed edges.

Dormant A condition of inactivity in plants usually occasioned by low temperatures.

Evergreen Term applied to a plant that drops its leaves gradually and replaces them through the year.

Exotic A plant not indigenous to the country in which it is growing, and which is unable to naturalize.

Falls Those petals that hang down, such as those of an iris flowerhead.

Fimbriate With a fringed margin.

Glabrous Smooth; devoid of hair.

Ground cover Thickly growing low shrubs or herbaceous plants that closely cover the soil which supports them.

Habit General appearance or manner of growth of a plant, e.g. upright, sprawling, creeping, etc.

Habitat Natural home or living area of a plant.

Half-hardy Term applied to a plant that needs protection in winter.

Hedgerow Essentially a hedge, some say with bank and/or ditch.

Herbaceous Term applied to a plant with soft or sappy, instead of woody, growth.

Humus Decayed organic matter- a soil conditioner rather than a fertilizer.

Hybrid Product of a cross between plants of different species, sometimes indicated by a cross, e.g. *Erica × darleyens.*

Lanceolate Term applied to a lance-shaped leaf, longer than its width and tapering at both ends.

Laying The process of hedge-making in which saplings are bent over almost horizontally and staked.

Limestone Underlying rock formation usually associated with a surface soil of high pH.

Linear Slender.

Loam Rotted turf; normally a soil mixture of sand, clay and humus but with no precise definition.

Marginal Term applied to a plant that grows in shallow water at the margin or edge of a pool or pond – 'emergent' to the botanist.

Marsh Land that is watery at all times.

Moraine A bed of small stones or grit, usually for growing alpines and usually watered from below, unlike a **scree** (q.v.).

Native Term applied to a plant or animal that is indigenous to a locality or country.

Naturalize To grow plants under conditions that are as nearly natural as possible; naturalized plants are those that were originally imported but have subsequently reseeded themselves in the wild.

Ovate Term applied to a leaf that is egg-shaped.

Oxygenating Term applied to a plant that grows in or under water, and which produces oxygen.

Palmate Term applied to a leaf shaped like a hand.

Panicle Flower cluster of several separate branches, each carrying numerous stalked flowers.

Peat Soil from boggy or swampy land. Moss peat comes mainly from decomposed sphagnum moss, whereas sedge peat comes from the roots and leaves of sedges.

Pedunculate Having a flower stalk.

Peltate Term applied to a shield-shaped leaf with a central stalk.

Perennial Any plant that lives and flowers for a number of years.

Pinnate Term applied to a feather-like leaf having several leaflets on each side of a common stalk.

Pinnule A secondary division of a pinnate leaf.

Pubescent Covered with fine hairs.

Raceme An unbranched inflorescence with flowers carried on equal-length stalks.

Radical Growing from the root.

Rhizome An underground stem that usually grows horizontally, producing shoots some distance from the parent plant.

Root ball A cluster of roots embedded in the soil.

Runner A shoot that roots at intervals along its length.

Sagittate Term applied to an arrow-shaped leaf with two lobes projecting backwards, giving it the appearance of an arrow-head.

Scree Similar to a **moraine** (q.v.), but usually watered from above.

Sessile Without a stalk.

Spadix A spike with a fleshy *axis* (q.v.).

Species A group of plants that resemble each other, breed together and maintain the same constant distinctive character.

Stolon A creeping stem that roots at intervals.

Taproot A straight root, thicker at its top than its base, from which subsidiary rootlets spring.

Tomentose Hairy, having a dense covering of short hairs.

Trickle irrigation A system using flexible small-bore tubing to drip or trickle water via adjustable nozzles to specific plants or pots.

Trifoliate Having three leaflets.

Triquetrous Triangular and acutely angled.

Umbel Flower clusters where the flower stalks all rise from the top of the main flower stem.

Variegation White or yellow spots, blotches or streaks on green leaves, arising from mutation, a benign virus or mineral deficiency.

Variety A group of plants within a species; any plant with distinctive characteristics but not worthy of specific rank.

Vernalization The exposure of a plant or bulb to low temperature to encourage early flowering.

GENERAL INDEX

PLANT INDEX

Italic type indicates illustrations.
Bold type indicates an entry in the
selective plant guide.

BIBLIOGRAPHY

Baines, Chris, *Wildlife garden notebook*, Oxford Illustrated Press 1984
Baines, Chris, and Smart, Jane, *A Guide to Habitat Creation*, Ecology Handbook No. 2, GLC 1984
Chittenden, F.J., *The Royal Horticultural Dictionary of Gardening* (5 vols), Royal Horticultural Society 1956
Clapham, A.R., Tuttin, T.J., and Warburg, E.F., *Flora of the British Isles*, Cambridge University Press 1985
Farrar, Reginald, *My Rock Garden*, Edward Arnold 1908
Fitter, Richard, Alistair Fitter, and Marjorie Blamey, *The Wildflowers of Britain and Northern Europe*, Collins 1985
Garden Plants Valuable to Bees, International Bee Research Association (with BSBI and RHS)
Gardening with Wildlife, The Royal Society for the Protection of Birds
Gilmour, John, and Walters, Max, *Wild Flowers*, Collins 1974
Grigson, Geoffrey, *The Englishman's Flora*, Phoenix House 1958
Heritage, Bill, *The Lotus Book of Water Gardening*, Hamlyn 1973
Hibberd, Shirley, *The Fern Garden*, Groombridge & Son 1879
Hillier & Sons, *Hilliers Manual of Trees and Shrubs*, Winchester
Hinckley Haufman, Ethel, *American Wildflowers*, Garden City Publishing Co. 1947
Hubbard, C.E., *Grasses*, Penguin 1954
Jekyll, Gertrude, *Wood and Garden*, Antique Collectors' Club 1981
Kaye, Reginald, *Hardy Ferns*, Faber & Faber 1968
Keble Martin, W., *The New Concise British Flora in Colour*, Michael/Joseph/Ebury Press 1982
Newman, L. Hugh, and Mansell, E., *The Complete British Butterflies in Colour*, Michael Joseph/Ebury Press 1968
Nicholson, B.E., Ary, F., and Gregory, M., *The Oxford Book of Wildflowers*, Oxford University Press 1976
Perring, F.H., and Farrell, L., *British Red Data Book 1: Vascular Plants* (2nd edition), Royal Society for Nature Conservation 1983
Phillips, Roger, *Wildflowers of Britain*, Pan 1983
Robinson, William, *The Wild Garden*, Century 1983
Rose, Graham, *The Low Maintenance Garden*, Windward/Frances Lincoln Ltd 1983
Rothchild, Miriam, and Farrell, Clive, *The Butterfly Gardener*, Michael Joseph/Rainbird 1983
Wells, Terry, Bell, S., and Frost, A., *Creating Attractive Grasslands Using Native Plant Species*, Nature Conservancy Council, Shropshire 1981

ACKNOWLEDGMENTS

The publishers would like to thank the following people for their help:

Mr Terry Wells of the Institute of Terrestrial Ecology (NERC), Monks Wood Experimental Station, for commenting most helpfully on the typescript, and in particular on the wildflower meadows chapter and the bulb planter technique. For the material on page 159 we are indebted to Emorsgate Seeds, whose wildflower meadow seed mixtures are based on information in *Creating attractive grasslands using native plant species,* by Terry Wells, Shirley Bell and Alan Frost, NCC, 1981. Mrs A. H. Bauerman, Mrs M. Huiskamp, Mr George Innes, the Hon. Mrs Lyttleton, Mr Ian Mylles and Mr Peter Baistow for their kind permission to photograph their gardens.

Susan Berry for initial work on the book and for editorial work; Joanna Jellinek for editorial work; and Leslie Johns for compiling the index.

Project editor
Alison Freegard

Art editor
Steven Wooster

Editor
David Black

Designer
Claudine Meissner

General editor
Pippa Rubinstein

Picture researcher
Anne Fraser

Photographs
ARCAID/Richard Bryant: 10; ARDEA: 77T; Peter Baistow: 62T, 66; Karl-Dietrich Bühler: 13, 14, 15, 48, 57, 59, 85, 101T, 103, front cover; Robert César: 9; Geoff Dann, 4, 11, 18, 20, 22/23, 25, 29, 35, 37, 45, 46, 54/55, 79, 82, 83, 87, 91, 95, 97, 100B, 109, 115, 120T, back cover; Henk Dijkman: 104, 113T; Inge Espen-Hansen: 1, 31, 34, 38, 49, 56, 96, 106B, 108, 110, 120B; Derek Fell: 19, 32, 61T, 68, 69, 72, 74, 114; Valerie Finnis: 7, 117; John Glover: 70, 76, 80, 119B; Jerry Harpur: 39L, 111; Pat Hunt: 40, 98, 100T, 119T; Jacqui Hurst: 12, 17, 21, 42, 47, 62B, 64, 65, 84, 86, 106T; Leslie Johns: author's photograph; Nature Photographers Ltd: 105T, 113B; Oxford Scientific Films/Stephen Dalton: 101B; Harry Smith (Horticultural Photographic Collection): 30; Ron Sutherland: 2, 28, 36, 43, 63, 71, 77B, 89, 105 (BL and BR), 112; George Taloumis: 8, 39R; Steven Wooster: 61B; George Wright: 53, 90, 118.

Illustrations
Angela Beard: 33; Jeanne Colville: 52, 75; Jane Cradock-Watson: 122; Fiona B. Currie: 7, 19, 21, 24, 26, 29, 37, 43, 53, 72, 76, 78, 85, 90, 94, 98, 102, 111, 114, 118, 121, 141; Will Giles: 123-140; Vana Haggerty: 142; Ros Hewitt: 16, 17, 41, 58, 59, 65, 67; Sally Launder: 31, 60, 73, 81, 88, 99, 107, 116; Andrew Macdonald: 27; Shirley Wheeler: 50, 51, 92, 93.

Garden designs
Anthony Paul 107; Robin Williams 73, 88, 116.

Cover border
Michael Craig

Typesetting
Chambers Wallace, London

Reproduction
Hong Kong Graphic Arts Limited

ADDRESSES

Specialist seed suppliers
Emorsgate Seeds, Emorsgate, Terrington St Clement, Norfolk.
The Seed Exchange, 44 Albion Road, Sutton, Surrey.
John Chambers, 15 Westleigh Road, Barton Seagrave, Kettering, Northants NN15 5AJ.
Naturescape, Little Orchard, Main Street, Whatton in the Vale, Notts.
Suffolk Herbs, Sawyers Farm, Little Cornard, Sudbury, Suffolk.
W. W. Johnson & Son Ltd, Boston, Lincs PE2 8AD.
Mr Fothergill's Seeds, Regal Lodge, Gazeley Road, Kentford, Newmarket, Suffolk CB8 7QB.
British Seed Houses Ltd, Bewsey Industrial Estate, Pitt Street, Warrington, Cheshire WA5 5LE.
Mommersteeg International, Station Road, Finedon, Wellingborough, Northants NN9 5NT.

Other useful addresses
Botanical Society of the British Isles, c/o Dept. of Botany, British Museum (Natural History), Cromwell Road, London SW7 5BD.

Local NCC Regional Office available from: Information and Library Services, Nature Conservancy Council, Calthorpe House, Calthorpe Street, Banbury, Oxon OX16 8EX.

Local Nature Conservation Trust available from: Royal Society for Nature Conservation, The Green, Nettleham, Lincs LN2 2NR.